BEING HENRY

BEING HENRY

THE FONZ . . . AND BEYOND

HENRY WINKLER

Written with James Kaplan

LARGE PRINT PRESS
A part of Gale, a Cengage Company

GALE
A Cengage Company

**LIBRARY OF CONGRESS CIP DATA ON FILE.
CATALOGUING IN PUBLICATION FOR THIS BOOK
IS AVAILABLE FROM THE LIBRARY OF CONGRESS.**

ISBN-13: 978-1-4205-1901-3 (paperback alk. paper)

Published in 2024 by arrangement with Celadon Books.

Printed in the USA
1 2 3 4 5   28 27 26 25 24

*It is with enormous gratitude,
love, and appreciation
that I dedicate this book
to my wife, Stacey,
for loving me, supporting me,
and standing by me
for our forty-seven years together.*

1.

It was the biggest audition of my life, and the sweat stains under my arms weren't just clearly visible, they were a cry for help.

I was in an office at Paramount Studios in Los Angeles. It was a sunny Tuesday morning in October 1973. About a dozen people were in the room, all of them seated except for me and one guy, the person I was supposed to read with. He, I would later learn, was a casting assistant named Pasquale. Seated on a couch were (I would later learn) the producers Garry Marshall, Tom Miller, and Ed Milkis, along with Garry's sister Ronny. Paramount's casting director Millie Gussie sat behind a large and impressive wooden desk. I believe several other important people were in the room, though I couldn't tell you for sure.

I was in an altered state.

I smiled. "Hi, how are you?" I said. Blank looks from the people behind the table.

"Okay, honesty is the best policy," I said. "So I'm just gonna tell you that the sweat under my arms is running like the Hudson River. These sweat stains under my arms are in direct correlation to the fear that is running through my body."

This drew faint smiles from the people who were there to assess me — but they had an expectant look about them. It was time for me to do what I was there to do. I had a couple of script pages in my hands (my palms were also good and sweaty): I had six lines to read. The show, titled *Happy Days,* was to revolve around a group of wholesome high school kids in 1950s Milwaukee. The character I was reading was the group's one renegade. His name was Arthur Fonzarelli, aka the Fonz.

This Fonz was supposed to be a knock-about guy, a man of few words, rough around the edges. Confident. A guy who could make things happen with a snap of his fingers. Someone his fellow teenagers would listen to and obey unquestioningly. If this wasn't the diametric opposite of who I was in the fall of 1973, it was pretty close. I was twenty-seven years old, soon to turn twenty-eight, a short Jew from New York City with a unibrow and hair down to my shoulders, confident about next to nothing in my life.

The one exception was when I was acting.

When I was on a stage, playing someone else, I was transported to another world, one where pretending made you successful. What I was miserable at was being myself.

I thought I had a vague idea how to play this Fonzarelli. I rustled the papers and cleared my throat. And somehow, at that moment, terrified as I was, I was able to make a firm decision. I decided that I was going to make this guy who was standing up and reading with me — Pasquale, though I didn't know his name yet — sit down. The force of my character's personality would give him no choice.

How was I going to accomplish this? I had no clue.

He read his first line. Something about how he'd been talking to the girls, trying to persuade the girls to come to this make-out party.

Then I opened my mouth, and something very odd happened. What came out was a voice that was not mine. One I'd never heard or used before, deeper and lower in my chest than my regular speaking voice. Assured. Authoritative. Rough around the edges. I pointed at Pasquale. "Ayyy," I said.

I had his full attention.

"Let *me* do it from now on," I ordered him, in that voice. "*You* don't talk to the girls. You have *me* talk to the girls."

He was backing up involuntarily.

"Got it?" I said. In that voice.

Now Pasquale was slowly lowering himself into a chair. I'm not sure he even realized he was. Now he was sitting down. Instead of reading his line, he just nodded. Silently.

Then I was done. That was it. I beamed at the people behind the table, tossed my script in the air, and sauntered out of the room, like the badass I was pretending to be.

Who was I really? That's always been the big question — and it's taken me fifty years to realize that there really is a me inside me. If you'd asked me back then, I would've told you all I knew at the time: Henry Franklin Winkler, formerly of 210 West 78th Street, Apartment 10A, New York, NY. The son of Harry and Ilse, younger brother of Bea. I had a BA in drama with a minor in psychology from Emerson College in Boston, one of the two schools of the twenty-eight I applied to that had accepted me. I'd somehow managed to scrape through four years of Emerson despite the fact that I couldn't really read. I mean that literally. Reading was not then, is not now, and never has been my forte. At Emerson I once wrote a report on a book by the French sociologist Émile Durkheim by looking at the chapter headings in the table of contents and channeling a sense of what he was talking about: I got a B-minus on the paper.

I was a terrible student as far back as I can remember; this was a real problem for my parents. From my earliest days, the only thing I wanted to do was act: now and then my mother and father pretended to indulge me. A charming childhood photograph shows a seven-year-old Henry on the telephone: the joke I made later on was that I was calling my agent. In my senior year at Emerson I applied to the Yale School of Drama, the crème de la crème of drama schools, despite thinking, *Oh my God. How could you possibly do this? It's Yale, you've been told you're stupid; it's Yale — it's not only the crème de la crème of drama schools, but of students from all over the world — how dare you think you can?* But finally I said, "I'm just going to — I'm just gonna try." It was the schizophrenia of: *Are you crazy? How dare you?* But finally — *Shut up and just try it.*

When I do speaking engagements, I say, "You can't catch a fish unless your fly is in the water."

At my Yale audition, when it came to performing the Shakespearean monologue I'd been told to memorize, I suddenly realized it had completely fallen out of my head. So instead I improvised something on the spot, something I thought sounded Shakespeare-ish, and, miracle of miracles, I got in. Into the Yale School of Drama! I mostly played fourteen-year-olds in student productions. (I was short and baby-faced.) But I got the chance to act in plays by Euripides, T. S. Eliot, and Eugene O'Neill. I was in the Greek chorus of *The Bacchae.* By my third year, I'd grown enough to play Albert Einstein in Friedrich Dürrenmatt's *The Physicists,* speaking in my parents' German accent and wearing a curly wig and my father's 1930s shoes, shoes that were so well made they were indestructible. . . .

My father had once dreamed of being a diplomat. Short, authoritative, always elegantly dressed, Harry Winkler spoke eleven languages and could be charming in all of them. He was good with people; I think I inherited that from him. He also demanded that you stand up when he entered the room. (I don't make that demand. Thought about asking my daughter's boyfriends to do it; didn't.) My mother was small, round, and often sad. I would gradually discover what she was sad about. She was also often angry. She was triggered by dust. And I don't mean dust on the floor. If dust floated by, she was off on a rant.

Harry and Ilse Winkler were refugees from Berlin. They managed to get out in 1939, just under the wire, with a subterfuge: my father, an executive in a company that imported and exported lumber, told the authorities that he had to go to the USA for six weeks, on business. He had a letter from two companies in New York wanting to buy the trees owned by the company he worked for, Seidelman. He told the same story to my mother, knowing she would never agree to leave Germany for good if her family couldn't come with her. Her parents and brother stayed behind, as did my father's brother and business partner, Helmut, who'd been just about to go with Harry and Ilse but changed his mind at the last minute. The Nazis murdered him, just as they murdered my mother's and father's whole families and millions of other Jews. I mourned that I never had relatives: my only relatives were faux — members of the German refugee community in New York.

There were a lot of lies in my family; this

13

big one that my father told my mother to get her to the United States was the most benign. Benign as it was, though, my mother never got over it.

Harry, a clever man, had brought the seed money for rebuilding his lumber business in the US by smuggling his mother's jewelry out of Germany. He'd bought a box of chocolates in Berlin, melted the chocolate down, then poured it over the jewelry and put the candy-coated jewels back into the box. When the Nazis stopped him and asked if he was taking anything of value out of Germany, he said, "No, you can open every bag; we've got nothing." After Harry and Ilse passed through Ellis Island, my father pawned the jewelry. It wasn't an easy decision to make, but he was later able to buy all of it back.

Many of the German Jews who stayed behind as World War II began remained in Europe because they felt they were *Germans* above all; their Jewishness came second. The Nazis begged to differ. But my parents, strangers in this strange land of America, in this new city of New York, really were German above all. Like many German Jews, they looked down on . . . well, nearly everyone, but especially all those Eastern European Jews who'd been flocking to America

14

since the 1880s. German Jews, and especially the ones from Berlin, the culture capital of the country, were just better: more cultured, more refined. Yiddish was not spoken in my household — not if Harry and Ilse could help it, anyway. German was spoken, though — it was my parents' life mission to teach me the language. I eventually learned four sentences in German, the only four German sentences I can speak today.

Harry's and Ilse's German was very expressive. Take the colorful nickname they gave me: *dummer Hund.*

It meant *dumb dog.*

I didn't find out I was severely dyslexic until I was thirty-four. For all the years before that, I was the kid who couldn't read, couldn't spell, couldn't even begin to do algebra or geometry or even basic arithmetic. If I bought a slice of pizza with paper money, I had no idea how much change I was supposed to get — nor could I add up the coins in my hand. When we read *A Tale of Two Cities* or *Ivanhoe* in tenth or eleventh grade, the only thing I read was the cover. I would sprinkle water on the book and let it dry, so the crinkled pages would make it look as if I'd been poring over that book — beating it into submission! I never read one classic — the closest I got were the *Classics Illustrated* comic books. (And even those I couldn't read — but at least I understood the pictures.) I consistently brought home report cards filled with Ds and Fs — first from PS 87, just down the block on West 78th, then, after I was twelve, from the private McBurney School. What did my parents make of this? They were embarrassed by it; *they* were diminished by it. Clearly I was just lazy, defiant, stupid — a dumb dog. So the lesson for my life was, when we are born into this world, we are separate beings from our parents, not extensions of who they want us to be. Stacey and I have a wonderful friend who is a pediatric neurosurgeon. He told us that at the beginning of his medical career he was convinced that the influence on a child was 80 percent nurture, 20 percent nature. Now, years and hundreds of patients later, he's convinced that it's 80 percent nature, 20 percent nurture.

I used humor to cover everything I couldn't do — which was most things. One day, in my Hebrew class at Habonim, the German Jewish congregation my family belonged to, the rabbi who taught us was handing out report cards when I made a silly joke. I don't remember exactly what I said, but the other kids thought it was hilarious. The rabbi gave a thin smile. "Let me have that report card back," he told me.

"No, I just got it," I said.

"Let me have it back," the rabbi said, and snatched it from my fingers. And ripped it to shreds.

This was business as usual for me: wandering attention, failing grades, making jokes; humiliation. And business as usual for my parents, who felt humiliated by every bad report card I brought home, and therefore felt the need (I guess) to humiliate me back. They were somehow convinced that the more they punished me, the better my grades would be.

[GERMAN ACCENT] "You are not trying hard enough. You are not concentrating. Stay in your room. You cannot go out on the weekend. You cannot go to the temple dance. No TV.

"Dummer Hund."

One of my father's favorite expressions was *le ton fait la musique* — the tone makes the music. Meaning, it's not so much the words that you say as the way you say them. Which, since he and my mother used to scream at me all the time, tells you a lot about my mother and father.

17

■ ■ ■ ■

Apartment 10A was a big apartment, with a wraparound terrace that had views of the Hudson River. The Winklers lived in fine style. We even had a country house, in Mahopac, New York, on a lake in southern Putnam County. From the beginning, my father's new business had some very good years. He also had some bad years — but he didn't talk about those. He preferred concentrating on his successes, and believing more of them would come.

I wouldn't realize for a long time that between the good years and the bad years, Harry was barely breaking even: we were constantly living beyond our means.

The apartment was big, but my room was small. And I mean *small.* Gray-green plaster walls. A bed that folded up against the wall when you weren't using it, a tiny sink like something you'd see in a train compartment, and a little closet that was probably meant for brooms — it had no depth. You opened the door and the wall was right there. I hung my clothes on a pipe. I didn't have space for a lot of ensembles.

My room was probably meant to be the housekeeper's room if a family had a live-in housekeeper; instead, we had a cleaning lady, Aury, who came in five times a week — fancy shmancy — so the housekeeper's room was all mine. After Aury came Rosalie, a big, wonderful woman. She was my solace. She taught me to dance at a very young age, in the kitchen. A swinging door led from the kitchen to the dining room, where my father sat at the head of the table and you did *not* sit in his chair. On the dining room wall hung a painting of some Flemish creep, whose eyes would move wherever you went in the room, always looking at you.

[GERMAN ACCENT] "Everysing was *severe.*"

My sister, who was four years older, had a real bedroom, with a real, non-folding bed, and drapes on the windows. Maybe it was because she was older; maybe it was because she was a girl; maybe my parents liked her better. I don't know. Now and then she took notice of me; usually she didn't. She used to have her friends over and they would listen to records and whisper together. I was the annoying little brother. Once she asked me to kiss her on the lips: she wanted to practice. Oh, that was horrible. I could just barely manage a peck.

My room was tiny, but it was my refuge.

For my fourteenth birthday I got a tan faux-leather Westinghouse record player with two speakers in front that you could lift off their hinges and pull out as far as the wires went. (Once I had a dance party in the living room; Suzy Rosenbaum was my date. And we listened to Johnny Mathis. Otherwise, the record player lived on top of the shelf above the bed that folded into the wall.) And when my parents were yelling and screaming in German about something and I had no idea why they were angry with me — which was often — I would go in my room, close the door, and listen to arias from opera. Yes, opera. My mother and father, if you can believe it, used to take me to the Metropolitan Opera when I was young. Ten years old, and I had to rent a tuxedo when we went on Monday nights. So when they were screaming at me, I would close the door and listen to arias. Tebaldi. Corelli. It didn't even have to be opera, as long as it was dramatic: *Finlandia*, by Sibelius. I would wave my arms, pretending to conduct. And sooner or later I would stop feeling bad.

Sitting in any class at McBurney School, I would start laughing to myself, because I would fantasize that my parents would move while I was at school, and leave no forwarding address. And I would figure out how to take care of myself.

I felt, when my parents were shrieking at me in German, or in English with their German accents, as though my brain were turning from pink to gray. As if the blood were draining out of it. And when I listened to music, it was like I was getting into an elevator in my brain and going down, down, level by level, like in a department store. And if the music really carried me away, I would reach the lowest level and my brain would turn from gray back to pink. The blood would start to flow, and I could breathe again. At those moments, I made a pact with myself that if I was ever a parent on this earth, I would be a completely different one.

I'm twelve years old, it's a Saturday night, and I'm grounded for the umpteenth time because of my latest report card. My parents are going out to play canasta with their friends. I'm supposed to stay home and do my homework: watching TV is strictly verboten.

I'm not supposed to watch TV, but they do leave me with a Swanson TV dinner. This is a very good thing: Salisbury steak or the turkey with the stuffing and the little apple cobbler with the tinfoil you peel back so it would crisp up in the oven. I put the frozen tray in the oven, and a half hour later I have a delicious dinner — in front of the TV, just the way Swanson meant it to be.

Our TV set is an Olympic television/radio/record player. Big console at the end of the living room. And Saturday night has three important Westerns on Channel 2 — *Wanted: Dead or Alive* at 8:30; *Have Gun, Will Travel* at 9:30; and *Gunsmoke* at 10.

My parents get home at 10:15. (So I never get to finish watching *Gunsmoke*.)

The second I hear the key in the lock, I move like lightning. They find me sitting at the kitchen table, conscientiously pretending to do my homework. The first thing my father does, even before taking off his coat, is put his hand on top of the TV set, to take its temperature. Still warm.

Grounded again.

The M104 bus went up and down Broadway on the Upper West Side; that was the bus I took every weekday morning from 78th Street down to the McBurney School for Boys at 63rd. Every weekday morning I would be on the bus going to McBurney in my gray slacks, blue blazer, and necktie, and if there was an empty seat next to me and someone was about to sit down, I would stop them and say, "Oh, wait a minute, wait a minute" — and then I would have a good discussion with my imaginary horse, George. "Please, George. No, no, no, no. Come on, be a gentleman. Get off . . . thatta boy. Step down. There you go. And yes, ma'am, it's all yours."

Because I was on the bus at pretty much the same time every day, it was usually the same driver — Sam. Once when I was late for my mid-term exams at McBurney, I got on and made an announcement to the entire city bus. I said, "Ladies and gentlemen, ladies and gentlemen. I am the future. And I am late for my midterms. I can't fail. Does anybody have to get off between now and 63rd Street? Can we speed down and get me to my exams on time? Can I see a show of hands?" We took a vote and everybody cheered. Sam complied. And I got there. Now, I flunked my midterms anyway, because I was in the bottom 3 percent in the country academically, but at least I flunked them on time.

I can't remember not feeling an intense need to perform. I recall putting on my sister's muumuu bathrobe, applying some makeup, and popping out into my parents' parties with little dramatic presentations.

I'd announce: "This is written by Henry Winkler, produced by Henry Winkler, and directed by Henry Winkler." Then: "And I'm thanking you as Henry Winkler." They all laughed, then they went back to their drinks and conversation.

Was my need to perform a desperate cry for attention? Did it stem, way back, from never really feeling seen or heard by my parents? Did I not feel seen or heard because I was constantly disappointing them?

Something like that.

I wasn't without friends. Lee Seides lived in my building, on the fourth floor, with his beautiful single mother. I used to take the elevator down and hang out with Lee. We tried making a rope pulley down the airshaft between his apartment and mine so we could send messages back and forth in a milk carton. Gerald Love — I would go over to his place after school; we'd eat cheese and crackers and listen to records: my favorite was Sil Austin, master of the melancholy saxophone. I liked songs that were sad and yearning — mournful, even: they completely matched the way I usually felt inside.

At school, where I was failing at everything, I was always running after the cool kids, trying to get into cliques, always just out of reach of making it. Harvey Joel Meyer; Bill Murphy — cool kids. I would go up to them at the beginning of the school year and say, "I've changed, over the summer. I'm better! I'm so much better!" Thinking about it now, they must have looked at me like I was an alien. *What the hell is he saying? Better than* what?

I was kicked off the swim team when I ate breakfast before practice one morning and vomited in the pool. I played left wing on the soccer team until it was discovered that I completely lacked foot-eye coordination. Sports were not going to make me popular.

Is this making you sad? Me too!

My miserable academic record at McBurney mostly disqualified me from participating in school plays, but I squeaked through twice: once in an eighth-grade production of *Billy Budd* (I played Billy), and then in my junior year, when I starred in the Gershwin musical *Of Thee I Sing* — which was a little ironic, because I couldn't sing. I sort of talked my way through my musical numbers. Like Rex Harrison, only not as good.

The drama teacher's name was Donald Rock. Mr. Rock was very flamboyant, so he was very wonderful. He was the one teacher at McBurney who encouraged me. "Winkler," he used to say, "if you ever do get out of here, you're going to be great." He was *my* rock, and I loved him deeply.

But I barely did get out of there: I failed geometry four times. My first geometry teacher at McBurney was Mr. Sicilian. Michael Sicilian. He was a former college wrestler with a crew cut and no neck — you didn't know where the head ended and the shoulders started. A tough-looking guy, but a kind man: Mr. Sicilian honestly wanted me to do well. He had a college ring with a red stone in it — and I got a permanent indentation in my head from all the times he would rap me with it. "Winkler! It's the Pythagorean theorem, Winkler!" He was warm about it — but it didn't make geometry one iota more comprehensible. Summer school was an annual ritual, from seventh grade to twelfth. Riverdale's summer school in the Adirondacks; Rhodes Prep School on West 54th Street.

Rhodes was when I lost my virginity. Kind of.

This is my senior year: if I don't pass geometry, I can't go to college. And I meet this girl at summer school at Rhodes. I unfortunately do not remember her name. But she invites herself over to my apartment.

We take the bus uptown. I'm looking at all the other people on the bus, thinking, *They have no idea what's about to happen to me.* I have no idea what is about to happen to me. We get off at 78th, walk over to my building, ride the elevator to the tenth floor. My parents are not home. My sister has long since gone away to college and gotten married: I've moved out of my tiny bedroom into hers. I now have floor space, the non-folding bed, the drapes on the windows.

My parents are not home. I am vibrating. And I don't know how to get undressed in front of her. So I go behind the drapes. And now I'm undressing — not so easy, behind the drapes! Meanwhile, she is very comfortable. Undressed, in the bed, smiling. Somehow I realize this is not her first time.

I have a condom.

Like every hopeful teenage boy in America, I have bought a condom and put it in my wallet, just in case. It's been sitting there for years, waiting patiently. And now Just in Case has actually arrived. And somehow, over the months and years since I bought the condom, the lubricant has leaked out, and the little envelope it's in is stuck in the compartment in my wallet where I kept it.

I finally manage to extricate the condom, and I take it out and put it on. And I am so

27

excited that I'm still a virgin when it's over, because I have never actually entered her body.

Did not know what my responsibility was. Did not know I could make her feel good. I didn't really understand any of it. I was locked inside myself, a victim of emotional dyslexia.

I passed geometry with a D-minus. I wish I could say the same for my virginity.

A word on shoes.

For the first twelve years of my life, I had to go around in heavy brown shoes with round toes and thick rubber soles that would never wear out — the cousins of my father's indestructible German footwear. You can imagine how much I loved that. And so my first pair of loafers, in eighth grade, was a very big deal, until I went to Riverdale summer school in the Adirondacks, where I stepped in mud and pulled my foot out without my shoe, and that was the end of my first pair of loafers.

My second pair was also a big deal. I was in my freshman year at Emerson, the year was 1963, and Bass Weejuns penny loafers were *the* shoe. People wore them forever; if they wore a hole in them, they'd tape it up with duct tape — it was a whole cult of Bass

Weejuns.

They were *the* cool shoe, but I didn't realize before buying them how painful it was to break them in. They didn't give, these shoes. I didn't know whether wearing them to break them in was even worth it — they should've paid *me* to wear that shoe.

Anyway, I'm wearing my painful new shoes and walking up the steps to Brooks Brothers in Back Bay Boston, just a couple of blocks from school. And I suddenly became 360-degree aware that I existed. It was like cellophane had all at once peeled back from my brain, and I was completely aware of being.

It was a bigger thought than any I'd ever had — or any I've had since, in whatever analysis I've ever gone through.

I paused on the steps for a second.

And the moment I began to explore the thought — *poof* — the feeling was gone. The cellophane came back, and I was just a human being walking around moving air on the earth.

I've given that moment a lot of thought since. They say that we're created in God's image, but we only use 10 percent of our brainpower. Maybe God is 100 percent of our brainpower. Maybe those people who are geniuses are just the ones who use more than 10 percent. I don't know. All I know is that the memory of that total awareness has stayed with me for a long time — and I've been looking for it ever since.

My father *really* wanted me to take over his business. So in the summer of 1966, between my junior and senior years at Emerson, he sent me to Germany, to work at a lumber mill. I did not want to take over his business. I did not want to go to Germany to work at a lumber mill. But that was the edict from Harry.

The town was Wiedenbrück, a picturesque village on the Ems River in the north. I lived at a small hotel in town; I became really close to the family who ran the hotel. I even met a German girl. And I worked at the mill.

I was an apprentice to *der Sägemeister,* the saw-master. I helped with putting these huge logs on the saw bed, slicing thin slices to make furniture veneer, changing the blade every three logs. Loud. Scary. Dangerous. I stood knee-deep in sawdust, which it was my job to clean up every day after the Meister went home. But the worst part was the Meister himself. I grew a beard that summer. And the Meister of the machine said to me, "Oh, you look like an old Jew."

"I am one," I said. That ended that conversation.

Needless to say, I was not cut out for the lumber business.

Back at Emerson, I was kicked out of acting class for not being able to memorize lines. My cognitive challenge would also get me in trouble at Yale. One of my teachers there was the great Bobby Lewis: cofounder of the Actors Studio, famed Hollywood character actor, legendary Broadway director, mentor to Marlon Brando and Montgomery Clift. And one day I made Bobby Lewis cry.

And not in a good way.

Bobby had an exercise. We each had to pick a figure in a painting, pose like the figure, then step out of the pose and create the person's character. The painting I picked was a famous one by Eugène Delacroix, *Liberty Leading the People,* commemorating the Second French Revolution of 1830. In the picture, a bare-breasted Liberty, holding a French flag high with her right hand and a carrying a rifle in her left, leads the revolutionaries through the smoke of battle, bodies lying at her feet. Next to her is a young boy with a pouch slung over his shoulder and a pistol in each hand. I chose to play a mash-up of Lady Liberty

31

and the boy, with a pouch over my shoulder, a gun in one hand, and a broomstick with a dish towel attached to it (that was supposed to be the flag) in the other.

I'd borrowed a toy rifle from the Repertory Theatre for the exercise. I'd hung a poster of the painting on the wall for reference. And as I struck the pose, I raised the flag with my left hand while I held the gun with my right.

"Is there any reason you're doing the pose completely backward?" Bobby asked.

"No!" I said, as I realized my error. Naturally, being totally dyslexic, I'd had absolutely no idea that I was doing it backward. Like lightning, I switched the flag to my right hand, the rifle to my left, and raised the flag high once again.

The class, some twenty-five kids, giggled.

And Bobby Lewis thought I was making fun of him.

He sputtered. "You take no care?" he said. "You just, you just make a mockery of my life's work?" His eyes glistening with tears, he ran out of the room.

I looked around. "Anybody?" I said. "Could anybody help here? Because I think I'm going to die. Nobody? Okay, fine."

My reputation may have preceded me when the great Stella Adler came to teach a class at Yale. Stella, of course, was also legendary — she had studied with Stanislavski himself! She was probably in her early seventies when she came to New Haven, and every inch the *grande dame* of theater. She once bragged to us that she poked her husband, the great theater director Harold Clurman, in the ribs while he was asleep, and said, "Stop sleeping like an important man!"

In Stella's exercise, you were supposed to get up and walk through a garden in your imagination, all the while describing what you were seeing.

My turn came. I got up, pushed open the imaginary white picket gate, and said, "And here —"

"Sit down! You see nothing!" said the great Stella Adler.

"Bluebells! I see bluebells!"

"You don't see anything!"

But I couldn't stop pleading my case. "Hey — the tulips over here, they're variegated!"

"*Down*, Winkler."

That threw me into a terrorized tizzy. I was sure I was going to be thrown out of school for going up against Stella Adler. And I was beginning to realize how much I hated not being seen or heard, especially

33

when I knew what I was talking about. I really *was* seeing bluebells and tulips; the tulips really were yellow and red! How did she know I wasn't seeing what I really was seeing? Even though she was the great Stella Adler?

My dating career, at Emerson and then Yale, was *not* stellar. In my sophomore year at college, I was madly in love with a girl named Susan Salter — she was a freshman and I was a sophomore. I used to leave class early so I could stand outside the class she was in and stare at her through the small square window in the door, just stand there and wait for the bell to ring. I used to write her letters every day — a hundred and fifty letters before spring break. I was like the guy in the cartoon, sitting in a pile of crumpled paper up to his knees, because I couldn't spell. And my penmanship was terrible; I had to cross out one word, then another, then throw away the paper, trying desperately to express the depth of my emotion, never feeling that I had gotten the phrase right.

Then it turned out that she had a boyfriend at BU. My song that year was "You've Lost That Lovin' Feelin' " by the Righteous Brothers.

At Yale I was living with five other people in a house by the beach on the Long Island Sound. One was a nurse, two were young lawyers, another was a psych student, one was an architect. A young lady I was dating came up to New Haven on the train. We drove to the house on the beach, very romantic. And after she'd been there for around an hour and a half, she said, "I have to leave. I can't be here for one more minute."

I asked her why.

"The way you are, it's horrible," she said.

What way was I? I had no idea what she was talking about. Which, of course, was at least half of the problem.

Around the same time, I went to a party and saw another girl. She was a dancer. And she was walking around on the furniture. I mean, from the chest of drawers to another chest of drawers to the desk, and I'm staring at her — oh my God, that face; those *legs* — and I can't breathe.

This was Lula. Of Alabama.

We start dating. She's in her senior year of college in Virginia, and I drive down to see her. When I come back, I write her letters every day, the same as I did with Susan Salter. Now she graduates, and starts teaching dance at a college in upstate New York.

Seven hours away. She drives down to see me. Whoa.

Then she's back in Alabama for the summer, and I go down there to visit her, at her parents' home. And I am a Northerner. And an actor. And a Jew. I remember her mother said to me, talking about Black people, "Oh, God bless that race, they got all the rhythm."

She didn't get around to telling me her feelings about Jewish people.

Then Lula wanted to make love to me while her parents were upstairs. Under the dining room table.

Oh my God.

Turned out this Northern Jew actor had zero sense of sexual adventure. And that was the beginning of the end for me and Lula.

Memorizing lines was supremely difficult, but not impossible if I read them over and over. And over and over again. It always helped a lot if the thing I was trying to memorize was well written. So I got my MFA in 1970, but more than that, I was one of only three people from my graduating class of eleven invited to join the Yale Repertory Theatre company.

Did this imbue me with ringing confidence? It did not. On June 30 of that year I began my professional acting career, earning $173 a week doing Story Theatre in East Hampton, appearing throughout the 1970–71 season in plays by Brecht, Shakespeare, and Terrence McNally.

Story Theatre was the creation of Paul Sills, one of the cofounders of the Second City, the great improvisational troupe in Chicago. It was akin to the "poor theater" of the Polish theater director Jerzy Grotowski: there's only a suggestion of scenery — the same set can be used for whatever the play happens to be — and there are no props at all; we would just pull them out of the air. If I needed a bow and arrow, I would create one using mime; when it was no longer needed, it vanished back into the air, and a paddle to take a trip down the river in a canoe would appear. It was so much fun, so exhilarating.

Carmen de Lavallade, the prima ballerina for the Alvin Ailey dance company before Judith Jamison, was part of the troupe that summer. I was in awe of her. We played one scene together where we both had to play a deer — I said to Carmen, "You are a prima ballerina; how could I possibly be a deer alongside you?"

She said, "Each of us is our own being, in

37

our own body — you will be a different kind of deer."

That unlocked a way of thinking that had never occurred to me and became one of my watchwords: *a different kind of deer.*

Cliff Robertson, a big-deal movie actor at the time, saw me perform in East Hampton and asked me to be in a Western he was about to star in, *The Great Northfield Minnesota Raid.* With real regret, I told Cliff that since there were no understudies in the Repertory Theatre, I couldn't just leave — especially after feeling so honored by being selected.

That really would have been a different life.

There was a Yale teacher who was part of the professional company: Betsy was her name. And one day during a rehearsal I was kidding around, doing shtick, being cute, making the rest of the company laugh — I was good at that. And Betsy turned to me with a frown and said, "If you don't stop joking around, I'm going to punch your teeth out."

It got my attention. And taught me a big lesson. Laughs were all well and good, but the work was always to be taken seriously.

In the fall of 1971 I was invited to be in the

cast of *Moonchildren,* a new and exciting play by Michael Weller to be produced at Washington, DC's Arena Stage. While I was in DC, an old friend from Emerson, Ceci Hart, invited me over for dinner — it was lovely to have a home-cooked meal while I was far from home. Ceci later married James Earl Jones, who became a family friend.

Moonchildren had a great cast, full of people who would become famous: Jill Eikenberry. Jimmy Woods. Ed Herrmann. Christopher Guest. The director was the semilegendary Alan Schneider. I wasn't fully baked yet as an actor, but I was finding my way. One day after three weeks of rehearsal, I went to Schneider and said, "I've solved the monologue in the third act." And he said, "You're fired."

At that moment, my brain became cream cheese. As if I were underwater, I said, "What?"

He said, "You're fired."

I put my snow tires back in my car. I said goodbye to the cast. They were all sad, or seemingly sad, to see me go. And I drove back to New York thinking, *I will never be hired again. My career is over at the beginning. Who's going to hire an actor who's been fired? I'm dead in the water.* I didn't know

39

what to do. Weeping up the turnpike, between Washington and New York. Oh my God. It turned out that Kevin Conway, the actor Alan Schneider really wanted for my role, was in a movie, and Schneider had hired me as a space filler. You know, like the seat fillers at the Emmys or the Oscars. When the star has to go to the bathroom, the seat filler fills in until the star comes back, so there won't be empty seats on camera. The minute Kevin Conway became available, I was toast.

What a shitty thing for Alan Schneider to do, you say? Well, Schneider wasn't just legendarily brilliant; he was also a legendary prick. I later found out that there were actors who put a clause in their contract if they were in a play: if the director was let go and Alan Schneider was hired, they could leave the play.

I dusted myself off and somehow got back on my feet. Back in New York, I sublet an apartment from the actor Lewis Stadlen at 72nd Street and West End Avenue — a bedroom, a living room, a little eating area, and a kitchen; $174 a month — and through Margie Castleman, a beautiful dancer I'd recently started dating, I got an agent, Joan Scott. Joan handled movies and theatrical. But another agent, Deborah Brown, began sending me on auditions for, of all things, TV commercials.

I auditioned the same way I'd tried out for Yale: winging it. A few people were annoyed that I wasn't saying the words that were on the page — "Excuse me, that's not what we wrote." I'd say, "I'm giving you the essence." Some were put off, but more of them were charmed.

I got really good at auditioning for commercials. And I started getting work! Sometimes I'd get two jobs a week. American Airlines! Sanka coffee! Talon zippers! It wasn't Shakespeare. For the Talon spot I was supposed to be an English gentleman wearing an ascot, sitting in a leather chair in his library — except that I was headless. This was somehow supposed to demonstrate that Talon zippers were invisible. I had to be fitted with a foam-rubber suit that covered almost my entire body; I could just barely see through the mesh in the costume's head. And once I was suited up, the producer on the shoot was so disrespectful and mean to me that — now that I *really* wasn't being seen or heard — steam began to come out of my ears. It was like some nightmare version of getting yelled at by Harry and Ilse.

Afterward, the prop person said, "Man, I

could *feel* your rage coming right through that rubber suit."

I'd stayed in touch with some people from Yale, and when they heard I was acting in commercials, they were scandalized. "We were trained for the *theater,*" they said. "What are you *doing,* doing *commercials?*" they said. And then their next question was, "How do you get them?"

I have to admit that I wasn't immune to guilt. In the eyes of Yale, I was prostituting my art. Still, I was making money, and that felt good. And my earnings allowed me to do plays for free for the Manhattan Theatre Club or the St. Clement's Church theater space, which also made me feel good.

I was also working on an improv show, *Off the Wall,* with four other people: Marc Flanagan, a friend from Yale; a couple, Mark and JoAnne Lonow; and a woman named Nikki Flax. In the evenings we would put together the show at Mark and JoAnne's apartment in Greenwich Village while their nine-year-old daughter, Claudia — who later became a successful actress, comedian, and producer — was instructed to remain in her bedroom. During the day I'd shoot commercials or go around to the various advertising agencies looking for work. And one day while I was making my rounds, I heard about a possible part in a small independent movie. I called my agent, and she got me in — the script was called *The Lords of Flatbush.* The setting was Brooklyn in the fifties; the protagonists were four leather-jacketed guys who were more interested in making it with girls than rumbling with other gangs. The part I was to read for was Butchey Weinstein, who pretended to be a tough greaser to cover up his true poetic nature. I went to meet with the director, Marty Davidson. He had three other actors — Sylvester Stallone, a couple of years before *Rocky* made him a superstar; a handsome guy named Perry King, who would also go on in TV and movies; and playing Sly's sidekick, Paul Mace.

I auditioned for Marty, jumping all over his couch with my freewheeling improvisation. Apparently I made a good impression: I got the part. A thousand dollars for eight weeks' work, but it was a movie! (I later heard I was replacing a soon-to-be-famous actor who'd been fired for not getting along with Stallone; it was the only time my career ever intersected with Richard Gere's.)

Suddenly I was shooting this picture every day from six in the morning to five in the evening, then going over to Mark and JoAnne's to work on the improv show from six to eleven. It sounds exhausting to me now, but I was young and filled with energy, excited about everything I was doing.

Not long after *The Lords of Flatbush* wrapped, I got a call about another independent film. The director was an Italian named Carlo Lizzani; the movie, *Crazy Joe,* was about the recently deceased real-life gangster Joe Gallo. It was a very short meeting: I shook Lizzani's hand and began to sit down; he said "Thank you" before my ass hit the chair. So that was that. But a week later I got a call: "Would you like to join the production as Mannie, the driver for Joe Gallo, and come in tomorrow for a costume fitting?"

Without saying a word, I hung up. I was sure someone was playing a joke on me: how could I possibly have gotten this job without even auditioning?

Then the phone rang again: same voice. "Do you want five hundred dollars a week?"

Apparently it was not a joke.

I was making money! I was making movies!

Sometime that year Joan Scott went to Los Angeles to open an office there, and I had a career talk with John Kimball, the agent now running her New York office. John was glad for my success, but he had a different idea. "If you want to be known to New York, stay here," he told me. "If you want to be known to the world, go to California."

2.

I'm a world-class agonizer, so I did what I was good at: I agonized. *Should I go? Could I — should I go to California? Oh, I can't go to California.* All the doubts swirling in my mind were about what I wasn't. I'm *not* tall. I don't *look* like a movie star.

But finally, as always happened (and still happens) when I spin my mental wheels like that: I got so fed up and bored with myself that I said to myself, *Just shut up and jump off the fucking precipice and FLY.*

I mean, you can talk yourself out of ANY-THING.

What are you doing? *Go. Just go.*

I'd saved a little over $1,000 from my TV-commercial earnings, and while it wasn't burning a hole in my pocket — I am naturally, shall we say, careful about money — my inner voice told me: *You have saved this money for a reason.*

And so, though I didn't know what was

going to happen — I hadn't even booked a hotel room — I bought a ticket to Los Angeles on American Airlines. Round-trip, just in case I failed — and there was a big part of me that was quite sure I'd be flying back home soon. I figured the thousand that was left after airfare would support me for about a month until I got acting work. This was the plan, such as it was.

On September 18, 1973, 10 a.m., I got on an American Airlines plane at Kennedy Airport and flew to Los Angeles. My *Lords of Flatbush* costar Perry King was traveling with me — Perry was also going out to try his luck in LA. Perry, I couldn't help thinking over and over, was everything I wasn't. *Was* tall. *Was* handsome. *Looked* like a movie star. (And Perry did — quickly — start to get TV and movie work soon after he arrived.)

Me, I got my two suitcases off the baggage carousel and took a taxi straight to Joan Scott's office. Marched in with my bags in my hand.

Joan, a friendly but no-nonsense lady, looked at me over her horn-rimmed glasses. "Don't you want to get a place to live first?" she asked.

I just stared at her for a moment. It's strange to look back through the lens of who

I am today, the me who started to be rescued by psychotherapy seven years ago, but the me of 1973 had absolutely no idea what Joan Scott was talking about. My epiphany in Bass Weejuns, my revelation on the steps to the Boston Brooks Brothers, was now years in the past. My sense of existing as a human being, with day-to-day concerns like other human beings, was virtually nonexistent. I could only think about one thing: hadn't I come all this way (and spent all that money) to find acting work?

"Maybe I should go out on an audition or two first," I said.

"Well, you know what?" Joan said. "I have to tell you, Henry, I didn't really agree with this decision. It's going to be hard to sell you here."

What she meant: LA was not New York. Which I totally knew before taking my cross-country leap of faith. Suddenly all the doubts I'd agonized over before coming out here popped back into my head, bigger and bolder than ever. This was a three-thousand-mile, thousand-dollar mistake I'd made. I just stood there as though somebody had smacked my face with a trout.

"Should I go back?" I asked her.

"I'd get a place to live before you make

any big decisions," Joan said.

I had literally given zero thought to where I was going to lay my head that night. But then I remembered: a girl I'd gone to Emerson with, Stephanie Axelrod, was in LA, working as the assistant to a studio executive's assistant, trying to move up the show-business ladder like so many others who'd moved to Hollywood. Stephanie had once said to me, "If you're ever in Los Angeles, you're welcome to crash at my place." It wasn't a romantic thing, just friendly. So I sat down in Joan's office and phoned Stephanie.

She sounded a little surprised to hear from me: maybe her offer had just been party talk? But now I asked her, "Would it be okay if I bunked at your place for a few days while I go out on auditions?" "Sure," she said. In retrospect I can hear the note of reluctance in her voice; back then, all I could hear was her yes. I picked up my bags and took a cab over to Stephanie's. "Henry!" she said, when she opened her apartment door. Was she a little horrified at the sight of me and my luggage? Probably! She had a studio apartment on Larrabee Street, a few blocks south of Sunset — a living room/bedroom with a little kitchen alcove and a bathroom separated from the living area by a tiny hallway with a door at either end. I could sleep in the little hallway, Stephanie said. Her boyfriend would be home in a couple of hours.

Stephanie's boyfriend's name was Francis Feehan — Francis X. Feehan. It turned out that Francis was a publicist, and a nice guy. How nice? He very kindly told me that I was welcome to make work phone calls from his office, which was just two or three blocks away. So for my first days in LA, I commuted by foot from Stephanie's place to Francis's office and sat on a couch next to a coffee table with a phone on it, making calls to everyone I knew in town — which was very few people. Mostly I called Joan's office to see if she had any auditions for me yet. She didn't. I left my work number (aka Francis's office) with Joan's assistant and hoped for the best. It was a little strange sitting in Francis's busy office without much to do. Sometimes I would pick up the phone and pretend to make calls — just like the seven-year-old in that picture I told you about. I was pinned to that couch: couldn't leave it during working hours — what if a call came in for me while I was gone?

Dinnertime at Stephanie's was the three of us sitting at the counter of her little kitchen alcove, making conversation that, I now see, was more than a little awkward. After a while I got sleepy and took the cushions from the couch into my cubicle and closed the door.

There were a couple of nights like this, the smiles at dinnertime getting more and more forced — and me not noticing. Then one night, a little too soon after I'd gone to bed, I left my little hallway to get a soda from the refrigerator and there were Stephanie and Francis X. Feehan. . . . Need I say more?

I closed the door very quickly. And left promptly the next morning.

That very night, as it happened, Joan Scott had a little get-together at her office, some of her clients and wine and cheese, and I met another actor named Charles Haid. Charlie was a graduate of Carnegie Mellon's drama school, Yale's rival. He was rough-around-the-edges looking, but super nice; he would become well-known in the eighties as Officer Andy Renko on the hit series *Hill Street Blues.* In the fall of 1973, he was just like me, another actor looking for work — though he'd already gotten a couple of TV jobs. Back then, the world of filmed entertainment was divided sharply between movies and television, the big screen and the small screen, and movie roles

were a lot harder to get than TV parts —
but TV parts were no piece of cake, either.
There were just the three networks, and a
couple dozen series, and all the struggling
young actors in town were looking for any
television work they could get. Charlie was
living at the Sunset Marquis, he told me,
with his actress wife Penny Windust, their
baby girl, Arcadia, and a golden Lab. It was
a cool place, he said — all the rock musi-
cians stayed there when they were playing
in town; lots of actors, too. "You could bunk
on my couch if you want," Charlie told me.
More party talk? How would I know? My
two big suitcases and I arrived at his place
that afternoon. Between Francis Feehan's
office and Charlie Haid's suite at the Sunset
Marquis, couches played a very big part in
my early days in Hollywood.

You may have noticed that I've now been in
Los Angeles for three days and I haven't
spent a dime on lodging. Something inside
me was pleased about this. I said that I was
careful about money: that's putting it very
mildly. From an early age I was obsessed
with not spending one cent more than I had
to. That old saying "penny wise, pound fool-
ish" could've been written specifically about
me.

Where did my frugality come from?

I mentioned that my family had a country house in upstate New York. It wasn't just any country house. It was a beautiful place, on three and a half acres right on Lake Mahopac. One of my earliest memories is stepping off the terrace and falling into the lake — tumbling down, down, deep beneath the surface, to the muddy bottom. One of my parents' friends, a distant Hungarian relative named Viggo (there was a whole colony of expatriate European Jews around the lake who Harry and Ilse socialized with), jumped in and rescued me.

I wonder if my father ever felt like that, sinking deep underwater. We had this beautiful country house and the big apartment in the city, full of heavy furniture. We had a Cadillac, after a long line of Packards. We went on cruises and trips to Europe. Only the best was good enough for Harry. How did we afford all this? I honestly don't know — besides "Could you please pass the mashed potatoes?" I asked as few questions as possible. But another memory I have — I must've been ten or so — is of overhearing my father on the phone in the living room, talking to a family friend, Carl Stohl, and begging him to lend him money. I knew it was Carl; I could hear both ends of the conversation. And my father — who was always dressed to the nines, who demanded we stand up when he entered the room, who had to sit at the head of the table — was weeping.

"Please, Carl," he was saying.

"I can't keep doing this, Harry," Stohl was saying.

One day when I was fifteen, in the upstairs hallway of the Mahopac house, outside my parents' bedroom, my father told me he needed my bar mitzvah money.

I'd put the money — about $375 and some savings bonds — into a bank account. "Okay," I said. "I can lend it to you. When will you pay me back?"

He stood up straight and gave me his most commanding stare. "I am your father," he said. "I have given you everything. I don't pay you back."

So — I was careful about money. And then some.

Not long after I graduated from Yale School of Drama, I was acting in a play for the Manhattan Theatre Club, *The Marriage,* by Witold Gombrowicz. I was doing the play for free, as my work in commercials allowed me to do. The other actors in the play had their headshots displayed in the lobby; I did not. My castmates said, "You have to put your picture out front, so when agents come to see the show, they'll know who you are."

"If they really like what I did, they'll find me," I said.

I was too poor — in my mind, anyway — to have a headshot made. Amazing that anyone ever hired me.

I'm not sure if Francis X. Feehan felt uncomfortable when I showed up again at his office, but he sure looked relieved when I told him I'd found another place to stay. And miracle of miracles, as I settled down on the couch, getting ready to pretend to look busy, the phone on the coffee table rang. I stared at it in disbelief for a couple of seconds, then picked it up.

It was Joan Scott's assistant. And amazingly, the assistant told me Joan had found me an audition. Even more unbelievably, it was for *The Mary Tyler Moore Show.* The part wasn't much more than a walk-on, the assistant said, but even that was a big deal, the assistant said, because *Mary Tyler Moore* was a big show. More than that. It was a powerhouse, one of the top ten highest-rated shows on TV.

All that, and I'd been in town for under a week. This was my chance to show Joan she was wrong about me, I thought.

The next morning I took a cab to the *Mary Tyler Moore* offices, in the CBS Broadcast Center in Studio City. A twenty-minute taxi ride, fifteen bucks — real money for me in the fall of 1973. And I was going to have to spend another fifteen to get back to the Sunset Marquis. I was saving money on lodging, but I couldn't keep taking cabs everywhere: my thousand dollars in American Express traveler's checks was starting to dwindle. What if I ran out of money altogether? I tried not to think about it.

I walked into the *Mary Tyler Moore* office — busy, bright, efficient; doing very well without me, thank you — and after pretending to read a magazine for a couple of minutes was shown in to meet one of the show's producers, Ed Weinberger. Ed was a menschy-looking young guy with long curly hair, and sad, kind eyes. "Okay, here's the part," he told me. "I don't have anything written yet. Mary's having a dinner party for a congresswoman — six people, and Mary's parties always go wrong. So one of the things that goes wrong at this one is that Rhoda brings you as an inconvenient surprise. You're Steve Waldman, one of her coworkers, and you've just been fired, so she feels sorry for you. But there's no room for you at the table, so she sits you by

56

yourself at a little table up by the front door."

I can see the whole thing right away — Weinberger is such a good writer that he's creating this gleaming, glowing little world, right there as I sit with him. But also, remember, I'd been doing improv with my friends in New York. So as Ed is describing the scene, I see a glass full of pencils on his desk. I pick up the glass, dump the pencils out, pick up one of the pencils, and tap it on the side of the glass — *ting, ting.*

"Excuse me," I say, as Steve Waldman. "Excuse me. Don't bother yourself, when you get a moment, could you please pass the salt?"

Ed Weinberger is smiling.

By the time I got back to the Sunset Marquis, I had the part. My first part in Hollywood.

Episode 10 of Season 4 of *The Mary Tyler Moore Show* rehearsed throughout the following week and shot on Friday night in front of a live studio audience. It wasn't my first rodeo — back in New York, I'd done an under-five (fewer than five lines) on the soap opera *Another World* — but it might as well have been. *Mary Tyler Moore* was top-of-the-line big TV business: everything about it was smoothly run, completely professional. And it was a funny thing: I felt both completely comfortable and like the rawest, tenderest newbie.

I was comfortable because I loved working in ensembles, the way I had at Yale and in theater afterward, and not only was this a great ensemble, but everybody in the cast and crew couldn't have been nicer. Mary herself was the leader of the set, but also warm and welcoming, and I fell in love with Ed Asner at first sight — he was the gruff, hug-you-around-the-shoulder father I wished I'd had. Betty White was bawdy, hilarious, and so kind. The show was run and written by two of the best, Allan Burns and Jim Brooks. The director, the multi–Emmy Award–winning Jay Sandrich, was totally encouraging — so much so that over the course of rehearsals, I felt confident enough to throw in a few ad libs, and when Jay and everybody else laughed, my extra lines stayed in the show. By the time we shot on Friday, my four lines had turned into eight.

But the insecure little boy in me also learned a valuable lesson during that week. After the first morning of rehearsals, which went very well, we broke for lunch — and suddenly, just at the moment when I needed all my new friends to pat me on the back, they vanished just like that. Suddenly I'm standing all by myself in the middle of the soundstage, with no idea what to do or where to go. I felt completely abandoned.

Now, nobody on that set had abandoned me: they'd all just gone about their business — scooted off to the commissary for lunch, or jumped on the phone to their agents. They were pros, acting like pros. And I was a big boy: I could have asked where the commissary was; eventually I did. But I made a vow then and there that this would never happen to another actor I was on a set with. Nobody I worked with would ever have to feel as alone as I did.

The shoot on Friday night went beautifully. Whatever nerves I had began to dissolve the moment I made my entrance onto the set — wearing a big smile, hair down to my shoulders, and my own tan suit — and said hello to Mary, who looked bewildered as she greeted me, then immediately pulled Rhoda aside and asked her why she'd brought me. Then came a knock on the apartment door, which I opened to admit Lou Grant (Ed Asner) and Murray Slaughter (Gavin MacLeod). I introduced myself ("Hi, I'm Steve Waldman"), and then, when

Lou asked how I was, said, "Oh, fine, fine — I just got fired."

Big laugh. Nerves: gone.

"You gotta have a car," Charlie Haid told me. "You can't not have a car in LA."

"I can't afford to buy a car," I said. "I only have nine hundred and forty-seven dollars."

"You don't have to buy a car — you can rent one."

"Isn't that expensive?"

"Not as expensive as taking cabs."

Not possessing an inner calculator, I had to hope he was right. Charlie took me to a car-rental place right next to Tower Records, the amazing store on Sunset that was then in full bloom, stacked with records from all over the world. The car-rental place had a lot full of used cars, and I saw one that — I thought — wouldn't make me look like a dork: a green 1970 Capri, a sporty fastback. All mine for $39.95 a week, and gas was on me. I peeled off another traveler's check, and I had wheels.

And within two days, another audition.

This was very nice, I thought. This must be the way things worked in Hollywood, I thought — you show up in town and (whatever Joan Scott had said) you get an audition, and then more auditions come your way.

What I didn't know was the way things really worked in Hollywood. The way things really worked (and still work) in Hollywood was all about connections and luck: in my case, an amazing piece of luck — my meeting with Ed Weinberger, quickly followed by my *Mary Tyler Moore* job — had led to a very important connection. The night after the *Mary Tyler Moore* taping, the show's casting director, Marsha Kleinman, had gone to a party. And at the party, Marsha had told someone how cute I was, and what a good job I'd done with my little walk-on. And that someone had told Millie Gussie, Paramount's casting director, about me, with the result that I got called to read for this new series, *Happy Days*.

Here's the amazing thing I said to Joan Scott when she told me about the audition. "I don't know," I told her. "I don't think I want to do a series."

"You what?" Joan said.

"I'm just not sure I want to get involved in a series," I said. What I wasn't telling her was that — with my commercials and soap opera walk-on in New York still fresh in mind — I was still under the weight of guilt from the Yale School of Drama. *Real* actors, I thought, didn't lower themselves to such things.

"Henry," Joan said, "let me tell you something, my dear. You've been in Los Angeles for less than a week. You've already gotten one big job, and you're being asked to try out for another. Other young actors would kill to have the kind of good fortune you're having."

"Oh, all right," I said.

If looks could kill, the look she gave me would have dropped me on the spot.

I prepared for my big audition, not only by memorizing the six script lines I'd been sent, but also by putting some dramatic photographs of me playing various roles at Yale in a brown paper Ralphs grocery bag. Why a grocery bag? Well, I was too frugal to buy the kind of leather portfolio actors carry their headshots in — not to mention too parsimonious to get a headshot. In my mind, it was very probable that I'd be flying back east when my money ran out, and shelling out for a pricey portfolio would only hasten that day. But what I would learn over time was that my Ralphs bag was a good conversation starter, and getting any kind of conversation going at an audition was a good thing. In later years I would tell young actors, "Get them talking. Pick something in their office that you like and ask them about it. Because we actors talk so much about ourselves, they'll remember you if you get them started on a conversation. Do they have a souvenir baseball? Maybe then they'll get to say, 'I got it when my daughter and I went to a Dodgers game and I caught a fly ball.' " So that's a tip I give to young actors. To young directors I say, "Comfortable shoes!"

And so I found myself strolling into a waiting room at Paramount Studios, brown paper Ralphs bag in hand, and seeing an amazing sight: sixty or seventy very hand-some young guys, a good number of whom I recognized from TV, all waiting to audition for this same role. For a minute, I was so incredulous that I walked around the room looking at them. "Hi, how are you?" I said. "Hello. You look very famous, even sitting down."

Then I finally walked to the far wall of the room and leaned against it. *Well, this is a joke,* I thought. *A lark. Here are all these guys — most of them taller than me, too — and here's me. The short Jew from New York.* The sheer impossibility of it liberated me — made me feel that once my name was called, I could waltz in and do anything at all. (Of course, this didn't stop those rivers of sweat from starting to flow under my arms.) The improbability of the whole thing gave me the nerve, I think, to find that voice deep inside me that I hadn't known existed — and the nerve, when I was done reading, to toss those pages in the air and strut out of the room.

Nothing in me was expecting anything to come of it.

Then I got a callback.

I returned to Paramount a week later, on a Wednesday morning — by now it was the middle of October; my month was almost up. I was shown into a wardrobe room, where a wardrobe lady looked me up and down, then handed me a pair of jeans, a white T-shirt, and a gray MacGregor golf jacket. I changed, and was then taken to a room with lighted mirrors, where the makeup artist — Bruce Hutchinson was his name — sat me down, looked at my uni-brow, and said, "This is going to hurt."

Boy, he wasn't kidding.

Bruce plucked every last follicle between my eyebrows, then he trimmed my mane and combed my hair into a ducktail, using at least a full can of hairspray. We both looked in the mirror at his handiwork.

"Beautiful," he said. "Knock 'em dead, kid."

Same script pages, same room. But this time there were only three people: Barry Diller, who was head of development for ABC (Paramount was going to produce *Happy Days* for the network), his second-in-command Michael Eisner, and Garry Marshall. I read the same lines in that same voice for the second audition, and again felt the voice's power. Garry grinned that beautiful Chiclet-y grin of his all the way through. Diller and Eisner, though, were stone-faced.

Afterward, I was walking down the street on the Paramount lot when Diller and Eisner drove by in a fancy Jaguar convertible, heading back to their office in Century City. They slowed down for a second, nodded to me, then drove off. I wondered for a while what that was all about. Michael later told me that Barry had said, "Should we give the kid a ride?" Then they looked at each other, said, "Nah," and sped away.

Garry later told me that the two network executives were not convinced about me after the audition — but he said, "Trust me. This kid is good. I'm going to use him." Garry, after all, had invented the show, and the Fonz was like any number of streetwise kids he'd grown up with in the Bronx. Garry's father had changed the family name to Marshall from Masciarelli — which wasn't so far from Fonzarelli. Garry knew this character, and something I'd brought to the audition had touched a chord.

And so it was that on October 30, 1973, my twenty-eighth birthday, I got the phone call from Tom Miller: "Would you like to play this part?"

I said yes, I would. I would like that very much — if I could show the emotional side of the character. When the Fonz is home and takes off his jacket, who does he have to be cool for?

Tom agreed. And I had the job.

When it came to living, I was usually a nervous wreck. But I always had the strength to stand up for my work.

I said that I got the phone call. I should elaborate. Staying on Charlie Haid's couch at the Sunset Marquis, I had no actual way of receiving telephone calls. But there was a desk clerk at the hotel who felt sorry for me and took messages for me. If he's reading this now, thank you! And about an hour after the big call, I got another message: my mother had phoned.

I phoned her back.

66

She was calling, not to wish me a happy birthday — had she forgotten? — but to tell me she and my father were going to go on a trip to Europe, and I must go with them, because they didn't know how long they were going to be around. As in, alive. "We're taking you, your sister, and what's-his-name," she said. They never called my sister's then husband, Donald, by his name.

They were going to go in December. The *Happy Days* pilot was going to shoot right after Thanksgiving. I told my mother I couldn't go with them because I had gotten this new job. It was really exciting, I said, and —

Ilse cut me off. "Yah, yah," she said. "Wait. Here. Tell your father — he'll be so thrilled." And she passed him the phone.

Birthday greetings? Congratulations on the big job? Ha.

I flew east for Thanksgiving, but then I committed another outrage — I told my parents I wouldn't be spending Turkey Day with them. Why wouldn't I want to celebrate this major holiday with my mother and father?

I think you can begin to imagine.

A few years earlier, not long after I graduated Yale, my classmate Jimmy Naughton had invited me to his home in Connecticut to spend a few days around Christmastime with him and his young family — he and his wife, Pam, had two little kids, a boy and a girl. So I drove the family Cadillac — the fancy car my parents could ill afford — up to West Hartford, Connecticut, and I got there, and everything in the Naughton household was warm and wonderful. Jimmy and Pam gave me a fried-egg sandwich on Wonder Bread, with mayonnaise — oh my God, the start of a lifelong relationship with that incomparable sandwich. I slept over, and when I woke up the next morning it was snowing out: a perfect country Christmas. We decorated the tree, the kids were thrilled, everybody was having a great time. Christmas music played in the background — to this day, "The Little Drummer Boy" always gives me goose bumps. I'd never done any of this before, and I was loving every minute of it.

I drove back home, filled with the joy of Christmas and Jimmy's family. I parked the car in the garage we used, a couple of blocks from the apartment, and as I walked through the streets, everybody I saw seemed to be in the Christmas spirit — there were garlands in the windows, and Christmas trees for sale on the street, with their wonderful aroma everywhere. And I walked into my family's apartment, and I was smacked in the psyche by Nothing.

True, we were Jewish, we celebrated Hanukkah, not Christmas, but there was *no* spirit in the apartment, Hanukkah or Christmas or otherwise. It had been the first time I was aware of how severe my house was. The heavy furniture: the couch, the two chairs. These weren't the kind of chairs you could pull up to get close to someone and have a heart-to-heart. These were big, square wooden armchairs — you'd get a hernia if you tried to move them. There was carved dark wood everywhere, a bookcase with doors and windows and carvings of great explorers — even the furniture was educational. And a big desk, also carved! And of course the desk chair was also big, and forget about wheels — no wheels on this desk chair.

Severe, severe, severe. And dark. Oh, very dark.

But there was another reason I couldn't spend Thanksgiving with my parents. I had a girlfriend I was in love with, Glenda Miller, a costume designer and stylist, and I hadn't seen her for more than a month while I was in California. Glenda had invited me for a cozy Thanksgiving at her place upstate. I couldn't wait.

I'd met Glenda soon after I moved to New York from graduate school, and I got her the job as costume designer for *The Lords of Flatbush.* In late 1972, soon after the picture wrapped, I went to Cincinnati to be in a production of Arthur Miller's *Incident at Vichy* at the Playhouse in the Park. And I missed Glenda and it was winter. I remember standing at a pay phone outside a bank in Cincinnati (yes, it was snowing) and calling her, and Glenda saying, "I just put a steak in, then I'm going to eat it — call me back in twenty minutes." I stood there, watching the digital bank clock, counting the seconds ticking off, freezing my ass off. After twenty minutes — exactly — I phoned her back. "I'm just finishing," she said. "Then I want to wash the dishes — can you call me back?"

Could I have read the tea leaves? Of course not. I couldn't read in any language.

My mother and father were incredulous that I was defying them, not only about the trip to Europe but about Thanksgiving, but there was nothing they could do about it. I went upstate.

To find that Glenda had also invited her best friend.

No, this was not a prelude to kinky fun. This was — what? Glenda being bored with

70

me? Not being able to stand being alone with me? Me having no understanding whatsoever about anything at all? Ever?

She always complained that my tighty-whities were too baggy. Was that the problem?

Back when I was at McBurney, I was a really good dancer. I couldn't play soccer or baseball or basketball, but I could dance: that was where I got some sense of self. I could foxtrot, I could do the twist and the limbo — I even won a school award for my dancing. And I would take my girlfriend at the time, Joanne, to dances at McBurney, and not knowing what I was doing, I would leave her standing against the wall, with her hands folded behind her, and I would have to flit from one clique to another to make sure I was still whole. To check with this group of guys and that group of guys and that couple of guys over there that they still acknowledged my existence.

All this, while I was completely ignoring Joanne's existence.

We shot the pilot episode of *Happy Days* in early December, on Paramount Stage 23 and the studio back lot: the set constructors built Arnold's Diner in a parking area; Jefferson High was just a sign put up on one of the administration buildings. I'd met all my castmates a couple of weeks earlier, and instantly liked all of them: Ron Howard as Richie Cunningham, Tom Bosley and Marion Ross as Mr. and Mrs. C., Erin Moran as Richie's little sister, Joanie, Anson Williams as Potsie, Donny Most as Ralph Malph. I especially clicked with Ron, who at just eighteen was a show-business veteran, having costarred as Opie in eight seasons of *The Andy Griffith Show,* played Winthrop in the 1962 movie of *The Music Man,* and of course recently had a major role in *American Graffiti.* Ron busted all the clichés about child actors and the troubles they have growing up: for all his accomplishments, he was just a solid young guy, modest, easy to be with, and wise beyond his years. We liked each other instantly.

With *American Graffiti* doing big box office and *Grease* a megahit on Broadway, ABC was eager to cash in on the fifties craze: the network picked up *Happy Days* quickly after screening the pilot, and we swung into weekly production. For all my misgivings about being in a TV series, I happily signed a contract which, like all series contracts, officially bound me to seven seasons, should the show last that long. Seven seasons! Who could imagine such a thing?

We were a friendly, happy cast, but one thing I'd learned at Yale was that an effective ensemble doesn't happen overnight. *Happy Days'* players all came from different professional backgrounds: Tom was a big star of Broadway musicals; I had seen him in his Tony Award–winning performance in *Fiorello!* before I ever got to Hollywood. Marion had been acting in movies and television since the early fifties; Erin, just twelve, had been doing TV for several years, while Anson and Donny were relative newcomers to the medium.

So was I! I'd done all those commercials and dipped my toe into soap opera, and I had those two indie movies on my résumé, but most of my acting experience, by far, had been onstage. I was a veteran of the Great White Way, having costarred with Regina Baff in a comedy called *42 Seconds from Broadway* that opened and closed in one night. And my Yale education and theater background gave me a lot of things — including that guilt baggage about doing TV — but one thing it hadn't given me was a big ego. At the Yale Repertory Theatre, individuals might stand out, but the ensemble was everything. When I was in the Greek chorus of *The Bacchae,* directed by André Gregory, weeks of rehearsal turned us into a group that was all but joined at the hip, physically and emotionally. Using all kinds of trust exercises, we bonded into a single organism: when we walked into a restaurant, people got up and moved to make room for us. We walked in together, sat down together, all got up together. There was a palpable force between us.

A similar kind of cohesion would develop over time with the *Happy Days* cast, but in the beginning there were growing pains. For all of us. In the pilot episode, Anson and I had a scene together where Fonzie shows Potsie and the guys how to undo a girl's brassiere in one smooth move, one hand caressing her face as you whispered sweet nothings to her and, with the other hand, reaching back and undoing the snap just like that. As the scene was written, Fonzie demonstrates this virtuoso maneuver to Richie, Potsie, and Ralph on a men's room radiator, Potsie being the one responsible for positioning the bra so Fonzie can demonstrate. But the way Anson first placed the brassiere gave me no leverage, so I said, "Let's put the snap right on the ridge of the radiator — that'll make it easier for me."

But when the time came for Potsie to place the bra on the radiator, Anson broke character and said, "I'm not sure I can do it."

My immediate reaction was impatience. "Please, Anson," I said. "You gotta help me with this."

I was harking back to my theater background, which had taught me a) that actors helped each other in performance, and b) that there was *always* a way. Theater is *so* live — you're constantly having to think on your feet. Improv is even more so. If something unforeseen happens during a performance, you just have to deal with it. When I was at Emerson I used to do children's theater on weekends: we'd travel all around the Boston area in two station wagons to put on these kids' shows, and some unusual things happened. Once we were doing *Rumpelstiltskin,* and a gunpowder flash effect as Rumpelstiltskin appeared set the king's throne on fire. I just picked up the flaming throne and blithely carried it offstage while saying my lines, and came right back on to continue the scene.

Another week I had what I thought was a cold, but which turned out to be debilitating pneumonia. Since there were no understudies, I had to go on. What was amazing: concentrating on telling the story turned out to be an unbelievable antidote to the illness — as soon as the performance was over, I passed out. That really defined The Show Must Go On for me.

But network television was a world unto itself. And what I wasn't seeing in the moment was that Anson and I were coming from two completely different places. Doing a sitcom was a brand-new discipline for me, and I had to learn how to meet my castmates in the sweet spot where everybody felt good about our work together. With a little give from Anson and a little give from me, the brassiere snap ended up on the radiator ridge, and I was able to unsnap it with one hand, maintaining the Fonz's cool.

I had more lessons to learn. Once, during the first season, I was doing a scene with Ron Howard, and there was a joke that I just couldn't make work. I tried a dozen different ways, and I was getting frustrated. "This, I can't make this work," I told Ron. And I started punching the script.

Now Ron Howard was almost ten years younger than I was. But Ron had been around the block a lot more times than me. And he put his arm around my shoulder and walked me to the back of Paramount Stage 24, across the street from the Mill, the place where they build all the sets. And he looked me in the eye and said to me, in the kindest and gentlest way possible, "You know, I wouldn't hit my script if I were you."

"But Ron," I said, "I can't make this work. This is stupid. What's written is stupid."

"Yeah, but the writers are working as hard as they can," he told me. "They're trying really hard."

I looked at him, and I suddenly heard him. "I understand that," I said. "I will never hit my script again as long as I live."

And so this wise eighteen-year-old taught this theater-seasoned but TV-ignorant twenty-eight-year-old a very important lesson for the rest of my career: a little tolerance, with a sprinkle of patience.

Charlie Haid's little family was adorable: his pretty wife, their cute baby girl, their golden Lab. The dog wagged its tail when I was around; the baby cooed at me. Penny smiled sweetly. That couch in their suite at the Sunset Marquis was a couch I enjoyed sleeping on. Was I reading the social cues? Not even close.

One day Charlie gave me a serious look. "You got to get your own place," he said. I believe Penny had read him the riot act.

Charlie and I drove all around West Hollywood, and finally we found a place for me, in a little two-story complex around a pool on North Laurel Avenue: 1560 North Laurel, to be exact, a stone's throw north of Sunset, just up the street from Greenblatt's famous deli and right around the corner from Schwab's Pharmacy, where Lana Turner was discovered. It was a cozy apartment — a living room, a bedroom, a bathroom, a kitchenette, and a wet bar with a half refrigerator under the Formica counter. I rented a TV set and a record player — careful about money! — and I drove my green Capri to Tower Records and bought some albums: Dan Fogelberg and Electric Light Orchestra. And I would smoke marijuana and listen to Dan Fogelberg and drift off to a place where I didn't worry so much.

What was I worried about? It was early 1974, *Happy Days* was on the air, I was earning a nice salary — $1,000 a week, as much per week as I'd brought out to last me for a month — and I was starting to get famous. Oh, but wait: not just famous. *Famous.*

3.

I had never encountered anything like this before. I had never *imagined* anything like this before. Back east, I would get recognized now and then by somebody who'd seen me in a play (or maybe a commercial for A&P supermarkets or Sanka coffee), but it was a rare occurrence. Now suddenly I couldn't go to Greenblatt's to buy my tuna sandwich and ambrosia salad or the two boxes of Almaden wine — one red and one white, to keep in my half refrigerator for guests — without getting stopped on the street and in the store, over and over again. Evidently, coming into people's living rooms at eight o'clock on Tuesday nights made them feel you were a friend of theirs — and not just any friend, but a close friend. It didn't help that my character seemed to grow more beloved after every episode.

Hey, Fonzie! Fonzie, over here! Hey, look who it is! It's Fonzie!

I began to stay indoors. A lot.

I could measure the Fonz's rising popularity by the volume of fan mail I got: very soon there were bushel loads of it. I had it all delivered to my apartment — boxes and boxes, literally thousands of letters. I read every one, opened every gift. There were hand-hooked rugs with my name woven in: HENRY WINKLER, SUPERSTAR. There was jewelry, there were little stuffed bears. Home-baked cakes. Even crucifixes.

Once I was relaxing in my place in my usual way when there was a loud knock on the door, audible right over Dan Fogelberg. Was I imagining it? Was what I was smoking making me paranoid? Then came more knocks, louder and louder. I opened the door a little nervously — liberating a WAFT of fragrant blue smoke — to find three large guys, who immediately identified themselves as plain-clothes policemen. One of them was holding a camera.

Oh my God, I thought.

But they were smiling. "We just wanted to say hello to the Fonz," one of them said. "Maybe get a picture — if that's okay."

"Sure!" I said, as I posed for a few snapshots with them, smiling my biggest showbiz smile and thinking the whole time, *Well, as soon as they're done with the pictures, they're going to clap the cuffs on me and haul me off to jail.*

Instead the cops left, still smiling. I was just beginning to learn that, along with its many downsides, fame offered a couple of nice perks as well.

For one thing, I noticed that though I'd never thought of myself as being in the same neighborhood as handsome, I had suddenly become *very* good-looking. By which I mean that girls — women — who would never have given me the time of day before I became the Fonz were now ready and willing to tell me what time and what day it was, and more, and more. . . .

Oh, you want to go out with . . . You're going to say yes, just like that? I don't have to . . . Oh, wow! That's nice!

Very nice! But then I had to worry: why are they saying yes? Is it because I'm such a cutie or because I'm a TV star? It was impossible to figure out.

I briefly dated the lovely Cindy Williams, God rest her soul, Shirley of *Laverne & Shirley,* which, of course, was a *Happy Days* spin-off. She made scrambled eggs — don't get any ideas, this was at night, after we'd gone to the movies. She had a white cat; I didn't like cats. It really didn't go much further than that — although the *National Enquirer* tried to make a thing of us, printing a mostly made-up story that said we went out for dinner and I asked for her credit card, because I was too cheap to pay. That was a little close to the bone, fictional though it was.

One night after finishing work I got back to my apartment, and as I was unlocking the door I heard the phone ringing. I picked it up on the fifth ring. It was Glenda.

We'd broken up after that fateful Thanksgiving — months before — but here she was again. "Henry," she said, "maybe we shouldn't do this. We've been together for a long time now; maybe we should try to make it work."

"Hmm," I said. Some totally unexpected part of me was rising in my brain, almost like when I'd summoned Fonzie in the audition. "No, Glenda," I told her. "Maybe you'll be completely available to me for the next three weeks. And then we're going to go back to exactly the way it was, and I can't do that again. So, thank you, but no. Oh, and by the way," I added, "my underwear is still baggy."

Was I suddenly becoming a grown-up?

Only for that moment.

I listened to my instinct when it came to

work, but when it came to living, I almost always smothered my instincts and let my fears and anxieties take over.

There was another young lady, very beautiful, someone I'd met while I was still in New York, and now she was living in Colorado. She found me, and I invited her to come down to LA for the weekend. And I can honestly say that along with being very nice to look at, she was a genuinely good person. I could tell from the moment she arrived that this was someone who truly cared for me. She was very giving.

And it was as if she and I were the opposite ends of a magnet. The more she gave, the more I pulled away. I was in no way, shape, or form able to accept her affection and generosity — they were so repellent to me. And it had nothing to do with her. She was being wonderful. But it's only now in hindsight that I understand. At the time I was a human from the bridge of my nose up, and the rest of me? The rest of me was a jumble. I could not wait for the weekend to end and for her to go home.

Things just got crazier and crazier. The ratings were coming in, and *Happy Days* was very quickly turning out to be an enormous hit. Garry and his writing staff were working overtime: we were shooting just two weeks ahead of airdates. And the writers were picking up on the Fonz's popularity: they were bouncing off me, and I was bouncing off them. In the pilot I had just six lines; soon I had a lot more to say besides my trademark *Ayyy,* and a lot more to do, too.

But those terrific writers probably felt frustrated with me sometimes, because a lot of what Fonzie was becoming came from me rather than script pages. My theater and improv background — and my dyslexia — caused me to make up a lot right on the spot. I knew how to get laughs, and I made sure to take care of my character. In one episode, I was invited for dinner at the Cunninghams'. As we sat at the table at the beginning of the meal, we all held hands and Mr. and Mrs. C. asked me to say grace. I took a moment, got very serious, and slowly, I looked up to Heaven. And I said, "Hey, God . . . *whoa!*" The words came out with reverence and appreciation. But apparently not enough for the showrunner at the time, Bill Bickley, who also happened to be a pastor. Bill went berserk at what he considered to be blasphemy. "You can't treat God like that," he said. I said, "Sir — what are you talking about? I said the prayer as my character would say it — with complete respect." The disagreement went on for an hour. In the end I had to acquiesce and say simply, "God, thank you." It is truly one of the moments in my career that still gnaws at me.

From the moment I was chosen for the role, I promised myself that Arthur Fonzarelli would never follow any of the greaser clichés: I would never roll up a pack of cigarettes in my T-shirt sleeve, for example. And when the pilot script called for me to comb my hair in the mirror, a much, much better piece of business came to me out of the heavens: I took my comb out of my pocket, looked at my reflection, mimed a *Whoa! I don't have to, because look at it, it's perfect!*, and put the comb back in my pocket.

The Fonz came together out of little details like that — small, unspoken things. He was a man of few words: he could say a lot with a look and accomplish a lot with a snap of his fingers or a bump of his fist. How do you smack a jukebox and start it just like that? How do you hit the side of an apartment building and make every light in the building go on? When you're camping with the boys in the middle of the forest and the chatter of the animals is making you crazy, how do you sit up and say, "Quiet!" — and create absolute silence?

Arthur Fonzarelli was magical. But his magic wasn't about showing off: it was about helping his friends. It was very important to me that the character portray loyalty. That in itself was magic. And more and more, everybody seemed to want more Fonzie in their life.

The question was, did *I* want more Fonzie in my life?

It was great to be working with an amazing cast, crew, and team of writers on a hit sitcom. But more and more of the press around the show — and there was a lot of press around the show — wasn't about Ron Howard's Richie Cunningham, who was after all the lead character and pivot of *Happy Days,* but about that laconic, magnetic guy in the jeans and MacGregor golf jacket who could make things happen with a simmering stare from under those tweezed eyebrows, a snap of the fingers, or a bump of his fist. Me. I mean Fonzie.

There was a little problem rattling around in my brain — well, there were a lot of problems running through my brain, but there was this one problem rattling like a dried pea in a tin can: I was still a Yale-trained theater actor, and I wanted the world to know about *everything* I could do besides say *Ayyy.*

Fonzie was a great character. I had created him, and with the aid of terrific writers made him subtle and funny and endlessly charming, but he was *so* great that I was worried about being typecast. More than worried. I had a total bug up my butt about being typecast. So when I was out in the world (which was less and less often), I made a point of being Henry at all times. People would ask for a little taste of the Fonz, just a word or two in that voice, and I'd smile and say something quietly — as Henry. When I did press interviews, I was careful to say great things about everyone involved with the show — which was easy, because that was how I really felt — but I spoke to reporters as Henry, not Fonzie. Quiet. Thoughtful. And, *Oh, you know I went to Yale School of Drama, right?*

I wasn't trying to be better than anyone else. I was just trying to be my best self. Which in itself was problematic, because I was, in my mind, always a little boy. Without any real handle on who my adult self was.

What a strange secret to be carrying around when you're supposed to be the coolest guy in the world.

■ ■ ■ ■

It was one thing not to be able to walk to Greenblatt's without getting stopped by fans. But a couple of months into the first season of *Happy Days,* I got my first taste of what was really happening out there in America when ABC sent Ron, Donny, Anson, and me on a two-week promotion tour to various cities around the country.

The first stop was an appearance at a women's fashion show at an amphitheater in a Dallas park. Ron had a commitment elsewhere and was going to join us in a couple of days. When the limo carrying Anson, Donny, and me approached the venue, we saw a huge crowd outside: our first thought was there must be some kind of rock concert going on.

But it turned out that we were the rock stars. It was just nuts — as our car pulled into the parking area, a horde of screaming teenage girls descended on us and began rocking the car back and forth. A bunch of cops had to push them aside so we could get inside the theater. And once we were miked up in the wings — we were going to take questions from the audience — I could see a line of cops standing at the foot of the stage to protect us from the crowd. The moment we walked out, the screams rose to such a pitch that I literally couldn't hear a word I spoke to Donny and Anson.

Insane.

There was a lot more insanity to come.

The summer after the show's first season — we'd already been renewed for a second — the network sent the four of us on another tour. This time we paired off, Ron and Anson hitting some cities, Donny and I going to others. That July, all four of us met in Dallas, this time at the Neiman Marcus flagship store downtown. We did a nice Q&A inside, in front of hundreds of people, but when we left the store, a crowd of more than twenty thousand, most of them screaming girls, was standing between us and our limo. The store's security team — this time there were no cops present — was helpless to get us to the car.

The girls were screaming *Fonz-eee! Fonz-eee!*

At each and every one of our events, I had talked to fans and reporters as Henry. Calm, reasonable, soft-spoken.

This, however, was an emergency. I summoned my character and raised my hands.

The screaming quieted a bit.

"Awright!" I said, in my Fonzie voice.

"Listen up!"

Suddenly you could've heard a pin drop.

"Dig it," I said. "There are twenty thousand of you and four of us."

"Fonz-eee!" one girl screamed. Somebody shushed her.

"There are twenty thousand of you and four of us," I repeated as the Fonz. "And we gotta get to that *car.*" I pointed to the limo. "You are going to *part* like the Red *Sea.*" I gave a *spread out* motion with my hands to show them how — and lo and behold, the girls started to back up, right and left. Miracle of miracles, an open lane began to form between us and our limo. The sea had parted.

"Awright," I Fonzed. "We are now going to walk to our car. And I say, thank you for coming here today. But do *not* touch the *leather.*"

This got a giggle, but the lane got wider. I nodded to the guys and we began to walk to the car. All of a sudden, a kid yells out, "He's so short!"

I whipped around and shot him a look. "Fuck you, I'm not short," America's best-loved character told this kid.

The kid grinned. "He's so cool!" he said.

My character had become bigger — much

bigger — than the character the show had originally been based on, and everyone in America knew it, especially Ron and me.

Please believe me when I tell you that as greatly as the Fonz phenomenon benefited me, it was not easy to take. I did not want to do anything to this man I loved, Ron Howard, that would hurt his feelings or cause him discomfort in any way. But I also knew that I had had a dream and I was now living this dream. It was very strange. On the one hand, I could never take it all seriously, could never believe I was as big a star as they said I was; on the other hand, I was loving that they — the fans, the media, the network executives — were saying it.

I was a star everywhere I went. And yet I realized I still couldn't do geometry. I was still short — I hadn't grown an inch. So (I thought) I'll let them think I'm a big star, but I'm not really a different human being. I cannot really be exactly what everybody is saying I am. There's a bit of a hollow sound inside.

At the same time, there were some very pragmatic benefits to my stardom. Thanks to my lawyer, Skip Brittenham III, I was earning a very nice living. If I wanted to see a movie, I could wait in the lobby and not in line. There were no more lines in my life.

The simplest things felt gigantic to me.

I'm pretty sure I never let any of it go to my head. The only time I got crazed with a fan was when someone didn't see me as a person or disrespected me. This still knocks my socks off: once I was in a men's room and somebody opened the stall and said, "Hey, could I get your autograph?"

"Do you know where we are?" I asked.

"I'm not going to get another chance."

"Could you please go and stand in the corner?"

But for the most part I was calm about all of it. I have very low blood pressure. And though I didn't buy into the hype, I let myself enjoy it a bit. If you don't nail your feet to the ground, you can just believe — and you want to believe. It's so enticing. It feels so good. You could just become a gigantic balloon in the Thanksgiving Day parade and float over everybody. Today there are only three basic reasons I won't interact with a fan: my wife and I are having a heated discussion; I am with my children or grandchildren; or I'm late for a plane.

Yale, the place that had meant so much to me, continued to loom large in my mind. I was so intimidated by the thought of how dedicated to the theater everyone there was, and so insecure about my new professional life. Robert Brustein himself, the dean of the Drama School and founder of the Yale Repertory Theatre, was quoted somewhere as saying, "Not only do I not applaud Henry, but I'm not sure he's doing the right thing."

Bob Brustein said this — and then, more than once, Yale classmates of mine would show up on the soundstage of *Happy Days,* looking to see if they could make a professional connection. And then Brustein asked me for money for the Yale Theatre. And then, mysteriously, I lost my checkbook. Looked everywhere — just couldn't find it.

One Sunday morning my phone rings, and it's Mrs. Rosenthal, whom I know from Congregation Habonim, my parents' synagogue on West 66th Street.

"Hello, Henry, this is Mrs. Rosenthal," she says. "From temple."

I am slightly unnerved to be getting this call. It isn't the first time since the beginning of *Happy Days* that I've heard from one of my parents' friends — or old acquaintances who have suddenly gotten a lot more friendly. "Hi, how are you?" I say. Carefully.

"Henry, I'm in Los Angeles, and I want to take you to dinner."

"I'm sorry, I can't do that, Mrs. Rosenthal," I say. "But I thank you so much. That's such a lovely invitation."

She tries a few different dates on me, until the message finally sinks in: there is no way I am going to dinner with her. Somehow I manage to get off the phone.

Then my mother calls. "Mrs. Rosenthal called," I tell her. "Did you give her my number?"

"Yah! It's Mrs. Rosenthal!"

"You can't give anybody my number."

"Yah, Mrs. Rosenthal from the temple!"

I said, "No, no, I'm saying to you, please. You *can't* give my number to all these people. I don't have the time to have dinner with all these people, I don't have the desire. I don't care."

"Yah, it's Mrs. Rosenthal from the temple."

And I said, "Mom, I'm going to change my number and unlist it. Do you understand what I'm saying?"

"Yah! It's Mrs. Rosenthal! From the temple!"

When I think of my bar mitzvah, I think of humiliation. It all still feels very fresh.

As you may know, this ancient Jewish coming-of-age ritual admits a thirteen-year-old boy (or, since the early twentieth century, thirteen-year-old girl) into the adult population of the synagogue congregation. The bar or bat mitzvah (literally, son or daughter of a commandment — or one who is now subject to the law) is called to the bimah, the raised platform at the head of the sanctuary, to read a portion from the Torah aloud, in a chanting voice: an accomplishment that marks him or her as a fully-fledged Jew.

My only problem was that I couldn't read in the first place, making learning to read Hebrew a total impossibility. Oh, and I also couldn't sing, making chanting an exercise in futility.

And standing in front of an open Torah scroll in front of the entire Habonim congregation was definitely one place where you couldn't say, "I'm giving you the essence."

How did I do it?

Barely.

Back in the day, the temple would give you a sad-looking old phonograph record in a brown paper sleeve with some cantor chanting your Torah portion. So I wore a groove in that record, playing it over and over and over and memorizing the whole thing phonetically. When the big day came, I got up there in my bar mitzvah suit and tallis and yarmulke, took the yod — the official silver pointer, literally a wand with a little pointing finger at the end — and pretended to read from the Torah scroll, pretend-chanting in a low monotone, and somehow bumbled my way through the whole thing, producing big smiles all around (except on my parents' faces, of course), smiles that I'm sure had more to do with relief than admiration.

Then came the reception. I had been to some of my friends' bar mitzvahs in fancy catering halls, with sculptures made of ice and chopped liver, with society orchestras and dancing and singing and lavish meals of many courses. This was not one of those parties. My reception was at the Hotel Olcott, a slightly seedy establishment on West 72nd, in a ballroom with faded burgundy carpets, bronze mirrors, dim lights, and a general air of seen-better-days. There were a ton of old people squeezing my cheek, some of whom I recognized, many of whom I didn't; a lot of German pretend aunts and uncles and other assorted characters from Germany; and about nine of my friends, including my then sort-of girlfriend Barbara Grant, and my best friends Gerald Love and

Lee Seides.

I remember thinking, *Wow, this is not the same as other bar mitzvahs I've been to.*

I did get a Polaroid camera, one of the first they made — it weighed around ten pounds — and some savings bonds and a bunch of envelopes of cash. Not big sums, but it all added up to that $375 I told you about, soon to vanish forever down the rabbit hole of my father's endless need. . . .

In the second season of *Happy Days,* disaster struck: we sank from the top ten in the Nielsen ratings to number forty-nine, largely because we were up against a hot new CBS sitcom, *Good Times,* whose star Jimmie Walker, with his catchphrase "Dyno-MITE!," had instantly become as beloved a character as the Fonz. We were on the verge of getting canceled. So Garry and the ABC brass decided to try something new and radical.

For almost two whole seasons, our show had been filmed with one camera, like a movie. If somebody blew a line or anything else unexpected occurred, the director could stop the camera and do another take. A laugh track was dubbed in while the show was being edited. But now our producers and the network wanted to give *Happy Days* a more immediate feeling — something more like *Good Times*. They decided to shoot an episode the way a lot of sitcoms were made, with three cameras and a live studio audience. And there was something else: they wanted to center this episode, for the first time, around Fonzie.

In Season 2, Episode 13, the Fonz shocks Richie, Potsie, and Ralph by announcing he's going to be married. But when I bring my fiancée to meet the Cunninghams, Mr. Cunningham recognizes her as a stripper who was the entertainment at a hardware convention he attended in Chicago. End of engagement; Fonzie stays single.

I loved working in front of a real audience, as I'd done so many times before: it got my adrenaline going, tickled all my improv instincts. It reminded me of the time when, at age eleven, I cut school and persuaded my sister to take me to the Adelphi Theatre on West 54th Street, to watch the live broadcast of Jackie Gleason's great sitcom *The Honeymooners.* The show had a studio audience, but you had to have a ticket to get in, and I most certainly did not have a ticket. "Oh, please," I said to the guard at the theater entrance, "I left my ticket in the cab. I can't believe it, I had my ticket. I really did. Oh my God," I said to my sister, "look in your purse again — do you see it anywhere?"

It was one of my earliest and most effective performances. At this point the guard was just shaking his head and waving me in, Best Young Actor in a Wheedling Role.

Wow. Wow. A big theater, facing that oh-so-familiar set, Ralph and Alice Kramden's cold-water Brooklyn flat — it looked so strange in color. Between the theater seats and the set were four enormous TV cameras, the first I'd ever seen, and the biggest I ever would see: little did I know then that these were special cameras that shot live video and 35mm film simultaneously, so that the show could later be rebroadcast in perfect visual quality. And little did I know that while none of *The Honeymooners* was improvised, Jackie Gleason kept rehearsing at a minimum so the performance would feel fresh — brilliant. Never mind the technical stuff (and never mind that those four cameras were so gigantic that a short person such as myself could barely see that beautiful set): this was actually *it,* the place where it happened! I was in heaven. And then, before the show began, the great man, Jackie himself (oh my God!), came out in his dressing gown and thanked the audience for coming to the show.

No, no, Jackie (I thought) — *thank* you. Could I have known then that someday I would follow in his footsteps? I'm not sure that I didn't have an inkling!

Anyway, here we were on Paramount Stage 19 with *Happy Days'* first-ever studio audience, and though I was excited, Ron Howard, who'd never acted before a live audience in his long career, was terrified. And there was something else. Fonzie had become more and more central to *Happy Days* over the show's first one-and-three-quarter seasons: it was clearer and clearer that Ron's Richie Cunningham, the character the show had been built around, was being overshadowed. Season 2, Episode 13 formalized it.

ABC liked the new format well enough that we were renewed for a third season and saved from the graveyard of canceled sitcoms. And the network was so impressed by all the Fonzie-mania our promotional tours had stirred up that the ABC brass made a command decision: in the new season, they were going to put Fonzie at the center of the show. My credit went from the end of the show to the beginning, with a picture of me over a revolving phonograph record.

Leonard Goldenson himself told me about it. Goldenson was the president of ABC-

TV, the guy who'd built the network up from practically nothing after merging it with Paramount Pictures in the early fifties, so his word carried weight. His whole self carried weight. When he walked into my dressing room and said, "Would you like to do your own show?" I shot to my feet. I paid attention. Too much attention. This was a man who had created an empire, who commanded the empire. What was I? Just talent. And I'd learned (and was still learning) that talent is interchangeable.

But at the same time, my work instinct — my producer's instinct long before I became a producer — kicked in right away. "Mr. Goldenson — sir."

"Leonard," he corrected me.

"Leonard," I said. "Sir. My first thought — and I know you've been in this business a lot longer than me — but my first thought is, let's maybe not fix something that isn't broken? I mean, *Happy Days* works."

He had to acknowledge that. He nodded. Meanwhile, I was thinking — I couldn't even imagine my own show. I couldn't imagine going *Ayyy* for half an hour. With a new cast? Impossible.

"I *exist* because of the Cunninghams and Anson and Donny," I told him. "Now all of a sudden we're going to change that and make something new? Oh my God — I have to say, that would not be good. For anybody."

"Well," Leonard Goldenson said, "I do want to change the name of the show." He looked serious. "To *Fonzie's Happy Days,*" he said.

Almost instantly I said, "Mr. Goldenson. Leonard. Sir. Okay, let me just say, I'm asking you not to do that. If you do that, it is so disrespectful to everybody else who has been doing *Happy Days* as a family together with me for two years."

He was listening.

"Mr. Goldenson. Leonard. How much more of a success can you make the show by changing the name to *Fonzie's Happy Days*? That would be so hurtful — just a slap in the face to everyone else in the cast. I cannot live on that set if you do that. I just wouldn't — couldn't — do that. It works so fine just the way it is."

He looked thoughtful.

"Leonard. Sir. I can't tell you what to do — or how much I appreciate what you want to do for me. It's your network. So I'm asking you respectfully, please, don't do that."

They didn't do it. I later learned that when Tom Miller and Ed Milkis, the show's producers, broached the title change to

Ron, he threatened to leave *Happy Days* and return to film school at USC, where he'd been taking courses to further his ambition of becoming a director. Our show's success and relentless production schedule had made going to college part-time an impossibility for him — but now he was ready to go back. He thought the name change was a cheesy idea, he told Tom and Ed. And it would also represent a very public demotion for both Richie Cunningham and Ron Howard.

But when Garry heard about the plan — and my reaction to it, plus Ron's reaction to it — he put his foot down. And that was that.

Now that I was a national celebrity, my parents finally had to admit that I'd done something with my life — although I think my father thought I might still come to my senses and take over his lumber business. They actually came to LA to visit: I introduced them to everybody on the set, and took a picture with them in character. My mother and father, short people with German accents, introduced themselves to everyone they met as "ze coproducers uf Henry Vinkler."

Cute.

It almost seemed they were finally proud of me. But the truth is, I didn't care. It was too late. They weren't proud *for* me. They were proud *of* me, like a possession. I'd needed them to be proud of me when everything was so confusing, and I was petrified, and trying to figure out how to make my way in the world. I could've used it then.

"Oh, your parents are so proud of you," people would tell me.

"Oh, really?" I'd say. "Lovely for them."

My mother asked me for a bunch of autographed pictures. I said, "You're my *mother.* What do you need autographed pictures for?" She was handing them out from the trunk of the family car. I guess I should've been glad she wasn't selling them.

My sister and brother-in-law, on the other hand, wanted to publish a book about me. "Only the good things," they promised. Nice memories of when I was a kid; bar mitzvah pictures. Stuff like that.

"Okay," I said. "I guess."

The book actually got published, a real (though pretty slim) paperback from a real publisher. That wasn't enough for my sister and her husband, though. They literally had a souvenir wristwatch manufactured, with a picture of Fonzie on the watch face. There was a man's wristband and a slimmer woman's wristband. Didn't sell a whole lot.

In the spring of 1976, just after we wrapped Season 3, I went to Australia to be a presenter at the Logie Awards, their version of the Emmys. *Happy Days* was a big hit there — I got a tremendous amount of mail from Down Under.

I'd never flown anything like fourteen hours, and practically the moment I stepped off the plane I had to do a press conference. And while I've always been pretty good verbally, I was so exhausted from the flight that I literally had no control over my mind and my mouth — I could not answer a single question coherently.

But I loved the Australians, who were so warm and down to earth. And they made it worth my while to have flown all those hours: my hosts took me on a tour of the outback, which was incredibly stark and beautiful. While I was there, I bought an artifact called a pointing bone.

I learned that the Aboriginal people make this pointing bone out of mud, human hair, and the bone of an animal that they've eaten. And what they believe is if someone upsets you deeply, you can (if the elders okay it) point the bone at that person and make them die. Even from miles away.

I still have my pointing bone. And I have to admit that over the years, there have been a couple of people I've been tempted to point it at.

Visiting the outback and learning about the Aboriginal people just opened my brain. You think you're living a life, worrying about money and status and Nielsen ratings, and here are these people who are just existing on another plane. Some Aboriginal people, if they feel like they're going to die and they're in a hospital, will crawl out of the hospital to die under the stars. All this amazing mythology was happening fourteen hours and thousands of miles away, and I've never forgotten it.

The name of the show didn't change, but the show did. The Fonz was now front and center in every episode, and very often the focus of the episode. Garry had hired new writers who sharpened the *com* in *sitcom*. All this, plus three cameras and a live audience, took *Happy Days* from being in danger of cancellation straight to the top of the ratings. The network was happy. The cast and crew were happy. It was a loose, easy, friendly set, with plenty of goofing around on rehearsal days. One of our favorite pastimes was tape-ball fights — throwing loosely wadded balls of gaffer's tape at each other.

Just before Christmas break in our third season, ABC distributed gifts to the cast. Ron, Anson, Donny, Erin, Tom, and Marion all got the exact same present: a very nice leather wallet.

I got a three-quarter-inch VCR. A gigantic machine.

This was late 1976, and videocassette recorders were a brand-new technology, and therefore expensive. I'm not sure exactly how much my present set ABC back, but it was probably somewhere in the low four figures. Wallets . . . probably a lot less.

When my castmates asked me what I got, I told them. I was kind of embarrassed about it, but I wanted to be honest with people I was close to.

They were pissed. Not at me (so much), but at ABC.

Was this petty and materialistic of them? Not at all. The network had — probably not intentionally but definitely not accidentally — sent them a clear message: *Henry is more important than you.*

Ron called ABC corporate and gave both barrels to the first person he talked to, a young executive named Bob Boyett. And he sent back his wallet.

Ron has said that that was a period when every interviewer he spoke with — and we were all doing a lot of interviews — asked him the same question: "How does it feel that Fonzie has taken over your show?"

It put him in a bad frame of mind. Others in the cast might've felt lesser versions of the same emotion, but it was especially tough on Ron. The camaraderie on the set dimmed a bit.

Garry Marshall, a sensitive and caring guy as well as an astute producer and businessman, quickly sensed the change. And decided to do something about it. What he came up with was genius: a *Happy Days* softball team.

It was nice and casual at first: Sunday games in the Valley against talent agencies and casts and crews of other shows, nothing superserious or hypercompetitive; just good team spirit and lots of laughs. At the same time, we had some pretty good players — Anson, Donny, Ron, Garry, Fred Fox, Brian Levant, Lowell Ganz, plus a couple of guys on the crew — and so did some of the teams we played. Everybody had fun, but everybody also wanted to win. Which posed an immediate problem for me — I'd never played the game before.

Harry Winkler was definitely not the kind of dad who was ever going to take me to the park and play catch. (The only connection we had with Riverside Drive Park was when he grounded me after my new Schwinn bike was stolen. "How could you be so irresponsible?" he said. I said, "A kid, he seemed really nice to me, asked if he could ride the bike. It never occurred to me that he would ride it back to the Bronx.") And while I had no eye-hand coordination — throwing, hitting, and especially catching were not my specialties — I was good at archery and riflery (I got certificates at summer camp), I was a pretty good swimmer, and I could water-ski (more on this later!).

Ron Howard gave me the first baseball mitt I ever owned. And Anson bought me my first bat.

And Ron's brother Clint, who'd been a good pitcher on his high school baseball team, made a project out of teaching me to pitch a softball. On the *Happy Days* set on Paramount Stage 19, there was a long area between the audience bleachers and the interiors of Arnold's Diner and the Cunningham living room: this was where the cameras operated on shooting days, and on rehearsal days, this was where Clint and Walter von Huene, our dialogue coach, gave me my pitching lessons in between scenes.

It turned out that the underhand motion of pitching a softball was something I was naturally pretty good at. This wasn't the super-fast windmill style of collegiate softball pitching, or the high-arc slow-ball style, but something in between. With Clint's and Walter's help, I got pretty good at hitting spots, especially high and inside on right-handed hitters. And eventually I pitched shutouts.

Catching was something else again. If there was a pop-up, I just walked off the mound and the second baseman (or woman) came in and caught it. And if the ball was hit straight at me, I turned sideways and my body stopped it. I would be black-and-blue on my left side for the next seven years.

And Garry had brought us back together as a team.

But even in the midst of *Happy Days,* at the height of my fame and success, I felt embarrassed, inadequate. Every Monday at ten o'clock, we would have a table reading of that week's script, and at every reading I would lose my place, or stumble. I would leave a word out, a line out. I was constantly failing to give the right cue line, which would then screw up the joke for the person doing the scene with me. Or I would be staring at a word, like "invincible," and have no idea on earth how to pronounce it or even sound it out. My brain and I were in different zip codes. Meanwhile, the other actors would be waiting, staring at me; it was humiliating and shameful. Everybody in the cast was warm and supportive, but I constantly felt I was letting them down. I had to ask for my scripts really early, so I could read them over and over again — which put extra pressure on the writers, who were already under the gun every week, having to get twenty-four scripts ready in rapid succession.

All this at the height of my fame and success, as I was playing the coolest guy in the world.

There was another young lady I saw in the early days of the show — a very nice young lady, pretty and smart and a talented actress. And one Sunday morning as I was leaving her apartment, quite pleased about all that had just occurred, she called out after me: "You know," she said, "you're a very selfish lover."

I'm afraid it says an awful lot about me at that stage of my life that a) I was shocked to hear that, and b) I had absolutely no idea what she was talking about.

But it stayed with me. Oh boy, did it stay with me.

One Saturday morning around that time, I was shopping for a sport coat to wear to a wedding — the first sport coat that I could buy myself, was the way I thought of it, even though now, in the fourth season of *Happy Days,* I certainly wasn't lacking for disposable income. Recently I'd even bought my very first house, in Studio City, in the Valley. So I was shopping in Jerry Magnin's shop, a very high-end, very fashionable boutique on Rodeo Drive. Browsing the rack, I saw one jacket I liked, then quickly saw another. Then I saw this beautiful redhead in purple parachute pants. "Excuse me," I called to her, then held up both garments. "Which one?"

"Get both!" she said. She had a nice smile, I noticed. She went back to looking at the clothes she was looking at.

Now, there were two immediate problems here. The first was that at that point in 1976, I was one of the most famous people in the USA. And this beautiful redhead in purple parachute pants shopping in Jerry Magnin's high-end boutique on Rodeo

Drive gave absolutely no indication whether she knew who I was — or if she did, whether she cared.

The second problem was that my strange relationship to money made me utterly incapable of buying two sport coats when I only needed one. Couldn't happen. So without knowing it, this redhead had thrown a wrench into the works. I bought one jacket — blue velvet with red piping — and left the store, a little discombobulated.

And I went back the next Saturday. Kind of thinking, hoping, that I would be so absurdly lucky as to see the redhead there again.

And there she was.

This time I went up to her. "Hi," I said.

"You again," she said. Smiling. A little sassy; pleasant but not over-friendly. Certainly not gushing, the way tens of thousands of other young women all around the country would be if I favored them with my attention.

"I'm —" I began to introduce myself.

"The two-jacket guy," she said. Did she know I was Henry Winkler? She had to. Was she being coy? She didn't seem like the coy type. At all.

"I'm going to a wedding and I need to buy a present from the silver store across the street," I told her. "Do you think that — do you maybe have a little time to help me pick something out?"

"Well," the beautiful redhead said, "I'm not a gift-buying service." At least she smiled when she said it.

"All right," I said, teasing. "So you can stay here, and I can go on my merry way."

She rolled her eyes and sighed. "Oh, all *right.*"

"And when we're done, would you like to go have a soda with me?" I asked.

She gave me a look that said: *Saw that one coming up Rodeo Drive.*

But she said yes.

4.

Her name was Stacey. Stacey Furstman Weitzman. That was her married name, but she was no longer married. Little did I know, as we talked and talked over our sodas that Saturday afternoon in 1976, that we would still be together four and a half decades later.

STACEY:

I was divorced, the single mom of a beautiful little boy — Jed, who had just turned four. And I was seeing somebody. I was what they used to call independent-minded — it was still a time when women were mostly supposed to be dependent. But after I divorced Howard, I wanted to make my own way — I didn't want my father, who was a successful dentist, to have to take his grandson and me to the grocery store to make sure we were eating well. So I got a job, as the assistant to a publicist here in LA, a woman named Joan Luther. Her clients were mostly restaurants — you know, she'd call *The Hollywood Reporter* and say, "Regis Philbin was in Spago last night."

It was interesting work, and soon I was meeting with clients myself, and even bringing in a few. But when Joan started to ask me to pick up her dry cleaning and bring the dog over, it got less interesting.

In the course of working for Joan, I'd met a guy named Jerry Magnin, who was from a very wealthy San Francisco family, the founders of the high-end department store Joseph Magnin Co. Jerry had come to Los Angeles to make his own way, and started his own clothing store on Rodeo Drive. We became friendly, and when I told him I wasn't loving working for Joan, he said, "Why don't you go out on your own? I'll be your first client."

That's why I was in Jerry's store the day I met Henry.

Of course I knew who he was; everybody knew who Henry was. Jed had just had a Fonz candle on his fourth-birthday cake. But I'd grown up around show-business people — a number of them were my father's patients. I went to school with many actors' children. So meeting Henry Winkler just seemed normal to me. And nice. I could tell right away that he was a sweet guy — cute, full of life, with a great smile. So when he asked me to go get a soda, I said yes — even though I wasn't looking to meet anybody.

I wasn't looking to meet anybody, exactly, but I was also starting to realize that I should not be with the guy I was seeing. So was I interested in Henry? Maybe a little.

We went to the Beverly Wilshire and had a soda, and we talked and talked — he was very easy to talk to. And smart, and very sensitive. Just nice. My ex-husband was a lawyer; every time we had an argument, he would go A, B, C — he argued like a lawyer. Henry was very different. And then he said, "You know, I just bought a house. Do you want to see it?"

"Where is it?" I asked.

He told me it was on Reklaw Drive in Studio City, in the Valley — which meant up and over the Hollywood Hills from where we were, and down the other side. Studio City was a nice area to live in. The Valley was down-to-earth. And so was Henry.

Of all the hundred different ways some guy I'd just met could ask me if I wanted to see his new house, Henry Winkler's way of saying it triggered no alarm bells. He was proud that he'd just bought his own place, and he honestly seemed to want me to see it.

Still. I excused myself and went and called my mother from one of the hotel's phone booths. (No cell phones in those days.) Jed was over at her house, playing. "I'm following this guy, Henry Winkler, the guy from Jed's birthday cake," I told her. "I'm going to look at his new house. In Studio City. If you don't hear from me, that's where I'll be."

I was joking. Mostly. Because I'd never met someone and then followed them home — that was a new one. My mother asked me the question she had to ask: "Are you sure you know what you're doing, sweetheart?"

I told her I did. What was more, I had a date that night, so I had to be home early to get ready. "This is not a problem, Mom," I said. "He really is a nice guy."

I drove my car, Stacey drove her car. We turned left just past the Beverly Hills Hotel and headed up Coldwater Canyon Drive, curving and climbing up that steep hill. At the top, where Coldwater crosses Mulholland Drive, there was a man selling flowers. I pulled off to the side of the road, and so did Stacey. I bought a bunch of flowers, brought it back to her car and handed it to her, then got back in my car and led her to Studio City. I showed her my new house, and we listened to music and talked some more. She told me about a book she'd been reading, *Ordinary People,* that she liked a lot; she told me about a new band that she liked a lot — Huey Lewis and the News. I asked her if she'd go out with me that night, but she said she already had a date. And that she had to go, to get ready.

The next morning, Sunday, I woke up and got ready to go see my friends Susie and Donny Zubowski, just down the road, for brunch, as I did most weekends. And when I got in my car, the book and record Stacey had told me about were in the front seat.

I was flabbergasted. I was amazed. How did those things get into my car? What time had she come and delivered them? How did she get into my *garage*? I went back into the house and called the number she'd given me, and it was busy. I'm so obsessive that I waited ten minutes and called again. Still busy. I drove over to Susie and Donny's house, and called again from there. Busy. I called every ten minutes for the next twelve hours. Busy, busy, busy. Crazy, crazy, crazy. The next day, I finally reached her at her office, and we talked some more. I thanked her for the book and record, and I asked her out, and she said yes.

Three weeks passed. Long weeks. As the night approached, I phoned Stacey and asked her what she'd like to do on our date. "Why don't we see a movie?" she said.

"I don't know, that might be a little hard for me," I said. I explained, as best I could, what happened whenever I went out in public.

STACEY:

I thought, *Oh, get over yourself, buddy.* Then I said, "Well, why don't we try?"

I'd asked her if she wanted to see Nicolas Roeg's *Walkabout,* which was playing at a revival house in Westwood. It was a dramatic piece about two white kids stranded in the Australian outback who are helped to survive by an Aboriginal man — a story which, after my trip Down Under, really resonated with me. I'd already seen the film once, but it was so amazing that I didn't mind going again. Stacey said, "Sure."

She was staying at her parents' house while they were traveling. I rang the bell and this little boy — Jed — opened the door.

"Fonzie!" he yelled.

Now, I didn't know that this kid had had a Fonzie figure on his birthday cake. I didn't know anything in general about kids. I looked down at him and said, "My name is not Fonzie. My name is Henry. Would you like it if I called you Ralph?"

And this little boy, having no idea what the hell was going on, ran away. It was a moment I would replay in my mind many times over the years to come.

I was very intense in those days, quite Germanic and serious (where could that have come from?), even though comedy was my beat. You wouldn't think it to look at me, but I was.

STACEY:

I had told Jed that I was going on a date with this man, Henry Winkler, and I explained to him that he was Fonzie on TV, but that he was really Henry Winkler. It didn't quite compute with Jed — he just got really excited that Fonzie, the guy from his birthday cake, was coming to see us.

So we went to the movie theater and I said to Stacey, "You know, I think it's better if we sit toward the back."

"Oh, come on — why?" she said.

So we walked in, went down toward the front, and sat down — and within two minutes, everyone in the theater got up and came over to say hello.

"Oh," Stacey said.

After the movie I took her to Le Restaurant for dessert. On the way, I kept waving out my car window. Stacey said, "*Who* are you waving to?" I said, "I have no idea — they're waving to me; I'm waving back to them."

We both smoked at that time, so we stopped at a 7-Eleven along the way to get a pack. All the magazines of the day were displayed on racks below the cashier. I was on the cover of most of them. It was exhilarating and embarrassing at the same moment. Stacey said, "Will you look at that!" And I just replied with a sheepish "Yeah."

I paid for the Tareytons and got out of the store as quickly as I could.

After a delicious chocolate mousse, we drove back to her parents' house. Jed was asleep; Stacey paid the babysitter. And as soon as the sitter left, I started to say good night to Stacey, and she said, "Oh, you don't have to go."

Then she said, "I didn't leave that door open."

The sliding glass door in her parents' living room was ajar. And I don't know where I got the nerve, but this short Jew walked out that door into the backyard. I looked around — then I turned and saw a guy sort of crouching in the bushes, wearing boxer shorts and a T-shirt.

"Hello," I said.

"Hi," he said — and raced by me back into the house.

This was the guy she was dating. "This is Terry, the man I told you about," Stacey said. She had told me about him. "You really have to leave now," she said.

"Okay," I said. Thinking she was saying it to me.

"Oh no, no — *he's* gonna go," Stacey said. And then, to the guy: "What are you doing here? How dare you?"

STACEY:

This was the guy I should've gone out with

in college, just to get it out of my system. Tall and blond, a jock, very Waspy — like the Swede in Philip Roth's *American Pastoral.* You know, there's a time and a place for the Swede, but in my life, it wasn't any longer. I think he was hiding in the bushes and waiting for Henry to leave, so we could rekindle. I made it very clear that that was not going to happen. And so he — Terry — left. And Henry and I began to see each other.

I saw that he was super popular, and very much in demand. But that didn't intimidate me, because he was so down-to-earth. And substantial. And really a total gentleman.

So he was terrific. And I just knew. I thought we had really clicked. But at the same time, there were so many things about his life that I didn't know. The hard things.

But with the things that were important to me, he had the right stuff.

After that first date, I wrote on a piece of paper: *I'm going to marry this man. I'm going to marry Henry Winkler.* And I put the paper in my mother's jewelry box. Because I just knew.

A year before I met Stacey, I went to a

Hollywood party where I met a most atypical Hollywood couple, Lynn Arost and Frank Dines. Lynn was a former inner-city elementary schoolteacher now working as a development executive at MGM, and later to become Jessica Lange's head of development. Frank, who'd grown up in Pittsburgh, was a psychiatrist. They were thoughtful, deep, and funny, and we hit it off immediately. If you'd told me then that we'd be friends for the next forty-six years, I wouldn't have been a bit surprised. And from the moment I met Stacey, I was dying to introduce this important new person in my life to Lynn and Frank.

Lynn invited the two of us to their apartment for dinner (coincidentally, their place was just a couple of blocks from my first LA apartment, around the corner from Schwab's Pharmacy), and, because worrying is my favorite indoor sport — along with volleyball — I instantly found myself worrying whether my friends would like this new woman in my life. The worry dissipated almost the moment we walked through the door. Stacey was nervous, but her nerves were for naught: the conversation started flowing at once — and hasn't stopped for nearly a half century.

Stacey grew up among show-business

kids, and so showbiz shop-talk was the last thing she was interested in. Instead, we spoke about family and friends and things that struck us as funny. The laughter came as easily as the conversation, and the food was delicious: Lynn made us her signature dessert, Sara Lee pound cake smothered in blueberry sauce.

We've been having dinner together ever since. Stacey and I are the proud godparents of Lynn and Frank's son, Matt, who was born within months of our Max; they're fast friends forty years later. And when Matt married the wonderful screenwriter Heather Regnier and they had a little boy, Ben, Ben became friends with Max and Jessie's daughter Frankie at almost the same age Matt and Max had become pals.

Our friendship with Lynn and Frank has truly yielded generational riches.

By the fourth season of *Happy Days,* everyone in the cast was clicking beautifully together, especially Ron and I. The two of us were having a great time. We could literally take a three-page scene, memorize it, improvise it, rehearse it, then shoot it three times in twenty minutes. There was a thread between us — the kind of thing you can't manufacture. It just exists. I was always careful not to do anything that might be seen as taking over, stepping on his toes, being disrespectful: all I cared about and all Ron cared about was making the show funny. There was no attitude, no star power. It was the same with Mr. and Mrs. C. — Marion and Tom — and Donny and Anson.

That season began with a three-episode subplot, "Fonzie Loves Pinky," in which the Fonz's old girlfriend Pinky Tuscadero (Roz Kelly) returned to Milwaukee for a demonstration of her motorcycle skills, and I drove in a demolition derby against the villainous Malachi brothers. We usually started the season at Paramount, but this year we needed to shoot the derby exteriors at a movie ranch in Malibu Creek State Park. I phoned Ron and asked if I could get a ride out there with him.

He picked me up early — he had a VW Bug, one of the originals — and we headed out there. We did a long day's work, then Ron and I headed back to LA. With each passing mile, I got more and more nervous. There was a question I'd been wanting to ask — that I'd been scared to ask — for three and a half years. I didn't know what was going to happen if I spoke my mind, but I couldn't put it off anymore. "Okay, I have to ask you," I said. "How are you feeling?"

"About — ?"

"You know," I said — though he didn't know. "Look," I finally said, "I know what's happening — everybody knows what's happening. The Fonz has taken off, and the show was designed for you to be the star. And they just gave me a big raise." I told him about the new deal I'd just made with ABC. "I don't know what's going on with your contract," I said, "but I want you to know how much I respect you. You've handled all of this incredibly well."

He looked serious. Thoughtful. "Well, it's good for the show," Ron said. "You're not doing anything, Henry — you're not letting this go to your head or change who you are. You're a great team player. What you've created is incredible and great for the show. But if I'm honest, I have to say it does hurt my feelings; more than that — it's made me angry at times. Because you're right — I was supposed to be the star of the show. But I was never angry at *you*, Henry." Marion had said the same thing, Ron said: that no one was angry at me as a person; it was just that Fonzie was sucking all the air out of Stage 19.

He told me about Tom Miller and Ed Milkis coming to him with the *Fonzie's Happy Days* proposal; he said that if it hadn't been for Garry's intervention, he might have left the show. I told Ron that Leonard Goldenson himself had brought that idea to me — after asking me if I wanted to have a show of my own. I said that, as respectfully as possible, I'd asked Mr. Goldenson not to change anything. "I'm only successful because I'm in the middle of *this* show," I said.

Ron nodded, taking it all in — and I could see he was feeling better.

"I don't want anything to change about our friendship," I told him. "I love you, Ron."

"I love *you,* Henry," he said.

And we both still feel the same. I'm godfather to Ron and Cheryl's lovely daughter Bryce, a very talented actress. And Ron and Cheryl have said to Stacey and me: "God forbid anything happens to us, would you take the children? You can bar mitzvah them if you want."

Before I met Stacey, I felt that I'd never want to marry a woman with a child — I was determined to start from scratch. Then I met an amazing woman who had a child, and everything I thought up until then went into the garbage bin.

We began to see each other exclusively. We were wildly attracted to each other. She was beautiful, she was kind, and she helped me learn to spell. She introduced me to good food. No more Swanson's TV dinners. (I have to admit, I missed them a little bit.) And she apparently thought a lot of things about me were pretty good, too.

But what she was seeing was on the surface. I looked fine on the outside, but if you opened the container, you saw that it had been sent from the factory without the jelly beans. To mix up the metaphor: what she didn't realize was that my real self was like a kernel of corn sheathed in yards of concrete — as insulated as the nuclear material at Chernobyl.

I don't think either of us realized that at first, because both of us were so busy falling in love. That's a time when you have stars in your eyes, which is a good thing. A necessary thing. And in falling in love with Stacey, I also began to feel closer and closer to Jed. My own childhood had been such a mess that I felt no natural pull toward children — I was almost intimidated by them. Certainly alienated from them. When Jed called me Fonzie the first time we met, all I could think about was myself and all my difficulties in prying myself — whoever that was — apart from the character I played on TV. Falling in love with Stacey, I understood more and more about who her son was as a human being: a lively, curious, affectionate little boy who missed his father, but had room in his heart for me. So I began to make room in my heart for him.

And then, room in my house.

After Stacey and I had dated for around a year, we made the big decision: she and Jed moved in with me. We had two bedrooms in my little house, one for us and one for him; we had one bathroom, with a mosaic on the floor of the phoenix rising from the ashes. (Could that have symbolized something?) And we had fun. But it wasn't uncomplicated.

For one thing (or two) there was Percy and Amanda.

Percy and Amanda were Stacey's Yorkshire terriers. I've always loved dogs, but I was convinced I wasn't a small-dog guy. There's a backstory here. When I was ten, I had an Irish setter named Dervin, and I loved her with my whole being. Dervin was a bright coppery red, and she was beautiful and amazing. When I went swimming in the lake at Mahopac, she would jump in the water with me to make sure I was safe. When I walked in the woods, she walked with me. One day I ran into the woods with Dervin at my side — and suddenly she was gone. I called and called for her, but she was nowhere to be found. I staggered back to the house, convinced she was gone forever; I sat on the grass and cried and cried. All at once, my mother opened the window. "What's the matter?" she asked.

I could barely get the words out. "Dervin ran away," I said, through tears.

"Ach!" my mother yelled, exasperatedly, and slammed the window shut.

Then, a miracle: as I sat there weeping, Dervin came up out of nowhere and laid her head on my hand.

And not long after that, my parents gave Dervin away. It would be better if she lived on a farm, they said.

That hole in my heart lingered into my adulthood, and I knew no little dog could ever fill it.

But Stacey's Amanda made quick work of me. She followed me everywhere. She sat at my feet when I was working at my desk. And as Stacey and Jed had already done, she moved into my heart.

STACEY:

I had stars in my eyes, too. When I met Henry, I thought — and I was stupid — that all he was was this great Jewish guy. Great energy. Just a really menschy guy who happened to be an actor. That was his job. And that idea, that acting was just Henry's day job, got reinforced when we moved in together. With the schedule he had on *Happy Days,* he practically could've been working at Douglas Aircraft. From Monday through Thursday, he was home every day at around six. There was a show every Friday night, then it was over until Monday morning. But we ate dinner as a family every night. That was very important to me.

And Henry was great with Jed. In many ways he was a much better parent than I was, because he was patient. He made plastic models on the dining room table with Jed; he painted Jed's face to look like Paul Stanley from Kiss. I was still feeling the aftershocks of my divorce from How- ard, still finding it hard to get emotional equilibrium. Meanwhile, Henry and Jed were winning each other over. It wasn't all smooth sailing. Jed would say to him, "Could you not talk as much?" — because

133

Henry could be very verbose, and Jed was four, and it got long. But Henry would smile, and tone it down a little bit. Until the next time.

Now and then, when we were all together — I mean with Howard, too, for Thanksgiving or some other social situation — Jed would pay more attention to Howard, and Henry was fine with that. Jed was able to take Henry for granted, because he felt safe. He didn't feel Henry was going to leave. When Howard married Margaret, things changed significantly. Margaret and Henry were the "strict team," and Howard and I tended to spoil Jed — I'm sure because of the guilt from the divorce.

I knew that acting was going to be the priority for Henry, over almost everything. I knew he needed that to be fulfilled — to feel alive. But I also thought that there was a separation between his acting life and his real life. It took me a long time to realize that that separation was a very elusive thing.

5.

Summer camp, like the rest of my boyhood, was rich with embarrassing problems. From ages nine to thirteen, I went to Secor Lake Camp, a half-hour drive from our house in Mahopac. I was a transient camper, which meant that they picked me up every morning and took me back home at night. This meant that I always felt I was missing out on all the important things that happened when I wasn't there. Could this have been to save my father a few dollars? At that age, you don't ask — you just go with the flow. I went with the flow.

The campers at Secor Lake were divided into tribes named after actual Native American tribes, and every Sunday night there was a tribe meeting. The counselors and the kids would tell stories, and we'd sing songs. And there was a ritual: if you got tapped on the shoulder, you were supposed to spend the entire week being silent. They gave you a lanyard with a twig on it to wear around your neck, and if anybody caught you speaking during that week, they would carve a notch into the twig. And if you got four notches in your twig, you couldn't join the tribe.

I never got into the tribe.

Verbose? Guilty. I talked too much when I was anxious, and I was anxious all the time. And, never really having felt heard, I had my own difficulty hearing others.

The summer after I turned fourteen, my parents tried to put some polish on me by sending me to a fancy summer school in Switzerland, Lycée Jaccard. Are you surprised to hear that I went to a lycée in Switzerland with the sons of barons and earls and captains of industry? Listen, I admit it: there is a split in my brain. For all the bad I've told you about my parents, I have to also say that I am grateful. Grateful that I lived in a nice apartment, that we had a beautiful country house, that we went on trips to Europe and South America. I was the beneficiary — I gained a lot from these trips. I saw the world. I think that traveling is the best education on earth. And my father was grooming me to take over his business, so I guess he didn't mind spending the bucks (money he probably didn't have) on a fancy summer school.

I was supposed to learn French at Lycée Jaccard — and, you guessed it, I wasn't going to learn French for all the tea in China. But I did meet some nice kids there, including the son of a sheikh from Kuwait. We were on the crew team together, until I turned an oar the wrong way and got flipped out of the boat.

I got kicked off that team, too.

As I grew older, though, I got a little more confident about myself physically. During the summers at Mahopac, water-skiing on the lake was a popular activity — everybody around the lake had a speedboat; you had to have a speedboat to keep up with the Joneses. But we did not have a boat: I had to depend upon friends who passed by our dock to pick me up. Nevertheless, I learned to water-ski, and pretty soon I was pretty good at it. Good enough so that when I was eighteen and got my first summer job (after working in my father's office filing letters about wood), as a counselor at Blue Mountain Camp in East Stroudsburg, Pennsylvania, they made me a water-ski instructor.

If you ever watched *Happy Days*, you might have an idea where this is leading.

As Season 5 approached, we had a slight ratings sag. So Garry and the other producers got the idea that moving the action of the show to California for a while might pep things up in general, including our numbers. And so they came up with a story arc that had a Hollywood talent scout thinking Fonzie might be the next James Dean. This plot line took the show to Hollywood, where, as it turned out, the Fonz failed his screen test and a new story arc for Richie developed instead. In the meantime, my father had kept saying to me, "Tell Garry Marshall that you water-ski!" And so sometime before the season began, I mentioned to Garry that I had once been a decent water-skier, had even taught it as a camp counselor. Garry's face lit up. "That's great!" he said. "I'm gonna put that in the show!"

Thus came about Season 5, Episode 3, the one where Fonzie accepts a challenge to perform a dangerous water-ski jump — over a shark.

Now, the whole storyline was pretty far-fetched — but with a long-running sitcom, the writers have to try all kinds of things. There are highs and lows: not every episode can be a masterpiece. There was a blip in Season 3 when Fonzie loses his job at the garage and starts selling encyclopedias door-to-door — I wasn't in love with that development. But little did any of us know at the time, or for years afterward, that the central scene of Season 5, Episode 3 of *Happy Days* would become a synonym for disaster.

The shark was a tiger shark, and he was caged — surrounded by netting on five sides, including underneath, but not on top. So, failing to execute the jump could, just possibly, dump the jumper into the drink with the shark.

Fortunately, I was not the jumper.

You hear that Tom Cruise always insists on doing his own stunts. Well, that's great for Tom Cruise — I have the highest admiration for his physical courage. But back in 1977, *Happy Days*' producers were not about to allow their star, their rainmaker, to risk getting injured, and I have to say, I concurred with them. So a stuntman did the jump.

But the scenes before and after, with me looking good on water skis in a leather jacket and swim trunks — boy, did I have great legs then! — were all me. And when I let go of the tow rope, glided up on shore, and stepped out of the skis with a big grin on my face . . . well, watch the episode. Half of that grin is the Fonz saying, *Ayyy, I did it! Come on — did you ever doubt it for a sec-*

ond? But the other half was me, Henry, thinking, *Oh my God, I made it.*

Was it a great episode? Maybe not. But years later, sometime in the mideighties, a University of Michigan college kid named Sean Connolly thought it was so bad that he started using the expression *jumping the shark* to refer to any outlandish development. Then, around a decade after that, Connolly's former roommate at Michigan, a comedy writer and radio personality named Jon Hein, started a website called jumptheshark.com — dedicated to those defining moments "when you know that your favorite television program has reached its peak. [Those instants] that you know from now on . . . it's all downhill."

Jon Hein made an entire industry out of that phrase — a book, a board game. Finally sold the website to *TV Guide* for millions. When I heard about it I thought, *This is really America.* Comes up with a phrase, all of a sudden it's a phenomenon. I was even a guest on Jon's show on Sirius Satellite Radio — a very lovely man. I don't begrudge him one iota of his success.

Even though some important people on *Happy Days* — specifically Ron and Don Most — thought that episode really was over-the-top, it wasn't anything like the beginning of the end for the series: in fact, it was just the middle. We would go on for six more seasons.

One day around Christmas of 1977, Stacey and I were in New York, walking down Madison Avenue, when I saw a very familiar face coming toward us — Paul McCartney. I'd never met him; I was a huge Beatles fan just like everyone else in the world. So I was thrilled just to see him, but I was almost speechless when he stopped, and in *that accent* said, "The Fonz."

The three of us stood and talked for a minute, and suddenly we were attracting attention, these two famous faces on a Madison Avenue sidewalk — never mind that at that moment I didn't feel like a celebrity: I was just another gushing fan. Fortunately (or unfortunately?) no one knew that but me. A woman comes up, wide-eyed, and says, "Can I just stand here?" And Paul says, "We're having a conversation. No." Then another woman comes out of the store we're standing in front of and hands us each a rose. And then Paul McCartney gives me his phone number. "Let's get in touch," he says. "Let's hang out." Then he leaves.

I just stood there for a minute, still vibrating. I looked at Stacey. "Can you believe that?" I said.

"Henry, you're famous," my matter-of-fact girlfriend said. "What do you expect?"

I did my very best to wait a couple of days — it wasn't easy! — then I called the number Paul had given me. I got an answering machine, and left a message.

No reply. (Like the Beatles song.) I waited a day, then called again.

No callback. (This was not a Beatles song.) I waited a couple of days, then called again. Same result.

I wound up calling seven more times. Or was it seventeen? In any case, I never heard back. And to this day, I can barely think about the whole thing without a hot blush, because I know I must have put that man off, acting like a crazed fan.

Maybe you thought that all celebrities know each other? That there's a secret celebrity handshake? Oh no. Oh no. While it's true that stars gravitate toward one another — even stars get starstruck — there are levels upon levels of celebrity, and all kind of unwritten rules about celebrity interactions. And of course, being dyslexic, I never read the unwritten rule book. . . .

The same thing happened when I met Mick Jagger. Twice. The first time was on a plane with the *Happy Days* softball team, flying to Miami to play an exhibition game at a Dolphins game. And there was Mick Jagger. I introduced myself; he was nice. He *seemed* to know who I was. He did *not* give me his phone number. (Maybe McCartney had warned him about me.)

And then the second time. It was years later, at Matsuhisa, the Japanese restaurant on La Cienega Boulevard. There was Jagger again, sitting with a woman. And I walked up after my meal and said, "Oh my God, Mick, it is so great to see you. I've got every one of your albums." I'm babbling like a nine-year-old girl; he's giving no indication of whether he remembers me or not. (I'm sure he doesn't.) The longer I stand there, the more embarrassing it gets, and I have no idea how to exit gracefully. *Can I show you a menu? Enjoy your meal.*

Finally I stumbled away. As I was leaving the restaurant, a couple at another table spoke to me. "You were talking to Mick Jagger!" they said.

"Yeah," I said.

"That was so cool," they said. "To see the two of you together."

The two of us . . . me and Mick. . . . And just for a second I felt less embarrassed, because they hadn't seen that I felt lower than whale poop on the bottom of the ocean.

Which was the way I felt for many years. I was still chasing the cool kids, never imagining I could be anything like cool myself.

Season 5 was memorable for more than shark-jumping. Around the time the writers began working on that year's episodes, Garry Marshall's young son, Scott — he was eight or nine at the time — said, "Hey, there should be an alien on *Happy Days,* and he should meet the Fonz — that would really make the show great."

Once again, Garry knew the right people to listen to.

He and one of the writers, Joe Glauberg, sketched out a story where an extraterrestrial from the planet Ork lands in Milwaukee and encounters Richie and the Fonz. Then Joe wrote the script, which was hilarious. The only problem was, the producers couldn't find an actor to play the alien. They asked some well-known people to try out: the British actor Roger Rees, the great Dom DeLuise, the impressionist John Byner. All of them had commitments and conflicts.

Every Monday morning at ten o'clock we'd start rehearsing that week's episode;

by Wednesday of that week we still didn't have an actor. Then around 11 a.m. on Wednesday, our casting director Bobby Hoffman brought a very shy young man to the set, someone I'd never seen before. His name was Robin Williams.

We later found out that Garry's sister Ronny, a producer on the show, had seen Robin doing comedy on the street and collecting money in a hat, and thought he was very talented. When Garry asked her why he'd ever want to audition someone who was working on the street, Ronny said, "Well, his hat was pretty full!"

It turned out that Robin had a memorable tryout. When he came in and Garry asked him to have a seat, he went to a chair and sat in it — upside down. Literally. A headstand in the chair. Later, when someone asked Garry why he'd picked Robin Williams for the character of Mork, the extraterrestrial, he said, "He was the only alien who auditioned."

So this long-haired young guy came onto the set, very quiet and polite, and shook hands with everybody. We all welcomed him. He picked up the script, and we started to rehearse. And within forty-two seconds, I knew I was in the presence of greatness.

The first scene we did was in Arnold's:

Mork had come to take Richie back to his planet so they could study him. I said, as the Fonz: "You're not taking him anywhere — you wanna rumble?" And instantaneously, without a millisecond of hesitation, Robin broke out a high-voiced couple of bars from *West Side Story*. And then and there I knew I had two jobs that week: one was to remember my lines, and two was to not constantly collapse with laughter. This truly was a life force from another planet.

Robin's first appearance on *Happy Days* happened toward the end of the season, in March 1978. His character made such an impact that by September he'd gotten his own show, the spin-off *Mork & Mindy,* starring him and Pam Dawber. They filmed just down the lot, on Stage 27, so I saw a lot of him. When I heard that besides making the show, he was doing stand-up comedy at nights, I was incredulous, and crazy enough to give the great Robin Williams advice. I told him: "You know, I don't think it's a good idea to do the stand-up. It takes so much energy to do your show all week — if I were you, I'd save up my energy."

It was my old advice-giving self, jumping right in where I hadn't been invited. Still, I really was concerned for him.

Robin didn't really answer; he just nodded. Here was a young guy who had the life force of fifteen people — who was I to give him career guidance? He just went on doing what he was doing. (And of course Stacey and I ended up in the audience of one of his stand-up shows.) Robin and I never became close, but I felt a warmth every time I saw him. I wonder if there was some part of him that knew he wouldn't have much time to be with us.

You remember that my father had always wanted to be a diplomat. So despite the many negative lessons he taught me, one thing I did learn from him was how to be socially charming. I could put up a great front, but it was just that, a front.

When Stacey and Jed and I first started living together, I was back in PS 87, emotionally speaking. I could be great with Jed — that was pretty easy. I could sit on the floor and build models with him; I could go to his T-ball and soccer games. And I loved Stacey, but that was harder. I didn't always know how to tell her, or even show her. I was afraid. Because this was a really adult thing we were doing, and I was not really an adult then. I was desperately immature and insecure.

Now and then back at the beginning, Stacey would write sweet little notes that she'd slip into the pockets of my clothing, or in my luggage if I was traveling: "I love you. I miss you. You're going to be great." But instead of being warmed by the notes, I was irritated by them. I felt smothered — I literally felt as if I had a plastic bag over my head.

"I need you to be intimate," Stacey would say to me. It didn't compute. I didn't even know the definition of intimate. Sometimes, in sheer exasperation, I would say, "What the fuck are you asking me? What? Tell me what 'intimate' means. And I'll tell you if I even know how to do it."

I said, "I'm earning a living; we're living in a nice house. I'm polite. What's the problem?"

I was unavailable. Not knowing I was unavailable. My insecurities were always threatening to run rampant. An early sign of trouble was a problem I imagined I had with Jim Brooks. Jim was the cocreator (with Allan Burns) of *The Mary Tyler Moore Show;* he would go on to codevelop *The Simpsons,* and write and direct movies like *Broadcast News* and *Terms of Endearment.* Jim was some kind of genius, and I got on his radar when I did my small part on *Mary Tyler Moore* — he even hired me for a guest spot on *Rhoda* after my first season of *Happy Days*. And a couple of years later, when Stacey and I had just begun living together, I said something (I think it was at some industry get-together) that, I thought, offended him.

Not only do I not recall where it happened, I don't remember what I might've said — I think that even back *then* I wasn't sure what I'd said. But once this worm of worry started burrowing into my brain, there was no stopping it. Soon I became obsessed. I couldn't sleep; I couldn't think of anything else. It was as if a python had wrapped itself around my body, and with every breath I took, it was squeezing a little more. There was nothing that existed on earth except this thing in my mind, this egregious affront to Jim Brooks.

Stacey, God bless her, was good at brass tacks. "Okay," she said. "Let's take care of this." Somehow I found out that Jim had gone to San Francisco for the weekend. So Stacey got on the phone and called every major hotel in San Francisco. By 11:30 that night, she had reached Jim Brooks on the phone. I got on the phone with him. And I said, "Jim, I'm so sorry. Did I offend you?"

"Man, what are you talking about?" he said.

"When I said what I said at that party."

"What? I don't remember you saying anything — no!"

"I'm so sorry to bother you," I told him.

"Have a great weekend, man!"

"You too, Jim. I will have a great weekend." And to this moment, I can still viscerally feel the way my entire body let go of this boa constrictor of guilt.

Was this a lesson to me? It was not, because had it been a lesson, nothing like it would have happened again. And it did happen again. And again.

And Stacey was starting to recalibrate her initial assessment of me. Remarkably, despite everything, she seemed to love me anyway.

We lived together for about a year, then, on May 5, 1978, at Habonim, the Upper West Side synagogue that my parents helped found, the temple where I'd been bar mitzvahed, we got married. The night before the wedding — Stacey and I were staying at the Sherry-Netherland — we had a tremendous argument about something or other: probably because I was just so scared. But in that moment of rage, I kicked my heel back and knocked the bathroom door off its hinge.

And I was so apart from myself that I

thought, *Wow, I had no idea I could do that.*

All four of our parents were there, and Jed, and my sister and brother-in-law, and my nieces. And paparazzi — lots of them. After the wedding we had a small party at the St. Regis for the New York contingent — we were going to have a bigger party in LA. And one of the paparazzi sneaked in, took pictures, and then sold them, after promising us she wouldn't. But it wasn't as if there was any scandal to stir up. It was a beautiful day, and Stacey looked incredibly beautiful. And my parents accepted her completely, and treated Jed as their grandson.

How could my mother and father, those terrible people, have been so loving and generous? All I can say is that life is complicated, and there can be good and bad on the same page. And that my parents would revert to form soon enough.

Back in 1975, at the end of the second season of *Happy Days*, I was asked if I was interested in being in a TV movie called *Katherine*, about a rich girl who gets kidnapped by revolutionaries — kind of like the true-life story of Patty Hearst. Katherine would be beautifully played by Sissy Spacek. I was to play Katherine's boyfriend.

I went to meet with the director, Jeremy Kagan, and the casting director, the famous Lynn Stalmaster. I thought the meeting went pretty well, though I was too nervous to know how it had really gone — I'm still the same way today. Afterward, Lynn walked me to the elevator, and I asked, "When will I know if I get this or not?" And Lynn put his hand on my shoulder and said, "I think you've got it."

Only at this distance can I hear the irony in his voice.

What I didn't realize — I was still naïve then — was that the reason they wanted me, pure and simple, was because I was the Fonz.

I was less of an innocent three years later when an amazing script landed on my desk, an autobiographical story by James Carabatsos, about a Vietnam veteran who comes home with PTSD — before there officially was such a thing — and escapes from a mental hospital and sets out on a cross-country trip to round up buddies from his old army platoon to help him start a worm farm. As in growing worms for fishing bait. It was a quirky, touching story, and playing Jack, the psychologically wounded warrior, seemed like a great opportunity for me to stretch artistically and show another side of me beyond the Fonz. What's more, I had enough professional leverage at that point to be able to pick my director and costars.

I asked Jeremy Kagan to join me on the journey, and we went to New York to cast the female lead, my girlfriend in the story. One of the first actresses to come in was a strikingly beautiful young woman with the odd name of Meryl Streep. At this point, Meryl (a fellow graduate of Yale School of Drama) was a complete unknown, but I instantly knew — and this is something I've felt a few times in my career — that I was in the presence of greatness. Her poise and her acting brilliance were off the charts.

And Universal would not hire her.

Why? She was nobody! *The Deer Hunter, Kramer vs. Kramer, Sophie's Choice* — all of those were in her future. Instead the studio approved Sally Field, who was just starting to leave behind her typecast image as the Flying Nun and blossom as a movie actress. And Sally was just great: it was a privilege to work with her.

Also in the picture, playing one of my former army buddies, was a young, very taciturn actor named Harrison Ford. When we first met, he told me he'd just finished shooting a movie in England, some science-fiction thing that was all green screen. He had no idea what to make of it or how it would turn out. That science-fiction thing was (you guessed it) *Star Wars.*

These days, if I ever happened to catch *Heroes* on late-night cable (I would never choose to watch it on purpose), I know I'd see that Sally was excellent, Harrison was very effective — and that I was painfully self-conscious. It was the beginning of a long period in my career when, whenever I tried to step outside of playing the Fonz, I just could not get out of my own way as an actor. That completely unexpected moment in my *Happy Days* audition, the moment when Fonzie's voice came out of me as if from another person, marked a professional fork in the road for me: playing him, I felt completely authentic. His certainty took me over, bolstered me. Protected me. Lifted me.

On the other hand, playing any other role, I would find my (confused) self constantly intruding. What you would see on the screen if you watched *Heroes* would be the real Henry Winkler (whoever he was), trying hard — and in vain — to inhabit another character.

What you would see if you watched *Happy Days* would be the character I loved — who had also taken over my professional existence.

But *Heroes* went with the mood of the time, and it was a big box-office hit, so much so that Universal sent me on a publicity tour to Europe, which happened to coincide with our honeymoon.

The movie's publicity wasn't the only publicity that touched on our trip. Stacey and I soon learned that while Jed was flying home from New York City with her parents, a hand holding a stuffed animal came through the gap between the seats. The hand belonged to a *National Enquirer* reporter, trying to charm Jed and Stacey's mom and dad so they would talk to him.

Meanwhile, at our first stop, in Stockholm, we were checking into our hotel when the guy at the front desk said, "Oh, your friends are here — they're at the bar." And Stacey said, "What friends?" And the desk clerk pointed to them, and she turned around, and instantly realized what was going on. And I'm telling you, I've never seen anybody walk that fast — it was as if the marble under her feet was cracking. She walked up to these two guys — one of them had a camera — and said, "How dare you? We're on our honeymoon! Who do you think you are?"

More people from the *National Enquirer.*

"We're so sorry, but it's our job," they

said. And Stacey said, "Give me your boss's name! Who's the editor?"

We called the editor from our room, and we made a deal with him. We told him that we would meet his photographer when we got to Paris, at eleven o'clock in the morning in front of the Eiffel Tower, and we would give the *Enquirer* exclusive pictures if they would leave us alone for the rest of the trip — and leave Jed alone for good. And he agreed.

And we went on to have a wonderful honeymoon, unbothered. The only intrusions into our total privacy were pleasant ones: *Happy Days* was now being televised in Europe, and I was recognized everywhere — but always with great affection. Nobody wanted to fight Fonzie; everyone just loved him.

After Sweden we went to Paris, then to London. And while we were there, I saw the Royal Shakespeare Company do *Henry IV,* with Alan Howard in the title role.

I'd never heard or seen anything like it in my life. Until that day, I don't think I had any idea what Shakespeare really was. I'd heard Americans *trying* to do it, but I couldn't follow it, it sounded pompous, and there was a lot of spitting. But Alan Howard and the rest of the Royal Shakespeare Company spoke to each other like they were having a conversation about a salami sandwich — it was just that natural. Truly great acting is such an awesome thing. As for me, I was just watching with my nose pressed against the glass.

I met Sir Laurence Olivier once. It was early in the third season of *Happy Days;* Olivier was shooting *Marathon Man* on the Paramount lot. I saw him as he was getting into his limousine — he was looking kind of frail — and I ran toward him, saying, "Wait, wait, wait — please, just wait one minute."

He stopped, stood holding on to the car door, a little stooped over. "Yes?" he said.

"I'm Henry Winkler," I said. "I'm an actor. And I've seen every movie you've ever been in and heard about you all my life — I needed to just shake your hand."

He smiled and we shook hands. "Thank you, dear boy," he said. Then he got into the limo and rode away.

Dustin Hoffman was Olivier's costar in *Marathon Man.* Dustin is a Method actor, which meant that when he had to play a scene in the movie where his character hasn't slept in three days, he actually went without sleeping for that long, so he could feel and look the way his character should look and feel. And there's a famous story, that Olivier said to Hoffman, "Why don't you just try acting?"

Dustin Hoffman is a real movie star and a tremendous actor. Years ago I saw the Broadway production of *The Merchant of Venice,* with Hoffman playing Shylock. The English actress Geraldine James played Portia, and she did that phenomenal thing that English actors can do — that salami-sandwich thing. And I want to tell you, Dustin Hoffman came damn close. I mean that as the highest praise.

One day very early in the show's run, Ron and I were sitting on the couch in my place rehearsing some lines, and he suddenly said, "Hey, what do you think about me directing?"

Now, something happened at that moment, something that, I'm pretty sure, had nothing to do with the joint I was smoking. (I had it all to myself — Ron didn't smoke.) I felt an energy coming off Ron, moving across the couch like the vapor from dry ice and bumping me. "Are you kidding?" I said. "I think you're so powerful — if you wanted to be a brain surgeon, I would be your first patient whether I needed brain surgery or not."

So during *Happy Days'* hiatus months, from April to July, Ron began to find his new calling. Working with the renowned B-picture producer Roger Corman, from a script Ron wrote with his dad, Rance, he directed his first feature, *Grand Theft Auto,* a fast-paced comedy-action picture with a *lot* of car wrecks, and, as Corman had stipulated, Ron himself in the starring role. The critics held their noses, but audiences loved it, and the film was a big commercial success — an amazing result on Ron's first time out, and by Hollywood's rules, his golden ticket for getting more work. He did a couple of TV movies, and then, immediately after *Happy Days* came to the end of its eleven-season run, Ron would direct his second feature and first big studio film, *Night Shift,* costarring Michael Keaton and . . . me.

But I'm getting ahead of myself.

6.

At the beginning of 1980, Stacey and I found out we were going to have a baby in September, and soon we discovered it was going to be a little girl. We were thrilled beyond words.

Not long afterward, I found that I'd won the Italian version of the Emmy, the Telegatto, for my work as the Fonz. Not only was this very gratifying — I'd been Emmy-nominated from 1976 through 1978, but my tush never left the seat (little did I know that it would be *forty years* until my tush left the seat) — but it also led, in the spring of 1980, to a beautiful trip to Italy.

Oh my God, I loved the Italians! One night in Rome, Stacey and I were walking down the street — it was around midnight; I had a full beard (which Stacey loved) and I was wearing a hat — and suddenly cars were backing up and stopping: "Fonzie! Bello! Bello!"

But what a great country, for many reasons beyond that. We got to spend a magical week at the majestic Villa Serbelloni, a grand hotel on Lake Como, and though Stacey caught a bad cold, an amazing thing also happened while we were there.

One afternoon, my publicist Richard Grant and I went out and bought ice cream and Italian hard sausages and cheeses and breads, and brought it all back to the hotel to have lunch with Stacey. And the three of us sat down in a big, lovely room lined with books to have some lunch. Just then, a woman came out and said, "Oh, this is part of my suite."

She wasn't being unfriendly. She was a pleasant, middle-aged woman, and after talking with her for a minute, I noticed she had a number tattooed on her forearm. I asked where she was from.

"I'm from the Carpathian Mountains, in Romania," she said.

"No kidding," I said. "My father has always talked about the Carpathian Mountains. He worked there in the lumber business as a young man."

"My father was also in the lumber business," she said.

"My father worked for Baron Von Gruedl, who owned forests."

"Oh," she said. "Baron Von Gruedl was my father."

Suddenly her eyes filled with tears, and in a moment she began to sob, gasping for air. When she regained her composure, she told us her story. Like my parents, she had lost her entire family in the Holocaust: for all her adult life, she had walked down the streets of various European cities, hoping against hope that she would recognize someone, or someone would recognize her. It never happened. She had felt so totally alone in the world, until this moment.

I walked her downstairs to the pay phone in the lobby, called my father in New York, and said, "I have Baron Von Gruedl's daughter here to talk to you."

I'm not sure which of them was more astonished.

In the weeks leading up to the birth of our first child, I said to Stacey, "Listen, make sure your mom is available, because if our baby is born on a Friday night, I can't be there."

"You what?" Stacey said.

"I won't be able to be there. I have to do the show — it costs over a million dollars to shoot an episode, and I don't have an understudy. And there's a schedule to get it on the air."

Stacey stared at me in disbelief.

She gave birth to Zoe Emily Winkler on September 30, 1980. It was a Tuesday. Luckily for all of us.

Jed was nine then, and he was amazing — he drove with us to the hospital in the middle of the night, sitting in the back seat with Stacey, who was starting to go into labor. "Mom, you're doing great, Mom," he kept saying. "You're gonna be great, Mom."

Then, when Zoe finally arrived, he said, "You know, could we put her back? I don't think I want a brother or a sister. I could go for an alien. But I'm not sure about a brother or a sister."

Now that there were four of us, we needed more space, so we moved into a big new house in Toluca Lake. That was a really beautiful house, designed by the eminent architect Paul Revere Williams, the only Black architect in LA — I got it in probate. I was bidding against this woman, and I couldn't look at her: it took everything in me to outbid her, and not just give her the house. Like the Fonz, I had a heart with a marshmallow filling.

Jed's room in the new house had bunk beds built into the wall and a ship's porthole for a window. His desk was built into the wall under the window, and his drawers were filled with multiple Walkmans from Howard, his Walkman supplier. And since at this moment in time Jed was obsessed with the British royals, his collection of souvenirs from Charles and Diana's wedding — commemorative magazines, figurines, drinking glasses, teacups, medallions, et cetera — was starting to overwhelm the limited shelf space in his room.

For the longest time, we did not want to break the news to Jed that he would never be a royal.

He knew he was an important guy, though. On the wall of his room was a photograph of — what doesn't belong in this picture? — young Jed Weitzman sitting in the front seat of a Jeep between Ronald Reagan, then the president of the United States, and the first lady, Nancy Reagan.

The backstory: the president's daughter Patti Davis had met Jed at a fundraiser on our lawn and thought he was such a personable young fellow that he should have the experience of spending the weekend with America's chief executive.

Stacey and I have had dinner with a president here and there, but we have never slept over at the Western White House. Jed did. Patti took him there when she went to visit her parents. And at the end of the weekend, Jed came home with stories about his new friends Ron and Nancy.

So now we were four, and things were a little more complicated. The baby needed a lot of attention, and Jed needed a lot of attention — for one thing, he had terrible problems with his ears, had to have tubes put in. We gave him medicine for his ear infections, but when he was at his father's, Howard didn't always give him his medicine. When Howard and Stacey talked on the phone, you could see veins pop out of her head that I didn't even know existed.

It was hard for Stacey, which was hard for me, and Jed was in the middle. And I can see from this distance that it confused him. So we said, "Look, the rules here are the rules here. And the rules at your dad's house are the rules at your dad's house. And whatever they are, that's what it is."

That helped, a little.

I was good at being patient with Jed, and I was good at being strict with Jed — one time he was being fresh at the dinner table, and I got mad and stood up, and he fell backward out of his chair. What I was not good at was being *with* Jed emotionally: still feeling like a boy inside, I was finding it difficult to be a dad. And the main thing was, I *wasn't* Jed's dad.

If he was feeling down, if Howard couldn't come and pick him up for some reason and Jed got upset, I could take him to the movies. And we went to the movies. But it was all so confusing, because I wanted to be let into the circle, and I couldn't find my way in. Once, when Jed was older, I think around twelve, and I was in a bad mood, he said, "You know, you could borrow my *Playboy.*"

The offer alone had raised my spirits. "Thank you," I said.

"By the way, I know what oral sex is," Jed said.

"Oh yeah?"

"It's when you talk dirty," Jed said.

Speaking of dirt . . . My love of gardening began with spider plants. When I grew up in Manhattan, our apartment had them on every windowsill, all of them the descendants of a single plant that Tante Anna — Aunt Anna — had smuggled out of Nazi Germany along with herself in, believe it or not, a coffin. When Anna and her plant reached New York City, everybody in this very tight circle of German Jews that my parents were part of got a cutting. And when I moved to Los Angeles, I took my own cutting with me.

My spider plant and its offspring occupied places of honor on the windowsills of my Reklaw Drive house; when Stacey moved in, we started to grow other things. We had a little forest of bonsai trees in front of the house, and the deck in back (we were on such a steep slope that there was no back-yard) was lined with clay pots containing all kinds of flora. I was fascinated with minia-ture ginkgo trees, so we had several: I clipped and watered them faithfully. To-gether, Stacey and I tended our forget-me-nots and ranunculi. I found that there was something wonderful about putting your hands in dirt, something that took my mind away from the everyday.

When we moved to Toluca Lake, the new house was on flat land, with a big backyard: this was where my passion for gardening really came into bloom. Soon after we moved in, Stacey gave me the gift of a rose garden: two dozen rose plants of different varieties, which she immediately put in their new bed. I could hardly wait until they started to bloom, in late March–early April. My favorite was (and still is) the Piaget: the fragrance is exquisite. We also had Elizabeth Taylors, Double Delights, and (Stella Adler should only have known) variegated red-and-whites. When we eventually sold the house to Andy Garcia and his family, one of the stipulations was to leave the rose garden as it was.

The new house also had a swimming pool, and with the yard and the pool, our real commitment to dogs began. Percy the Yorkshire terrier had passed on, and Amanda, now with gray hair on her muzzle, spent a lot of time napping. Our home clearly needed some puppy energy, and Waffles, a wheaten terrier, came along to fill the bill.

Or so it seemed at first. Waffles, it turned out, had just one goal in life: to run around the pool at top speed, whether someone was in it or not. He wouldn't even slow down to be petted. Jed, now ten, needed a dog he could interact with.

Enter Tootsie Annamarie, a beautiful black Lab. When Jed and I played catch (and as Waffles zoomed around the pool in the background), Tootsie played outfield. If Jed or I missed a catch, she brought the ball back to me, nicely coated with saliva, and politely dropped it in my mitt.

Simple pleasures. So important.

There was a pay phone in the corner of Stage 19 at Paramount that I used now and then to make calls, but there were only two occasions in the entire run of *Happy Days* when I *received* a call on that phone.

The first time was when I stopped a kid from committing suicide.

I'm being serious now, because this was a very serious matter. I was in Fonzie costume, in the middle of dress rehearsal, when somebody called me to the phone. On the other end of the line was a police officer from Indiana. "We have a young man here who's out on the ledge of a building," he said. "But he wants to talk to you."

He had my full attention.

Someone handed the phone on the other end to the kid on the ledge in Indiana. "Hi, this is Henry Winkler," I said.

"Hi," the kid said. His voice sounded quavery. I could hear the wind blowing.

"So, tell me first of all, what do you do?" I asked.

"Well, I'm an actor," the kid said. "And I'm —"

I interrupted him. Gently. "How old are you?" I asked.

"Seventeen," he said.

"Seventeen," I repeated.

"Mm-hmm," the kid said.

"Okay," I said. "Number one — you should know that I didn't get the Fonz until

I was twenty-eight. So there's plenty of time for you. So get the hell off that ledge."

All I heard on the other end was the wind blowing. For a moment I thought he had jumped. "You there?" I asked.

"Yeah."

"Okay, then here's number two," I said. "Do you have a record collection?"

"Yeah," he said.

"Great. Would you just go downstairs and sign the record collection over to me, so I can have it after you jump?"

He was quiet for a second. "Are you serious?" he asked.

"I am," I said. "I love music. And I don't know, you've got a whole collection. There might be something in there that's gold."

Now, where did I come up with the gall, the chutzpah, to think I was saying the right things to this kid? To think he wouldn't just jump while I was talking to him? I really had no idea. All I really had was the feeling that he liked me and wanted to talk to me. And that if I could keep him talking, maybe he'd change his mind.

And he did change his mind. After we'd talked for a few more minutes, the next voice I heard was the cop's. "Thank you," he said.

■ ■ ■ ■

In the late seventies, Bob Daly, the head of CBS Entertainment, along with his then-wife Nancy and their children, Bobby, Brian, and Linda, invited Stacey and me to a Christmas party at MacLaren Hall, a facility in El Monte for children who were abandoned, abused, and neglected. A bunch of celebrity actors and athletes who these kids knew from seeing them on TV traveled by bus to MacLaren and spent the day with the children.

The first child I met was Edward. Edward was five; I visited him in his dormitory room. I sat on a little chair, and Edward climbed into my lap and started to hit himself in the head. "Edward," I said, "that probably doesn't feel great. Why don't we find something else to do besides hitting your head?"

"I'm bad, I'm bad," Edward said.

"Why are you bad?" I asked.

"If I wasn't bad, my parents wouldn't burn me," Edward said.

Oh my God.

Afterward, my wife said, "We can't just do this on Christmas; we have to do more." And so Stacey and Nancy Daly joined

United Friends of the Children, a nonprofit dedicated to improving the lives of kids in facilities like this in every possible way. For MacLaren Hall, they raised money to put in a pool, to install computers, to build a library. They got artists from around Southern California to paint beautiful scenic murals on the walls so the kids didn't have to look at just brick. And though MacLaren Hall itself would later run into some bad scandals, the organization Stacey joined took hold. Stacey eventually became president of UFC, and she and Nancy went to Los Angeles City Hall and got the city government to separate children's services from elderly services and make it its own entity. They would call state senators, posing as Bob Daly's and Henry Winkler's secretaries, inviting them on our behalf to visit these institutionalized kids in order to get more services for them. (Of course, when the senators showed up, Stacey and Nancy would tell them that Henry and Bob were both on set working.)

United Friends of the Children continued and still continues to work for kids like this in the Los Angeles area. And inspired by Stacey's example, I began to go out myself to work with challenged children. As the Fonz, I started to visit severely disabled kids at Rancho Los Amigos Hospital in Downey; I began attending Special Olympics events and getting to know those amazing athletes. Each one of them thought they were meeting the Fonz. I was getting an education in giving back.

And soon after I met Bob Daly — who would go on after CBS to lead Warner Brothers and then the Los Angeles Dodgers — he became an important friend and advisor. Bob was salt of the earth: born in Brooklyn, raised by his mom and sisters, he started out selling individual cigarettes on the street, and rose from office boy at CBS to the top ranks of the company. But no matter how powerful he got, he never forgot the lessons of his humble beginnings; his understanding of the human condition and the right behavior was unequaled. From the start of our friendship, I would ask for his counsel and learn.

One night many years ago, while Stacey and I were having dinner at Bob and Nancy's house, a mutual friend who wanted to make a deal with Bob came over. This man gave Bob the contract in an Hermès bag that was so beautiful — I mean, made of leather that you didn't even know existed on the earth. And Bob handed it back and said, "I cannot take this contract inside a gift."

It's 9 p.m., we're inside Bob's home — who would ever have known if he had taken the bag and given it to his wife? Instead, the friend had to take the contract out of the bag and give Bob the raw paper. I will never forget that.

(Though Bob did gratefully accept Stacey's no-strings-attached gift of two hooded nuns, a breed of pigeon, to add to his collection, which harked back to the roofs of his boyhood in Brooklyn.)

I never worked for Bob, I only enjoyed his friendship, and that of his children and grandchildren. Both he and Frank Dines, my two closest male friends, are incomparably wise, and both have been important advisors to me for over forty years. Both have a deep understanding of the human condition, and both have given me — and continue to give me — invaluable perspectives and guidance.

The next time I was called to the pay phone on Stage 19 was a few years later, on a Friday morning in the fall of 1980. It was the beginning of Season 8. I'd gotten to work early, and we were about to start rehearsal. And the phone rings, and someone says, "It's for you, Henry." I had no idea what it could be. I flashed back for a second to that kid in Indiana. . . . Was it another emergency?

But this time the voice on the other end was Ron Howard's. "Hey, Ron!" I said. "How's it going?" Then, "Where the hell are you? You're supposed to be here!"

"Henry, I wanted you to know — it's going to hit the press in about ten minutes, but I wanted to tell you first — I'm leaving the show. I'm going to direct full-time."

I was completely thunderstruck. I was devastated, I was scared — you name it, I was feeling it. It was shocking.

Ron said more. He told me how disrespected the network had made him feel — financially and personally. "You know," he said, "ABC just really doesn't care about me." He mentioned his salary; he even mentioned the wallet the network gave him for Christmas, when I got that fancy videotape player. Bit by bit, all of it had chipped away at his good feelings about the series — and, finally, pushed him over the edge.

I understood completely, but my feelings were very mixed. On one hand, I was wishing Ron good luck; I thought, *Well, this is something he's got to do.* We'd talked about it for years; he'd already gone off and directed the Roger Corman picture, those TV movies, and some short films that his family helped him make. I thought, *This is his destiny. He's got to do this.*

But on the other hand, I was scared and sad. I didn't know what was going to happen. My acting partner in most of the scenes on *Happy Days* was leaving! My entire character was based on being Richie's big brother; everything else was ancillary. How could I ever find somebody I felt this connected to?

All these things were swirling in my brain. But mostly I felt, *I love you; I want you to go out there and be unbelievable; possibly cast me. . . .*

So Richie Cunningham got drafted into the army, and of course Ron *did* go out there and *was* unbelievable. (And did cast me.) Both directly and indirectly, ABC's rudeness turned Ron Howard into a billion-dollar director and a major player in the movie business.

Scott Baio had come onto the show during that eventful Season 5, playing Fonzie's cousin Charles Arcola — Chachi. He was just sixteen when he started, but he was dripping with charisma and acting talent, and at the same time, to his great credit, he was a real team player.

A quick aside about one actor who wasn't.

There was a kid who joined the cast during the late seasons of the show — and I won't say his name, but he had a moment. By which I mean, he started to get kind of popular, was getting written about, et cetera — all of which was lovely, and, in the team-spirit sense, great for the show. And the kid began to get fan mail. And then more fan mail. And he got very excited about it. All of which was fine.

But the thing that was less than fine was, he began to *flaunt* his fan mail. Started to talk about it, a lot. On the soundstage. In a surprised and happy way, but also in kind of a braggy way. Kind of obliviously to the feelings of those around him.

I took him aside. In a friendly way.

"You don't want to be talking about your fan mail on the soundstage," I told him.

He nodded, seemed to understand. Then he kept doing it anyway.

And I'm not saying that it was because of that, but it wasn't long before his character got written out of *Happy Days*.

Scott was not like that. He was cute, young girls loved him — he could even sing! — and he got very popular right away. He got *lots* of fan mail. Which he did *not* brag about. He didn't brag, because he didn't have to. After Ron left, the writers started to write a lot of scenes between Fonzie and Chachi, because Scott and I had chemistry — not the same as the chemistry between Ron and me, but in its own way just as strong. And of course the rest of the cast kept being great. After seven seasons, you might expect a series to go on autopilot: *Happy Days* never did. The final four seasons of the show were filled with a sense of fun and discovery, and the people kept watching. And a lot of it had to do with the fact that — to my great good fortune — Scott Baio stepped up.

While Stacey and I were dating, I took her to meet the cast and crew of *Happy Days.* As with every other studio in Hollywood, there was a gatehouse at the entrance to the Paramount lot, with a gate — a long bar that went up and down, operated by the guy in the gatehouse: in those days, it was a nice old guy, Mr. Hawks, who'd worked there for fifty years. And as the Fonz, I'd always get a big smile from Mr. Hawks as he raised the gate and admitted me to the lot. And I would smile back at him: it was a great feeling to be known, and liked, and let in.

That day, Mr. Hawks leaned down and

peered into my car window as I proudly introduced Stacey to him, and he gave her a big smile, too. "You're a lucky fella, Mr. Winkler," he said.

"Don't I know it," I told him.

But as we drove onto the lot, I said to Stacey, "Never think for a moment that there's not going to come a day when the nice old man at the Paramount gatehouse, whoever he is then, doesn't automatically let me through. That day will come."

Ron has said that I did him a major solid by agreeing to appear in *Night Shift,* and I understand the truth in that: movies don't get made unless the people you ask to back them feel they can make money, and one of the best ways to get distributors to fork over is to sign a big name to your project. And in 1981 I was a big name, thanks to *Happy Days.*

But I also felt (and still feel) that Ron did *me* a big favor by asking me to participate, and by giving *me* the chance to be directed by *him. Night Shift* was a darkish comedy about two morgue attendants who decide to make some side profits by opening a house of prostitution in the morgue. One of the attendants is a mild-mannered, milquetoastish guy named Chuck; his coworker,

Bill, is a take-no-prisoners wild man. Ron told me, "You can play either role." And I thought, *Well, the Fonz is pretty flamboyant. I'm gonna play Richie Cunningham.* Directed by Richie!

We saw every actor in town for the role of Bill, and then Michael Keaton came in. Michael was still just a journeyman then, working his way up the Hollywood food chain with a lot of TV parts, but he had a real presence about him, and he could really nail that crazy-eyed thing, and so he was just right.

But the one who was *truly* just right was Ron Howard. Poor Ron was so nervous about taking on his first big-time feature. *Grand Theft Auto* had been a great start for him, but Roger Corman movies were shoestring affairs: everyone working in them, from cast to crew, was just trying to rack up some experience. *Night Shift,* though, was a Warner Brothers picture — this was the big leagues. "Oh my God," Ron said to me. "Everyone in this crew has been in the business for twenty-five years, they've all made a thousand movies, and I'm brand-new — are they even going to listen to me?"

"Yes, they will," I told him — and I wasn't just blowing smoke. I knew Ron. I had felt the quiet force of his personality. And from the jump, his crew felt that same force. It was really remarkable: when a question came up on the set and Ron said, "Let me think about that," the place went dead silent. Everybody was like, "What is Ron going to say?" He had their complete respect. He was smart and passionate; he really knew what he was doing, and everyone knew it.

And as an actor himself, he really understood acting. I took home movies of the making of *Night Shift,* and there's footage of Ron directing me. I'd make a choice for my character and say, "Can I do this?" And he'd say, "Well, if you did that, I'd probably print it." And I'd say, "Oh, okay — got it. I'll do that."

And all of that (and much more) is why Ron Howard went on to become a great director.

From the beginning, I'd loved Ron like the younger brother I never had. One of my favorite scenes over the whole course of the show was in Season 5, when Richie lay unconscious in a hospital bed after being in a motorcycle accident and Fonzie stood beside the bed crying, praying he'd be all right.

Ron returned for a guest appearance in

the final season, for a two-episode arc in which Richie and Ralph come home to Milwaukee after being discharged from the army. When Richie tells his parents he's planning to move to LA to become a screenwriter — the writers were definitely inspired by Ron's actual career choice — Howard and Marion disapprove, but Fonzie tells Richie he has to follow his dream. In Episode 238, Ron's final appearance on *Happy Days*, Fonzie says goodbye to Richie at the door of the Cunninghams' house, and starts to cry — and the tears in my eyes were real: that was really Henry saying goodbye to Ron.

Ron had gone out and made his way in the world. Now it was my turn to do the same. The only problem was, nobody wanted me.

What that really meant was, nobody wanted me to be anything besides the Fonz.

Baby Henry in all his moods.

Calling my first
agent. I couldn't
get him on the line.

TOP: At McBurney's School for Boys, I won the prize for best dancer that night by doing the limbo.

LEFT: My high school graduation picture.

Memorizing *Peer Gynt* at Emerson College
was one of the most difficult things I've
ever done.

My first headshot
taken at Yale
Drama School.

A Yale Reparatory
Theater production.

Robin Williams, Cindy Williams, Ron Howard, Pam Dawber, and Penny Marshall. We all owe a tremendous debt of gratitude to Garry Marshall.

My parents sitting in the lobby of the Breakers Hotel letting everyone know they were my parents.

Ladies and gentlemen, my wife.

Magic and me, nothing more needs to be said.

BELOW: Jed and I meeting the GREAT Mohammed Ali.

An incredible
moment
in my
Hollywood
life: joining a
history I had
heard about.

(Courtesy of
MediaPunch Inc.
/ Alamy Stock
Photo)

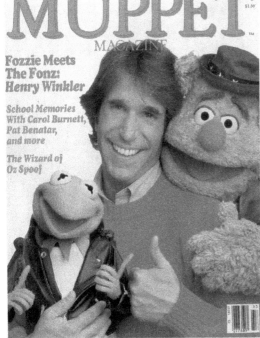

FALL 1983

MUPPET

MAGAZINE

$1.50

**Fozzie Meets
The Fonz:
Henry Winkler**

*School Memories
With Carol Burnett,
Pat Benatar,
and more*

*The Wizard of
Oz Spoof*

How lucky
am I? I got
to meet the
Muppets.

The first
television
movie I ever
directed was
for Dolly
Parton,
*A Smoky
Mountain
Christmas.*

I won my first daytime Emmy directing
All the Kids Do It, an afterschool special
starring Scott Baio.

The young fam.

Stacey and I with my parents,
Harry and Ilse.

With my buddies Allan King, JoBeth Williams and Billy Crystal – my first directorial feature, *Memories of Me*.

Making *The Waterboy* with Adam Sandler. We always had a pasta bar at lunch.

I'm pretty sure I was a Viking in a past life. (*Better Late Than Never* with Bill Shatner, George Forman, Jeff Dye and Terry Bradshaw.)

TOP: The cast from the television show inspired by Hank Zipzer, my children's novels with Lin Oliver. I play Mr. Rock, my actual music teacher from McBurney's.

LEFT: Ron and "I" meeting up in Milwaukee.

Jessica ALWAYS brought the funny and
I, of course, knew EVERYTHING about
the law!

The fam again, all grown up.

Apart from family and my profession,
fishing is my passion.

Our girls Maisie and Sadie.

The ever-growing Winkler clan.
I love them all.

7.

Sometime between Seasons 4 and 5 of *Happy Days,* the talent agent and producer Allan Carr came to me — wearing a caftan, something he was famous for — and asked me to costar in a movie he was coproducing, a little thing called *Grease.*

The film was to be an adaptation of the Broadway musical, then in the midst of a monster eight-year run. The part was Danny Zuko, the story's singing, dancing greaser hero. With fifties nostalgia in the air — a cultural trend *Happy Days* had contributed to big-time — the movie was almost guaranteed to be big.

I turned down the role.

Didn't want to be typecast. "I've been playing the Fonz for four and a half years now, and I don't think I can do it," I told Allan Carr. "But thank you so much." Then John Travolta did it — and did it perfectly. The joke I always make is that I went home and had a ginger ale; John went home and bought a 747. (He literally did.)

For a long time, people tried to cobble up some rivalry or bad blood between me and John. It began after *Happy Days* had been on the air for about a year and a half, when John first got famous as the greaser Vinnie Barbarino on *Welcome Back, Kotter.* Vinnie versus the Fonz. It was baloney — there was nothing there. I don't know John well, but he has never been anything but warm and wonderful with me. He has done very well, and *zei gezunt* — he should live and be healthy.

For ten years I did everything I could to avoid being typecast. When fans or reporters met me, they always wanted just a little taste of the Fonz — everybody loved that character! — and I always held back. I was Henry, a real-life person and a trained actor, and I wanted people to know it. If I came off as a little overserious or pretentious, so be it. Once I was offered $10,000 — something like $30,000 today — to go on some variety show and give lessons on how to be the Fonz. It was supposedly all in good fun, but I wouldn't go anywhere near it. Instinctually I knew that no matter how much money was on the line, you couldn't do that: it would be like a magician showing how he does his tricks.

But of course keeping Fonzie magical only enhanced his aura, made him more unattainable — and therefore more sought-after and beloved.

What happened when he wasn't there anymore?

I had become a prisoner of my own creation.

Where typecasting was concerned, I thought I was going to beat the system. I thought — this is going to sound arrogant, and maybe I was a little arrogant then — I was a big enough international star that I could go from mountaintop to mountaintop in my career. I would beat the system of being typecast.

What I learned: there is no beating the system.

After *Happy Days* ended in 1984, I found myself not on top of a mountain but lying in the valley, with grass stains on my jeans. I thought the acting offers would come rolling in; instead, my agent would say things like, "Oh my God, they *love* you. You're so *funny*. You're *such* a good actor." And then: "But you were the Fonz."

I could not — as they say — get arrested.

A new series? My agents wouldn't call me — I had to call them. Every pilot season, it was, "No, there's nothing. I've read every-thing. There's nothing for you."

A movie role? Remember, this was still a time when movies were considered a big step up from television. And I hadn't exactly distinguished myself with my movie work so far. The truth was that, the Fonz aside, I was half-baked as an actor. Self-conscious.

Now, it wasn't as if I was hurting for money. *Happy Days* had made me comfort-able. But I was uncomfortable. We now had three kids — our son Max was born in August 1983 — and a big nut to cover. We were good for the present and near future, but if we wanted to keep living the way we were living, I didn't have enough for us to live on forever. And I could never shake the memory of overhearing my arrogant father weeping on the phone to his friend Carl Stohl, begging for money. Or of my arrogant father coming to me and demanding my bar mitzvah money. I couldn't dismiss my growing-up feeling of living beyond our means. Was I living beyond my means now? Would I be in five years, or ten?

My father had a saying (he had a lot of sayings): *Make hay while the sun shines.* Had I made enough hay?

I was terrified of being a flash in the pan. A one-hit wonder. Was I?

186

Between my money neurosis and my feelings of abject misery and worthlessness when I wasn't working, I was an extremely unhappy camper.

I loved working. (Still do.) I hated not working. (Still do.) When could I, how could I, work again? And would I ever again have anything like the impact I had during the charmed decade of 1974 to 1984?

Meanwhile, for the next seven years, I was living in the Valley of Career Death.

I had an office at Paramount, a place from which I would (theoretically) conduct post–*Happy Days* business. And I remember sitting at my desk in my office, paralyzed, my mind weaving bleak scenarios. *I can't get hired. I don't know what to do. I feel rudderless. I don't know if anything is going to happen. How am I going to take care of my family?*

I had no plan B. I had just lived my plan A.

I've already mentioned my lawyer Skip Brittenham, the dynamic young guy Joan Scott had sent me to while I was still doing *Happy Days.* I was his first client. His full name was Skip Brittenham III. Sounds like someone to the manor born, a snotty prepschool jock — Skip was anything but. He was warm, he was smart, and he was in my corner from the very beginning. And he said to me, "I'm going to start a production company for you, Henry."

"Skip, I'm dyslexic," I told him. "I couldn't do that — I don't know anything about business."

He said, "You'll learn."

But even before we started my production company, Skip did an amazing thing for me. He took us fly-fishing in Montana for five days.

Now, I'm from the Upper West Side — I don't know the first thing about Montana or fly-fishing. But Skip and an amazing literary agent named Leonard Hanzer took Stacey and me to Helena, Montana, where we floated down the Smith River and I learned how to fly-fish . . . sort of.

Let the rod help you make the cast. You bring it up to twelve o'clock, hold for a second, and let the line load behind you. Then you move the rod forward with a gentle whip, to two o'clock, and the line floats like an angel onto the water.

The wind, the water, the trees, and that big, big sky — I could feel my blood pressure dropping with every cast.

The leaders of our little trip were John and Mary Smith — was the river named after them? Anything seemed possible in that glorious landscape — and there was a group who went ahead of us and set up lunch, then after lunch they went ahead of us and set up our camp for sleeping.

Oh. My. God.

That big sky, the stars, and the sound of the water and the trees . . . I caught three fish in five days. Didn't care.

Got back to Los Angeles in a Zen state of relaxation. Then, as Skip began to introduce me to potential production partners, I repressurized. Fast. The plan was that I was to be the name and the face of the company, and my partner would sell the shows we developed. That was the plan — but even though I knew nothing, I knew I could never just be a name and a face. So that was a little bit of built-in tension right at the get-go.

The first guy we hired — I won't say his name — was a reasonably successful show-runner, and he was very abrasive. Not only that, but we didn't sell anything for a year. So I moved on.

The next guy was actually lovely, and he was running a show that was doing well, so there was a shot. But again we didn't sell anything, and I moved on once more. And then, in 1985, I was put with a man named

John Rich. And John Rich was a very famous TV director, a multiple-Emmy winner for *The Dick Van Dyke Show* and *All in the Family* — Norman Lear loved him, but I think he was crazy.

Rich was sixtyish, with white hair and dark eyebrows, and carried himself like a tough guy. A big star in his field, with an ego to match. I was still south of forty, and (in his eyes) merely a TV star. *Not* a producer. A creature of some lower stratum, with — by definition — nothing of substance to contribute to the enterprise. Window dressing.

We pitched two shows to ABC. Actually, we were a step above just pitching, because the deal Skip Brittenham III had crafted for me included (no small thing) two on-air commitments from the network. It was like a gift from heaven. It meant that if I brought them a show and they liked it, we didn't need to shoot a pilot — we could go straight to series.

The first show, *Mr. Sunshine,* was a comedy about a blind college professor, created by the wonderful Gene Reynolds, who'd been the driving force behind *M*A*S*H.* ABC ordered eleven episodes, and we went to work. Jeffrey Tambor played the professor to perfection, the show was wonderfully written and very funny, and John Rich was very much in charge.

My everlasting memory of *Mr. Sunshine* is of Rich sitting at the studio control panel looking at the playback, and me standing behind him. And as we were watching the videotape, something occurred to me, and I said, "Oh, I have an idea."

Zero reaction from John Rich. He doesn't pause, he doesn't turn around; apparently he didn't hear me.

The assistant director then says, "Oh, Henry has an idea."

"I don't give a shit what he thinks," says John Rich. He continues to watch the playback. Then, a couple of seconds later, he turns around. "Oh, Henry," he says. "Come with me. Let's go talk to the key grip."

As though nothing had happened. No transition. Not even a flutter in the water.

Rich had a habit of dressing down crew members at the drop of a hat. He would scowl and say, "You're an asshole," right to their face.

"What?" the crew member would say.

"He said you're an empty vessel," I would say. Half of my time on that show was running around putting Band-Aids on the wounds this guy had left. Really — and I do not exaggerate — John Rich was one of the worst people I ever met in any country in all my years. But you know what? I was part of the problem. I had so little sense of myself that I let him walk all over me.

ABC did not pick up *Mr. Sunshine* after the first season.

The other show we — I — sold them was *MacGyver.*

MacGyver was the brainchild of a young guy named Lee David Zlotoff, who was doing a lot of the writing on the NBC show *Remington Steele.* Lee came to us with the idea of a secret agent who was an ultimate fix-it man, someone who fought with his mind instead of weapons. A guy who, when all else had failed, could do as much with his Swiss Army knife, duct tape, and matches as anyone else could do with guns, bombs, and martial arts. A fun, brilliant idea.

MacGyver, as Lee conceived him, worked for the Phoenix Foundation, a shadowy, mysterious organization headed by Pete Thornton. And we found our Pete Thornton immediately, in the person of the terrific actor Dana Elcar. Dana was a major find. But we spent most of our time auditioning a lot of handsome men for the title role.

Then Richard Dean Anderson came in.

There must have been ten or fifteen men out there in the world who were just ugly because Richard Dean Anderson got all the handsome. Richard Dean walks in — and we've now seen a *lot* of handsome men — and has to look for his glasses in order to read the script. Literally cannot read the script without his eyeglasses, and can't find them.

He was good, but he wasn't perfect. But he was perfect because he was imperfect. Does that make any sense? Remember when I talked about the Ralphs grocery bag I used to carry my headshots in? *Have a conversation starter* is some of the advice I give to young actors. And Richard Dean Anderson's missing eyeglasses — not to mention the fact that this off-the-charts-handsome guy *needed* eyeglasses — were a great conversation starter.

The conversation continued. And as you know, he got the job.

MacGyver first aired in September 1985 — right around the time Brandon Stoddard became head of ABC. And Brandon Stoddard did not like *MacGyver.* But here's the thing: the show had great ratings, for two reasons. One, people liked it. And two, it was a perfect lead-in or lead-out for *Sunday Night Football.* And one thing network executives never argue with is great ratings. *MacGyver* was good television, not great television, but you could not kill it with a stick. And so it stuck around for seven seasons. And — John Rich notwithstanding — it made a producer out of me.

Every episode had a teaser at the beginning, and early on there was a teaser with MacGyver racing down a beach on a white horse. He's being chased by forty Middle Eastern nomads also on horses and brandishing swords — and out of the mist comes a helicopter that flies over MacGyver's horse and drops a hook. He hooks it onto his saddle, and the helicopter picks him and the horse up and flies back into the mist, and the nomads are befuddled. Brilliant.

So I needed forty horses. ABC wanted to give us twelve. I called our executive at the network, Peter Roth, and said, "Peter, we need forty horses. The bit doesn't work with only twelve. I need those horses."

Peter said, "No, no, no, it's not in the budget."

I said, "Peter, I will give you my salary. Please."

"We can't take your salary, Henry," Peter said.

We got the horses.

During the same period Rich and I produced a TV movie called *Scandal Sheet,* a dramatic piece about the down-and-dirty underbelly of a fictional celebrity-gossip newspaper something like the *National Enquirer.* We thought Burt Lancaster, then in his early seventies but still a Hollywood icon, would be terrific as the fictional paper's diabolical publisher. ABC offered to pay him what I thought was an amazing amount of money. I got Lancaster's phone number and called him.

"No, I'm not interested," he said. "It's not enough money."

"Can I just send you the script?" I asked. "I'll bring it to you personally."

"No, thank you," Burt Lancaster said.

"All right," I said. "This is how much you'd be making" — I mentioned ABC's offer again — "and this is how much I'm going to add to it. My producing fee is fifty thousand" — which was a lot of money in the mid-1980s — "and I'm going to add that to the pot. I'm *giving* you my fee."

He said no again, but I thought I could detect a slight wobble in his resolve.

Remember, this was still during the period when I was lost. When psychologically I did not exist. But I stood my ground. I was relentless. And Burt Lancaster finally said yes.

And in that moment, I said to myself, *Yes, you have earned the title of producer.*

I learned on the job. I was good with the talent. (I knew talent from both sides of the equation.) I was good at casting. I was good at editing. And John Rich kept being an asshole to me for eleven hours and fifty-five minutes of every twelve-hour day. There were maybe five minutes in there where we got along. But the rest of the time, he was remarkably consistent. And I didn't have enough inner strength to stand up to him. Soon after *MacGyver* went on the air, the two of us did an interview for one of the morning shows — you can find it on You-Tube if you look hard. And what you'll see is a very confident John Rich sitting next to a very young-looking Henry Winkler who looks like a poster child for Stockholm syndrome.

I had a minor pang of conscience the other night. I thought, *Should I be talking about these bad guys like Alan Schneider and John Rich? They're dead, they can't defend themselves. Should I talk about the dead like this?*

And out of the ooze in the Magic Eight Ball comes the answer: *Yes, I should, because they were the worst.*

I was earning a living, but I was an actor who wasn't acting, a terrible thing to be if you're an actor. Still. If people couldn't see me as anything but the Fonz, I thought, what about doing some acting where I wasn't seen? If the voice that had come to me out of nowhere had made me a star, maybe my voice could do things for me again?

I knew that a lot of very successful actors did very well on the side by doing voice work for animated features. Why not me?

But breaking into voice acting proved to be no easier than breaking into any other field. There was an elite cadre of people who did the work, there were voice casting directors, and I was saddled with the age-old chicken-and-egg problem: how could I get hired for the first time if I hadn't done the work before?

I got lucky. Jerry Bruckheimer's wife, Linda, told me about an animated series she was trying to get off the ground with Bill Melendez, the creator of the *Peanuts* animated specials. It was about a third grader named Molly, and some of the hard things in her life. The first episode, "Happily Ever After," was about her parents' divorce, and I'd be playing Molly's dad, Carl. Linda had already cast some very big names for the show: Carol Burnett as the narrator. Carrie Fisher as Molly's mom. And Danny DeVito and Rhea Perlman. It was flattering to be in their midst, but it was also intimidating.

The whole thing was scary at first. You go into a studio, there's a soundproof booth, and the director and the engineer are at a control panel in another booth. And you go into your booth and close the door, and it's just you and a microphone. And you then have to put everything you use on a sound-stage or a theater stage — your use of your body, your use of movement, your use of facial expression — you have to put all that into your voice as it comes out of your body into the microphone. I had to go back to one of the lessons I learned at Yale: Relaxation-Concentration. If you can find relaxation, concentration will follow.

But relaxing in that soundproof booth was anything but easy. I was so dyslexic that there were times when I screwed up a line twelve times in a row, in rapid succession.

" 'He went to the market, and he —' "

"Sorry."

" 'He went to the market —' "

"Sorry, Henry."

" 'He went to the market, and he couldn't find that —' "

"Sorry."

" 'He went to the market, and he couldn't find the mayonnaise —' "

"Sorry."

" 'He went to the market, and he couldn't find the jar of mayonnaise so that he would have a sandwich —' "

"Okay, could you do it again, Henry? That's 'so he *could* have a sandwich.' "

"Of course I can," I would say. "Of course I can."

People were so patient with me. Sometimes, if there was a paragraph to get through, it was like climbing a mountain. But slowly, slowly, I made it up each hill. And though the Molly series didn't get off the ground, slowly, slowly, I began to get more voice work.

One day in 1982, I walked up to the commissary on the Paramount lot to find the *Happy Days* triumvirate Eddie Milkis, Tom Miller, and Garry Marshall standing outside engaged in an intense discussion. "What's up?" I said.

They told me that they needed a director for the twelfth episode of the *Happy Days* spin-off *Joanie Loves Chachi,* and they couldn't find one.

"Hey, I'll do it," I said. Joking.

"Okay," they said. Serious.

Now, I had never directed anything — not even traffic. But apparently Eddie, Tom, and Garry had been around me enough by that point to feel I really could get what was necessary from the actors. So I went out and bought a red sweater to emulate our great director Jerry Paris, who wore his good-luck red sweater every Friday night for more than 230 episodes of *Happy Days.* And I went in there and did the job.

Was I scared? I'm always scared. I only had the most basic instinct when it came to cinematography. I knew that if we were shooting a joke, I wanted to see both characters in the same shot, as opposed to: cut to a close-up, cut to a close-up. Fortunately, I had wonderful professionals to help me. I could tell the director of photography, "This character wants this from this guy; this guy wants this from her — I want you to show me that on camera."

What I felt confident about from my own acting experience was that I could help the actors to live in the moment, to create the emotion and the tension of the story. To tell the story. I led Scott Baio and Erin Moran through the episode, and everyone was happy with the result.

So I had a credit, and in 1984, just after *Happy Days* ended, I directed a *CBS Schoolbreak Special* — and won a Daytime Emmy. It wasn't exactly a second career for me, but I enjoyed it and was good at it. Two years later, I got the opportunity to direct the great Dolly Parton on a TV movie for NBC, *A Smoky Mountain Christmas.* Her manager, Sandy Gallin — he also represented Michael Jackson, Barbra Streisand, Cher, and Mariah Carey, among many others — was an enormous help with every detail of the production, and later became a very close and wonderful friend until his untimely death.

During the making of the movie, I learned a very big lesson.

First of all, just getting to work with Dolly was a lesson in itself — I think she's some kind of genius. She cowrote the story, in which she played a version of herself: a country singer who gets sick of the grind of touring and performing and escapes back to the Tennessee mountains she came from. In the piece, Dolly's character's handlers initially think she's been kidnapped, and the cops come to her apartment to investigate. And my old friend from Yale Marc

Flanagan, who was playing one of the cops, had an idea that his character wanted a souvenir from this great country singer's place. But a cop can't just take something, because that would be stealing. So I turned to the crew. "Okay," I said, "if somebody wanted a souvenir but couldn't steal anything, what could it be?"

Suddenly the boom man spoke up. "Hey, maybe there's a lot of songs she didn't like or rewrote, and she crumpled up the first versions of them and threw them in the trash can. That's garbage — he could take one of those."

I snapped my fingers. "And so it will be!" I said.

And here's what I learned: the myth is that if you're the director, you have to know everything. Bullshit. If you take an idea from the crew, you're still the director. And the boom man who came up with that neat little idea is now holding that boom with pride. He's part of the process. He feels great. I feel great. Marc Flanagan feels great, because his idea has come to fruition. Everybody wins, instead of, *I am the director, and nobody has an idea but me.* Because as a director, you have to answer nine hundred questions every thirty-two minutes. If you can't work cooperatively, you're dust.

Fun facts: Paula Abdul, who had just been the choreographer for the Laker Girls, choreographed the opening dance number of the movie. And Jean Howard, Ronnie Howard's mom, also joined the cast.

And *A Smoky Mountain Christmas* turned out very well. The morning after it aired, I was dropping Max off at preschool — the same preschool, it happened, attended by the daughter of Brandon Tartikoff, the head of NBC. And I got out of my car to walk Max to the door just as Brandon got out of his car to walk his daughter Calla, and he said, "Oh, good morning, Mr. Thirty-four Share."

A thirty-four share, in Nielsen audience rating terms, being a nice, fat hit.

As much as I loved everything about the holiday of Christmas — the sounds, the smells, the lights — it was so difficult for me even to think about having a tree in my own house. Stacey, on the other hand, loved the idea and wanted a tree for years: her family had always had one when she was growing up, even though they were Jewish.

But finally I was able to ease my rigidity. And Stacey bought a tree. And started her lifelong quest for ornaments that represented every family member. There were

203

trout, trucks, ice cream cones, donuts, unicorns, a six-pack of Coke, Santa, birds. A representation of every dog in the house. And every year the tree got taller, until ladders got involved. And runs to the hardware store for more lights. Every year, the tree stood proudly side by side with the menorah my parents had brought from Nazi Germany. And there were presents around that menorah and under that tree. And we had to be very careful, because even our grown children would eye each other's presents to make sure everything was equal.

Even though I had given in on the tree, for years I felt a slight misgiving at going against the tradition I had grown up with. But what I came to realize, watching our grandchildren, Indya, Ace, Lulu, Jules, Gus, and Frances, taking turns lighting the candles on the menorah and reading aloud about each night of Hanukkah — and then joyfully ripping apart the packaging of their dual-holiday gifts — was that the sheer ecumenical pleasure of the occasion was more important than my holding on to any one-sided view. And our religion did not drift away because of the presence of a (sublimely fragrant) pine.

Meanwhile, my acting career was still

flatlining. I pestered my agents about the offers that weren't coming. And meanwhile, I kept driving Jed and Zoe and Max to school — and kept driving Stacey crazy with my worries about never working again.

I worked hard to be a good dad. Every day, growing up, I'd thought, *I am going to be a different parent than my own parents were.* As I tried to put that into effect, first with Jed, then with Zoe and Max, there were some hiccups. On the one hand, I really made sure that I was present. On the other hand, I was infamous, at home and elsewhere, for being willing to give advice about almost everything at the drop of a hat. As our children grew up, I could practically see them thinking, *I know this. Why is he telling me this again?*

And it's hard to be a parent when you don't feel fully adult inside.

STACEY:

I remember very early on in our marriage, Henry would say, "Zoe really hurt my feelings." And I would say to Henry, "But she's three."

When it came to parenting, Henry needed hand-holding and patience. But I have to admit there were times when I thought, *What the fuck? Now I have another child?* It took me a long time to understand that the need that makes someone choose to be an actor, to put themselves out there, meant that his life, our life, constantly depended upon people — strangers — liking what he did. It wasn't always easy.

I always thought it was important for our kids to have chores. Nevertheless, all three of them were great negotiators: I did their chores. And things were never simple with my very feisty daughter. Once I planned to take the three of them to a Dodgers game, and after extensive talks, I got Zoe to agree to pick up her room — a disaster area — before we left. The time came to go, and a glance into her room told me she hadn't held up her end of the bargain.

"Zoe, come on," I said. "You gotta put some of that clothing back on the hangers. You can't just leave it all over the floor. Just put it on the hangers and then we'll go."

She grumbled what sounded like a grudging yes. And we left. Got to Dodger Stadium, sat down — and suddenly my face is on the Diamond Vision mega-screen. All at once, fifty-five thousand people start chanting, "Henry, Henry, Fonzie, Fonzie!"

"Dad, it's so cool," Zoe said. "Can you hear them?"

"No, I'm a mirage," I said. "What do you mean, can I hear them?"

Finally, my image left the screen, the ball game was about to start, but the chanting didn't stop. People, lots of them, surged around our seats. After a few minutes more of this, the security people had to come and escort us out of the stadium. And now we're back in the car, going home. I let Jed drive — he's now eighteen. And we're listening to the ball game, the game we were supposed to see, on the radio. Zoe and Max were not happy. Jed, at the wheel, took on the role of family sage, discussing their father's fame with them. "Listen," he said. "Some people will want to be friends with you because of Dad. Some people will want to be friends with you because of you. You'll know the difference."

We got home. I walked by Zoe's room and saw that it was still a mess. "Zoe," I said, "we made a deal. You were gonna hang that stuff up before we left."

She looked me in the eye. "If that crowd knew who you were, they wouldn't even whisper your name," she said. "I will never cheer your name."

We stared at each other for a second. "Okay," I finally said. "But anyway, hang up your clothes."

Zoe had a bunny: she named him Mister. Once, while Stacey and I were in our bathroom, Zoe came in. And I said, "Zoe, did you feed your bunny?" And Zoe looked at my wife and said, "Why did you marry him? I can't listen to his voice anymore."

In 1987, a year after the success of *A Smoky Mountain Christmas,* I got the chance to direct my first feature, a comedy-drama called *Memories of Me.* Billy Crystal cowrote the script with Eric Roth, and starred, playing a stressed-out heart surgeon with JoBeth Williams as his understanding girlfriend and Alan King as his father, the needy "king of the extras," and the source of much of his stress.

Memories of Me was a touching, funny script, Billy and Alan were a joy to work with, and I had a great time. The movie did not do well at the box office — stuff happens — but I was pleased with it, and as long as I wasn't acting, I was happy that people were also thinking of me as someone who could do this other thing.

Someone sent me a screenplay called *Stella,* an update of *Stella Dallas,* the classic

1930s weeper starring Barbara Stanwyck as a young woman from the wrong side of the tracks who marries a rich guy, then sacrifices her own happiness for her daughter's. The brilliant Bette Midler wanted to star, and I really wanted to direct. I understood this movie — I loved the idea of this woman on the outside wanting to be on the inside. It just sang to me. I went to New York to meet with Bette, and it went very well. I was happy. I was excited — so excited that I decided I'd buy myself something nice to wear.

So I went downtown to Barneys, the original store at Seventh Avenue and 17th Street. "Select, don't settle" — its motto. And I'm walking through the aisles, looking at the nice clothes and humming a little tune to myself, when a security guard, a woman in a gray uniform, comes up to me and says, "Mr. Winkler, there's a phone call for you."

A phone call for me? In the aisles of Barneys? My heart started thumping. Had something terrible happened to someone?

"It's Mr. Katzenberg," the security guard said.

Oh. Jeffrey Katzenberg. The head of Disney's motion-picture division, the most successful studio in Hollywood. So — nothing terrible, maybe something very good. How did he find me? It turned out that he'd called my home and Stacey told him where I was. I followed the security guard to a store telephone and picked it up.

"Hi, Henry, how are you?" Jeff Katzenberg said.

"I'm fine, thanks, Jeff — how are you?"

"Great. Listen — what are you doing now?"

"Right now? I'm shopping for clothes at Barneys."

"I mean, are you directing anything?"

I told him about *Stella* and Bette.

"No," Jeff Katzenberg said. "Forget about that. I want you to direct *Turner & Hooch.*" And he told me what it was: a buddy movie, with Tom Hanks as a cop and an adorable dog as the buddy. Jeff was very pumped up about this movie. "It's a great script, it's going to be huge, and it'll be very, very good for you, Henry," he told me. "And you're gonna love Tom."

Well! This was something! Maybe I really was a director — I mean, a capital-D Director — after all? The *head* of Disney just called me in the aisles of a clothing store. The head of Disney wanted *me.* All of a sudden, my capital-E Ego, a great feathered creature in my head that emerged very, very seldom, was battling somewhere in my midsection with my stomach, that powerful feeling in my gut that *Stella* was the perfect project for me. Meanwhile, my nonexistent sense of self was a passive onlooker.

Jeffrey *Katzenberg.* The head of *Disney.* Me.

I couldn't say no. I actually thought there might be a clause somewhere in the bylaws of Hollywood that made it illegal to say no to Jeffrey Katzenberg.

Meanwhile, he's still on the other end of the line.

"Wow," I said, in a stunned voice. "Wow. Okay. I'd have really liked to direct *Stella.*" But I knew as I was speaking that I'd already given it up.

"I really think you would be perfect for this, Henry."

That did it. That broke the camel's back. I was a goner.

"Okay," the great feathered creature in my head told Jeff Katzenberg. Which was the usual thing that people said to Jeff Katzenberg.

So I started on the journey of *Turner & Hooch.* As my producer I took along Michael Hertzberg, who'd produced *Memories of Me.* I moved into a nice new office at Disney. And I immediately started to form a relationship with Hooch, a French mastiff puppy with an adorably wrinkled face — actually several French mastiff puppies, because each one was going to learn a separate trick. I went and visited these dogs, I worked with the dogs, I watched them learn tricks. I developed a relationship with these dogs. I loved all of them.

And I met with Tom Hanks. I'd actually met him before — Tom appeared on *Happy Days* in 1982, when he was just getting started and couldn't get a movie yet. He played an old nemesis of Fonzie's who'd become a martial-arts master: we had a kind of non-battle in which Tom's character mostly busted up a lot of furniture, then finally kicked Fonzie through the front window of Al's diner — the first person who'd ever bested the Fonz. We were gracious and supportive of Tom on the show, and he was very charming in the role. And that role got him noticed at Disney, which put him in *Splash* — directed by Ron Howard — which made him a movie star.

Tom and I met in my Disney office. We had a nice meeting — while we were talking, he built a plastic model of a plane. I had him sign it. I still have it. We talked about casting, and he went for Mare Winningham as his costar. Lovely, down-to-earth actress — a good match for Tom's all-American charm. He and I went to Big Sur to scout locations with our director of photography, a big, nice Israeli guy named Adam Greenberg. Then we drove back to LA, and bright and early the following Monday, I began directing *Turner & Hooch.*

From the start, I knew in my gut that something was wrong. Deep down, I didn't understand the movie. I didn't know how to tell that story. Of course I couldn't let on to anyone that I felt that way — and I also had the thought, *Maybe this is just your insecurity talking. Maybe I just need to fake it till I make it.*

But one immediate problem was that I talked too much. As we've noticed, I had a tendency in the first place to be verbose; when I was anxious, my verbosity increased. I would eventually learn that a good director needs to say very little to the actors: they've been cast by smart people, they know what they're doing — all you really have to do is massage them a little bit.

I was massaging a *lot.*

One day there was a scene where Tom and Mare come down the stairs, and — in my mind, the scene had a certain rhythm, and the rhythm wasn't right — I asked them to do it several times. In retrospect, it was a few times too many.

One day a couple of weeks later I'm called into Jeff Katzenberg's office. I sit down, and Jeff shakes his head. "You know, Henry, it's not in the dailies," he said. "It just isn't in the dailies."

"What isn't — ?" I started to say.

"We're going to have to let you go, Henry," Jeff said.

I was devastated. I called Stacey — she was back East; she'd gone on a trip to Connecticut with an old friend — and told her.

"What happened?" she asked.

"I don't know," I said. She got on the next plane.

The next call was from my agent, Jim Wiatt. "We're going to lunch," he said. "We're going to the Palm." It was a fancy restaurant on Santa Monica Boulevard in Beverly Hills.

"Why are we going to the Palm?" I asked.

"You need to be seen," Jim said. "After what just happened to you, it's important that you be out and about."

My call was for 7:30 the next morning. I went to the set to say goodbye to the crew and to get my things out of my trailer. Thinking the whole time: *Here I was, directing a major motion picture. And my career is now over.* It was humiliating, and then

214

some. My face was hot with shame.

A Brit, Roger Spottiswoode, wound up directing *Turner & Hooch.* I didn't know at the time, but apparently he was on the set for days before I was fired, meeting everybody, getting the lay of the land. Maybe they wanted to make sure Roger was on before they let me go. I don't know. And I never found out.

8.

My father didn't like the way Stacey held her coffee cup.

I'm not kidding.

STACEY:

I liked to put my hand around the cup, because the warmth felt good. And my father-in-law would look at me and make a face. "Ugh, this is not the way you hold a coffee cup," he would say. "A real lady, a proper German lady, is supposed to hold the cup by the handle, maybe even with the pinkie extended."

Excuse me, Henry's father. I'm not a proper German lady.

My parents would come out to visit us, and they would make trouble. Every time. I could never believe how much damage they could do. It was like the entire house was made of china. And by the time they left, everything was broken. Every time. And yet, they had to keep coming.

STACEY:

At first I couldn't understand how, after so many years, Henry could still feel so resentful. For a long time I didn't understand the depth of what they had done to him, growing up. The disrespect, the failure to acknowledge him. It took me a long while to get my head around that.

So for years, I thought: *It couldn't have been* that *bad.* Also, I was raised in a family where every Sunday, we went to my father's mother's house or my mother's mother's. That was what you did with parents, and grandparents. And so Henry's parents kept coming out to see us.

My father-in-law had always been extremely disrespectful to my mother-in-law. He was utterly disrespectful to women in general. He thought he was better than other people. Like a dandy or something. Vain. Entitled.

But what happened with Henry's parents was, as they got older, they switched roles.

217

And my mother-in-law began to brutalize Harry. She did not treat him nicely. She only wanted to be with Henry. And the heartbreaking thing was, I believe she only wanted to be with Henry because he was now famous.

Now, all at once, my mother seemed excited to see me. She would give me a hug and a little peck on the cheek. *Piefke,* she called me — little pipsqueak. *Schnuckiputzi* — sweetie pie.

Sometimes when I do speaking engagements, I show a picture of me giving my leather jacket — Fonzie's jacket — to the Smithsonian Institution in 1980. And I always say, "Hey, look who's sitting behind me. The two short Germans. Who didn't want me to be an actor, who didn't support me being an actor, who hated the fact that I was going to be an actor instead of taking over my father's business.

[GERMAN ACCENT] " 'Why do you think I brought the business over here?'

"And I said, 'Besides being chased by the Nazis, Dad? Was there a bigger reason than that? Because I'd like to know.' " It always gets a big laugh. Oh my God.

STACEY:

We flew them out, flew them back. First-class, always — of course. And if there was anybody well-known on the plane, my mother-in-law would march right up to them and ask, "You know ze Fonz? Zat is my son!" One day she phoned and said, "Yah, Shirley MacLaine sends her best to you."

"How do you know her?"

"I saw her on the plane!"

It was hard for Stacey to say no to them. "They're your *parents,*" she'd say.

"I'm telling you," I said. "You know what happens when they come here — do not do this. They can come for five days. Six days, tops." And then Stacey would take up the banner for their side. She felt sorry for them.

"Henry, they're making the trip," Stacey would say. "They're old. Let them stay for two weeks."

Once, when we lived in Toluca Lake, my Yale friend Marc Flanagan was staying in the pool house, so I put my mother and father up in a hotel — the Sheraton Universal. Nice hotel, beautiful, just around the corner from us. Stacey or I would go and pick them up at 7 a.m., bring them over for breakfast. They'd stay all day, have dinner with us, then I'd take them back to the hotel to sleep.

Then Marc left. And my mother said, "Yah, so, the time we were in the hotel doesn't count. We're here for two weeks."

It was impossible to get rid of them. And they would cause so much tumult. So much friction. Not only between Stacey and me, but with our children. Once, when Zoe was three, my father was trying to discipline her about something, and he slapped her in the face. And Zoe, feisty Zoe, slapped him right back.

I yelled at him. He was outraged. He said, "She slapped me in the face!" I said, "So what? You must have deserved it!"

It never even dawned on me to tell Zoe at the time that you probably don't want to slap adults. But we didn't punish her. I thought, *Wow, slapping Harry! Isn't that just what I always wanted to do?*

STACEY:

My mother-in-law had no boundaries. She would walk by people and just bump into them. We had French doors leading into our bedroom, and we never locked them.

The first time they came to stay with us, Ilse marched right in and got into bed next to Henry. We locked the doors after that! And whenever Henry's parents visited, we would watch from our bed as the door handles jiggled. It was like a horror movie.

In 1989, my mother had a stroke. Stacey convinced me that I had to go see her, so I went. My mother was in my old bedroom, which had originally been my sister's room, in a bed in the corner. She could talk, but her words were a little slurred. Mostly she just stared into space.

I didn't know what to say to her. So I just made myself busy, organizing the top drawer of the dresser, which was full of things from Berlin — old letters and German money and stuff like that. Part of her was still back there, with her disappeared family. I looked at her, lying in bed, and realized that part of her had always been back there. After she died I found out that when I was very young, she'd been hospitalized for depression. Of course no one ever talked about it. She never got over the lie my father had told her to get her to leave Germany. And after that there were many more lies.

The fury between Stacey and Howard had

calmed to a very lovely co-parenting situation. Margaret, Howard's second wife, and I got along famously, as did Stacey and Margaret. The two of them put together Thanksgivings that you could only dream about: delicious, family-filled. And when Jed was accepted to Georgetown, it was decided that the four of us would take him to Washington to start his college career.

We pooled our resources and rented a three-room suite at the Four Seasons. Max and Zoe, now six and nine, along with Howard and Margaret's six-year-old son, Arman, made the trek to DC with us. The trip was fun, but the fun had a bittersweet tinge: Jed was really a homebody, suffering the honest anxiety of starting a new adventure at a brand-new school in a brand-new city.

The hotel suite was lovely: the Weitzmans were on one side, the Winklers on the other, a big living room in the middle. We went to dinner, we did a little shopping, we toured the school. We came back to the suite, and Jed squared his shoulders and announced, "I'm going to the dorm."

We were all hugging and yelling, "Congratulations, you're gonna be great!" Then Jed picked up his bag, walked out the door, and the door clicked shut.

Reader: count to three.

Stacey dropped to the rug and started sobbing inconsolably.

Everyone knelt down to try and comfort her — I could still kneel at the time. We got her a pillow from the bed so she could at least be comfortable in her sorrow.

Stacey understood why we were in Washington. She was calm throughout the entire thirty-six hours before Jed walked out the door of the suite. But the idea that her firstborn was leaving the nest was just too much for her.

We all sat on the couch and the two armchairs for a while as Stacey continued to weep. We then retreated to our rooms to start packing to go home — and Stacey was still crying. Finally, I said, "Stace, it's time."

Now the sobbing turned to sniffles. "Okay," Stacey said. She stood, and we were all able to leave Washington together — though intermittently she would start weeping again. We got home, and as any good mother would, she wanted Jed to be comfortable and not miss California too much. So she FedExed him care packages five times a week.

If a *Sports Illustrated* came for Jed, it went in the envelope. He loved the tacos from Henry's Tacos, right down the road from us

— and so several tacos, wrapped in aluminum foil and insulated with dry ice, went into the envelope. Other treats and reminders of home went into the envelopes. This continued during the entire first semester.

Stacey finally got a phone call from the dean of students at Georgetown. "Mrs. Winkler," the dean said, "we are so sorry, but we must take action. We think your son is a drug dealer."

Stacey was outraged. "What do you mean?" she said. "Our son doesn't take drugs!"

"No, he gets four or five Federal Express packages a week, more than any other student on campus."

"No, no, no, you don't understand — those are tacos!" Stacey said. "I just don't want him to miss home too much!"

Finally, an acting offer came.

Absolute Strangers was a TV movie, not a feature, but I was thrilled Gil Cates asked me to do it. Gil was not only a director; he was the head of the Screen Actors Guild. A smart, solid guy. And this was a serious drama, based on the pro-choice/antiabortion debate: the story revolved around a comatose pregnant woman who could be saved if the pregnancy was terminated. I played the husband who had to make the decision. It was my first chance to act since *Happy Days* had ended, and what I discovered was encouraging.

One thing I'd learned back at Yale was this: you do a play, let's say in repertory theater, then you put that play away after you've done it, and you get a chance to do it again a year later. And what you find is that the character has grown in you during the time you haven't done the play.

That's what happened with me and acting. I hadn't done it in seven years, but it had grown in me over all the time I was away from it. I had moved just an inch along the line. It wasn't much, but it was something.

MacGyver came to an end in 1992, after seven seasons — the milestone required for a series to go into syndication. This was good for me financially (though nobody, especially Stacey, could have convinced me that we weren't just two steps away from ruin), and especially good for me personally: it marked the official end of my business relationship with John Rich. The actual end had come a couple of weeks earlier, when I finally worked up the courage to tell him, "I can no longer look for a new key to open the new lock to our offices every day, and then have to reintroduce myself to you. There is no continuum between us. There is no respect. There is no warmth. I must go now."

"Oh, okay," John Rich said, as though I had told him I was going out to buy a pack of chewing gum. What a prince.

But I quickly found a much better producing partner in Ann Daniel, the ABC executive who had bought *MacGyver.* Ann had come aboard a couple of years earlier, when Rich and I decided we needed a head of the company. She was perfect: as a former network insider, she knew all the ins and outs of broadcast television (which is all there was in those days), and everything there was to know about how chilly this business is. She was amazingly diligent and productive — but she also understood that if the room doesn't fill with celestial sunlight when you're trying to make a sale, you're going to go home empty-handed.

A TV writer named Linda Moulton Howe had brought Ann the idea of a documentary series based on all things paranormal, all around the world. Ann then came to me with the idea, which we sold to Fox as *Sightings.* Ann and I came up with what I still think was a terrific concept: we got Dale

Timothy White, the news anchor at Fox's Washington, DC, affiliate, to host each episode in the most serious, newsman-like way ("This is Tim White. I don't know if what we're about to tell you is true, but we're going to discover together whether this woman, Molly Sims, was taken by an alien"). And with the producer Steve Kroopnick running the show brilliantly, *Sightings* also ran for seven years. I loved that material. Ever since I was young, I'd always had the feeling that if aliens ever landed on earth, they would land somewhere in my vicinity.

Two whole years went by before I got my next part. *Absolute Strangers* hadn't exactly put me back on the map. But then another TV movie came along. And this time I got to do something I'd never done before: play the bad guy. I was the dangerously disturbed ex-boyfriend of John Ritter's character's ex-wife. It was fun to play dangerously disturbed, but I don't think I knocked anyone's socks off.

The best thing about *The Only Way Out* turned out to be getting to work with the very lovely, very gifted, very much missed Mr. Ritter. John and I had first met in 1976, while I was making the third season of

Happy Days. One night I saw a commercial for a new ABC show called *Three's Company,* in which John did a daring and unexpected thing: he took a pratfall and tumbled right out of frame, something very few, if any, actors in the business would have had the nerve (and lack of vanity) to do. Then, as fate would have it, we had our own minor slapstick at ABC's twenty-fifth anniversary celebration. John was sitting directly behind me, and when I moved my chair back from the table to get up, he was also moving back, and we bumped right into each other. When he turned around to see who the klutz was, I apologized — then I recognized him.

"Oh, wait a minute," I said. "I just saw you on a commercial for your new show — it's going to be great, because — wow, the way you fell out of frame."

He smiled. I smiled. And we became friends. Very wonderful friends. We did the television movie together. We did animation together. We did Broadway together. And for ten years we raised millions of dollars for cerebral palsy, doing a telethon together. John could do anything, comedy or drama. He was handsome enough to be a leading man, but funny enough to fall on his ass. Ron Howard's former costar Don Knotts once called John the best physical comedian on the planet. It was true. He made me laugh morning, noon, and night.

Six of us — Ron and his wife, Cheryl; John and his first wife, Nancy; and Stacey and I — used to go out to dinner on Mondays, the night when we'd be least likely to get bothered in a restaurant. We called ourselves the Monday Marauders. Oh boy, we had a lot of laughs. It's so funny about time — you get into these nice little grooves with people you love, and you think it'll go on forever. But time goes so fast, and nothing goes on forever.

Not only did I get another acting job right after *The Only Way Out,* I got the chance to work with Katharine Hepburn. The TV movie *One Christmas* was based on a Truman Capote short story, and it wasn't just Hepburn who made the cast amazing: Swoosie Kurtz, Julie Harris, and Pat Hingle were also on the show. I wish I could say I was anywhere near their level. At the time, though — this was 1994 — I just wasn't.

Instead, I had burdened myself with the worst enemies an actor can have: self-consciousness and self-doubt. I was outside of myself. I was never in the moment. Why? I was more worried about the perception everyone would have of me than being immersed in telling the story. To do the real work of acting, you have to abandon yourself completely. That was a lesson I wouldn't learn for a long time.

I was overawed just to be in Katharine Hepburn's presence, but at the time, she was at the end of her great career. She had a longtime reputation for being as disagreeable as she was great, but I think she had mellowed by then. I literally held her lines on a piece of cardboard in front of my chest. Between takes one day, we got to talking about John Wayne, and when somebody spoke of him in the past tense, Hepburn said, "Oh, John Wayne — did I know that he died? Did I know him?" And her friend the TV journalist Cynthia McFadden, who was with her on the set, said, "Yes, you did, Katharine."

"Oh, sad," Hepburn said.

I never felt complacent about the crazy level of fame I had while I was still playing the Fonz. I was always amazed (still am!) when people recognized my voice on the telephone. And I was doubly amazed when people I considered great not only acknowledged my existence, but did it in a welcoming way. At *Night of 100 Stars* in the early eighties, Orson Welles said to me, "Finally we meet, Henry."

"Wait a minute, what?" I said.

And that same night, I went up to Marcello Mastroianni and shook his hand. "Hello, my name is Henry Winkler," I said.

"You do not have to tell me who you are," said Marcello Mastroianni.

Did he see me on Italian TV? I wondered. (When I won the Telegatto, I got the chance to see *Happy Days* on Italian television: everything was dubbed except the *Ayyy!*)

And then there was Bette Davis.

Once, while I was still doing *Happy Days,* Bette Davis called me up and said she wanted to take me to dinner.

This was when Stacey and Jed and I were still living on Reklaw Drive in the Valley. And on the appointed evening, Ms. Davis showed up at our little house, where we had two couches and a chair, sat down, and lit up a cigarette. We actually had an ashtray — I was still smoking then — but ashtrays weren't for Bette Davis. The ashes just went wherever they went. And I thought, *You know what? It's Bette Davis. That's the way it is.*

We went to a French restaurant on Ventura Boulevard, La Serre. I drove; Ms. Davis was in the passenger seat and Stacey sat in back. The restaurant put us in a private room. Did I feel self-conscious in the presence of this great star, this Hollywood icon? Of course I did. Was I awkward? Of course I was. But Bette Davis picked up the slack — she kept the conversation flowing; she was lovely. And her cigarette ashes, being Bette Davis's cigarette ashes, went wherever the hell Bette Davis felt like putting them.

Remember I told you how Hollywood works? Despite my less than sterling track record as a director, I got another chance, through Ron Howard's company, Imagine. The story, titled *Cop & 1/2,* was about a little boy who witnesses a murder, but refuses to testify unless he gets a chance to be a policeman. And he's teamed with the police detective who's investigating the killing, who hates kids.

I had a meeting with John Candy to play that role, and I had a lot to say about what I thought about the character. After the meeting, Ron called me. "Candy passed," he said.

"Oh," I said. "Why?"

"Apparently you talked too much in the meeting," Ron said.

Would I ever learn? Evidently it was taking me a while.

But when I met with Burt Reynolds, I did

my best to keep my lips zipped. And Burt took the part.

Burt Reynolds was well over fifty at the time: *Deliverance* and *Smokey and the Bandit* were far in his past, as was a full head of hair. But even though not a lot of leading-man parts were coming his way, he was still every inch the big star. As a matter of fact, in his contract, he had a new hairpiece, called "The Unit," delivered to the set each week. He wanted to shoot *Cop & 1/2* in Tampa, on the west coast of Florida. Why? Because he had rented a house in Clearwater, just a couple of miles away. Fine with me.

A couple of nights before we started shooting, Burt had a party at his house. Everyone was there, all the actors, the stunt guys, everyone. Like the star he was, Burt took his time about making his appearance. Finally, he walks down this grand staircase, chewing gum like a tough guy, and announces, before he even reaches the bottom, "Winkler, I just got off the phone with Ron Howard. He said I can fire you any time I want."

I looked up at him, and in front of everybody I said, "Oh, good! Let me know as soon as possible. I've got another movie lined up right after this one — I can get started early."

I have no idea where that came from — it shot out of my mouth like it was a hockey puck. But it actually stopped Burt in his tracks. He thought about it for a second. He descended the rest of the staircase, walked up to me, and said, "This is how you direct me: you just say, 'Louder.' 'Faster.' 'Slower.' "

"Okay, I can do that," I said.

"Oh, and by the way — I direct the kid," he said.

We began shooting. Burt seemed pretty angry at the director most of the time — there was a lot of yelling. And in my calmest voice I'd say, "You know what? Let's try it again." Then we'd try it again, and I'd say, "All right. I think we've got that one." He used to call me Thumper the Bunny, after the sweet-tempered rabbit in *Bambi,* because he could never get me angry.

Staying calm wasn't always easy on that picture. One day, the mother of Norman Golden, the little boy who costarred with Burt, came to me and asked, "Why do you only do two takes with Burt and ten takes with my son?"

For a moment I was so stunned, my brain almost stopped. Then I gathered my wits. "Let's see," I said. "Burt will only do two takes. It's your son's first movie. He forgot a line. I think he can do better. He's very talented. And he's seven. I'm going to try and get his best. But if you have a thought about that, please let me know." She backed off.

One day we were doing a big fight scene in a bar, and Burt reminded me that he directs the kid. Now mind you, this is the first time he's ever exercised that right. Norman, the kid, is up in a window, talking to Burt, who's out on the street before he comes into the bar. We rehearsed the scene; we're about to shoot, and I whisper to Burt, "Excuse me, I don't mean to interrupt, but I believe it would be better if Norman pauses between his first and second lines."

Burt then yells up to the kid: "Hey! Pause between your first and second lines!"

The scene continues, and in between takes, I whisper to Burt once more: "Excuse me, I don't mean to interrupt, but I think that Norman should get a little feisty when he says his next line to you."

Burt yells up to the kid, "When you're saying, 'I'm not going with you,' get a little feisty!"

I am now directing the child through Burt.

One weekend, Burt invited me to stay overnight at his house in Jupiter, Florida, where he lived with his beautiful wife, Loni Anderson, and their four-year-old son, Quinton. I didn't know how to say no to the star. When I got there, I realized I've been invited to the house to be the playdate for Quinton. I go swimming with Quinton. We have a tuna-fish sandwich with the crusts cut off. And finally, I get to have adult time at dinner, after which Burt asks Miss Anderson to take me to her private collection of Disney figurines. And she shows me hundreds of these porcelain Snow Whites and Goofys and Mickeys, and then I get to go to my room.

So now shooting the movie is done; we're all back in LA, and now we're in looping — rerecording all the dialogue that was ruined by some noise that happened during the making of the film. Burt comes into the studio with a small bottle of water. I remember what he told me about how to direct him: slower, faster, louder, softer. We have to redo a line that he spoke when there was noise on the set. He does the line. I say, "All right, let's try this again" — and he throws that little bottle of water right at me. I duck out of the way just in time. "You are so fucking lucky that you're so short or I'd rip your head right off your neck," he says.

"Burt," I say, "I have never been so happy

to be this short in my whole life." Then, "Okay, let's move on."

"Did I get it?" he asks.

"Well . . ."

"I want to do it till it's right," Burt says.

We eventually got it right. And I emerged with my head still in place.

PS: *Cop & 1/2* was a big box-office hit. But I decided to give directing a rest for a while.

I loved every nook and cranny of our Toluca Lake house. I loved its brilliantly colorful interior design, created by our dear friend Maxine Smith. I even loved the fact that Bob Hope lived around the corner — I never met him, but I was happy he was there!

Nevertheless, one day Stacey said to me, "You know, the air here in Toluca Lake is not great — I think we should move."

"But I love it here," I said.

"Yes, but the air here isn't great for the children," Stacey said. "Let's just see what would happen if we put this house up for sale."

In the interest of domestic tranquility, I decided to agree with my wife. More than that: we went out and bought a statue of St. Joseph and buried it upside down in the garden, amongst the irises — a traditional good-luck ritual if you want to sell a house.

Within a week, we had several bids, and our migration to the Westside began.

We first bought a house in Bel Air, but it needed work, so we rented a place nearby. And one day in January 1994, the Northridge earthquake happened — the biggest quake ever to hit Los Angeles. Zoe was screaming from the other side of the house; the walls were cracking, Stacey's prized collection of mercury glass was shattering all over the floor. And as the house shifted, the front door became lodged in place, unopenable.

I rammed it with my shoulder, and I don't know how, but it flew open. I have never been that strong again in my life.

My family had always laughed at me for making survival bags. Each bag contained a little cash, some medicine, bottled water, dehydrated food for five weeks, some warm clothing, and heavy wool socks. I grabbed our bags as we ran out the front door, and now, as we all sat in the family car, I handed out the clothing, and no one was laughing.

One small problem: I hadn't updated the bags for a while, and when Max put on the sweatpants I packed for him, they were now shorts.

After a while, we drove over to check on Stacey's mom and dad. Everyone was still shaken — literally and emotionally — and Stacey's mom suggested we light a fire in the fireplace in order to get cozy. Instantly, the same light bulb flashed over everybody's head: earthquake; broken gas mains. We all screamed "NO!" at the same time.

In 1993 Jed graduated from Georgetown and moved to New York City, where he got a job as an intern at *Saturday Night Live,* working for Lorne Michaels. Now it was just the four of us, and my darling daughter had entered adolescence as though fired from a cannon. From the moment she started to talk, Zoe had never taken any prisoners.

At the time — I was working during the day; Stacey was on a commission downtown for the rights of abused and neglected children — we were lucky enough to have a couple helping us in the house, and the husband, Terry, would drive Zoe to school and pick her up. And Zoe — she was maybe fourteen at the time — being Zoe, would convince Terry to lie down in the back seat of the car, and she would drive around Westwood, the home of UCLA.

Zoe at the wheel. As she was with so many things.

Around then, life taught me another big lesson. Marc Lawrence was a very young, wonderfully funny, and inventive writer — he used to work on *Family Ties* with Gary David Goldberg. And Marc sent me a pilot script, *Monty,* and I laughed out loud when I read it. It was about a Rush Limbaugh–like talk radio host (to be played by me) who has a gay daughter, and I loved it . . . but. I called Marc and said, "This is too controversial — can't do it."

"Just give it another read," Marc said.

I did. Laughed out loud a second time. Thought to myself, *Oh my God, don't you dare. This is just too controversial — you can't do it.*

I read it a third time. It was so funny. I called Marc again and said, "I can't do this, but I can't not."

Touchstone Television, the TV arm of Disney, was producing the show. And we sold it to NBC. Made a pilot, directed by the multitalented John Pasquin. Wonderful cast: Kate Burton, Cynthia Nixon, David Krumholtz as my youngest son — David was like a heat-seeking missile to a joke at age thirteen. Fun fact: this was one of the first jobs for both Jack Black and Gwyneth Paltrow, who were day players — just one scene apiece. NBC sent me my ticket to go to New York for the upfronts — the annual event where the networks offer all the advertisers the chance to buy commercial time on the new shows. And all of a sudden NBC dropped out. And asked for my plane ticket back. Warren Littlefield, the head of the network, had said yes to the show, but it must've finally dawned on somebody at GE, which owned NBC, what kind of political waters the network would be wading into with *Monty.*

Jeff Katzenberg, now also the head of television at Disney, was undeterred, and determined to sell it. So we sold it once more, this time to Fox. And very quickly, the show transformed from Rush Limbaugh having a gay daughter to Rush Limbaugh having a son, David Schwimmer, who went to college to become a lawyer, and now wants to be a chef. Transformed, in other words, from something sharp and fresh into a run-of-the-mill sitcom.

Marc's original concept was unbelievably funny, and it came straight from his heart. He had a gay sister. He understood the material. He was passionate about it. It was brilliant. And suddenly, it was . . . mush.

This was when John Pasquin dropped out.

And the big life lesson I should have learned was: if you say yes to something because it is exactly right, and they change it, go home. Do not walk; run.

I did not go home. We made thirteen episodes of *Monty,* until it died the death it deserved. No one's career was enhanced, least of all mine.

It was the second time, after *Turner & Hooch,* that I went completely against my gut instinct, and once again I was hit in the mouth by a two-by-four. When I give talks these days, I say, "Your head knows some things; your tummy knows everything." I say it to kindergartners, I say it to seniors. I say it to everybody, because it is the law of living.

Tootsie Annamarie, our beautiful black Lab, was now in her golden years, and Max was now ten, the same age I was when I got — and then lost — Dervin. Our next dog was a King Charles Cavalier. We named him, optimistically, after the TV show I'd just started: Monty. Unfortunately, after the show was canceled, I would feel resentful every time I called Monty's name. And you can't change a dog's name. (And unlike Tootsie, Monty's version of playing ball was just watching the ball roll by him, never leaving his seated position.)

Our next puppy was Charlotte, a black labradoodle, our first. Charlotte was a love, and highly intelligent. Together we invented a game where she would guard an open doorway, any open doorway, as if she were a goalie on an Italian soccer team. Charlotte always won. She was a better athlete than I could ever dream of being.

I loved all our dogs *so much* — I still do. But the difference between then and now is that I've finally come to understand how the dogs allowed me to express the love that I found so difficult (except with our children) to express otherwise.

My father died in 1995, a month after his ninety-second birthday and — his birthday was the day before mine — a month after I turned fifty. Fifty years old, and my acting career was still more or less dead on arrival. My producing career, pulsing weakly. And Harry Winkler, this tiny man who had loomed so large in my life — and the vast majority of the time in such a dismissive and disrespectful way — was no more. Only Ilse, now a mere shadow of herself, remained.

"We have to go," Stacey told me. Meaning, to the funeral.

Almost anyone else wouldn't have thought twice about it. A parent dies, you go to the funeral. But it hadn't dawned on me that I actually had to go to New York and *be* there at my father's funeral. I literally thought, *Okay, he's dead, and my sister is there, and that'll be that.*

I didn't say anything to Stacey. "We have to go," she repeated.

"I don't think we do," I said.

But of course I surrendered to necessity. It wasn't easy.

As we've discussed, I have an idiosyncratic relationship with money. Largely thanks to the guy who had just died.

But even more idiosyncratic was my relationship with him. Harry would often travel on business, alone, when I was small. He always brought back presents. I liked the presents! I remember a gift he once brought me from Honduras: a native headdress and a suction-cup bow and arrow. But I also remember there was this sense at home that on that trip and others, he was away for too long. Like, way too long.

A couple of years ago it occurred to me: could there have been another woman? Maybe even another family? I've thought about that.

But I just don't know.

■ ■ ■ ■

Another acting gig came my way: another television movie, *A Child Is Missing.* I played a mountain man, a hermit, who stumbles upon a child who's been kidnapped, then becomes a suspect in the kidnapping. I did the movie because, once again, I was trying to show the world I could do something different from the Fonz. I channeled Daniel Day-Lewis in *The Last of the Mohicans* — the way he ran through the forest, carrying his musket low to the ground.

But I wasn't anything close to Daniel Day-Lewis. I was the 1995 version of Henry Winkler: I strained, I pushed and pulled, but I was so disconnected as an actor that I couldn't access the kernel of authenticity deep inside. I did everything I could to find myself inside of myself, but the real me was still locked away, sheathed in yards of concrete. I knew it was in there somewhere — I just couldn't get to it. It was my life's ambition to jackhammer through the concrete shield that girded that spark of reality.

And that was most of my life until around seven years ago. Only now do I understand that things come in their own time. That you couldn't have known then what you know now. That only the process of living gets you there: you must do the work in order to eat the fruit of growing — of being. In my late seventies, I am trying very hard to live in the moment and enjoy every moment. I'm thrilled, elated that I'm here now, at a kind of new beginning. But I am also incredibly frustrated that it took me until now to get here. There are other actors — look at Anthony Hopkins! Jack Nicholson! — who were able to do it from the very start. Not me.

After my stint as a self-conscious mountain man, Wes Craven got in touch with me. He wanted to have lunch. Great! I didn't know anything about horror films, but I certainly knew of Wes Craven, the master of *A Nightmare on Elm Street.* We met at Iroha, a sushi restaurant on Ventura Boulevard, and we hit it off right away. He was lovely: professorial. Tweedy. Gentle. Soft-spoken. Thoughtful. And from that mind came terror. So we had lunch; we chatted — and then he said, "Look, I'm doing this movie *Scream.* I've got a small part I'd love you to play — the principal of the high school. Would you do it?"

"Of course I would," I said.

So I went to Santa Rosa, where they were

shooting the movie, and worked for a week. In the story, I am killed by the guy in the mask. I had tubes full of prop blood inside my clothing, and the blood would shoot from the tubes when I was stabbed. We did a take, and Wes said, "Do you think it might be a little more excruciating?"

"I do," I said.

"Do you think that you could scream a little louder?" he asked.

"I will!" I said.

So they cleaned me up, re-tubed me, re-dressed me, refilled the blood capsules — and this time, as the knife was plunged into me multiple times, blood shooting all over the place, I screamed louder than I believed any human could. Then I lay on the floor with the camera lens very close to my eye — it took two hours to get the reflection of the mask in my eye just right. What you learn is that a horror film takes more cuts than your usual film, in order to build the tension. I hadn't known that.

Anyway, I finish my little bit, and the movie gets done. And the executive in charge of the production company says, "We cannot put Henry's name on the movie. We can't put Henry's picture on the poster. He is the Fonz. He will knock the balance of the horror off."

Wes told me about it himself. I was a little hurt; he apologized. But that was the movie business — I understood.

Now the movie is tested: shown to test audiences who write all their comments on cards so the film can be reedited and improved. But what the producers did not anticipate was that at every screening, there was big applause when my character walked on the screen. And the executives from the production company who had made the very thoughtful decision not to put my name on the film or the poster now asked my agent if I would do press for the movie.

I extended my middle finger in the privacy of my own home — and went out and did press for *Scream.* Why? Because it benefited my friend, who had asked me to be in it, and it benefited me. It became a story that I still have in my life. People now talk to me about *Scream.* I did not need to put my name on the movie or on the poster. I am now forever associated with the first *Scream.* I am asked to sign every piece of *Scream* memorabilia at every Comic-Con anywhere in the world.

The moral of the story? Keep working!

My mother died on September 22, 1997. This time I realized that as little as I wanted to go to New York, I had to; we all had to. I spoke at her funeral. I made a couple of jokes about her. I said that she used to ride a white horse around the apartment, making sure everything was spotless. I said that when she came in to check on my homework, she was wearing a Prussian uniform. I was joking, but I was really just saying the truth about who she was and how she was to me. I pulled no punches; I had no grace. I only had extraordinary anger. My sister came up to me afterward and said, "That's not the mother I remember."

"Okay," I said. "You had a different experience. That's *exactly* the mother I remember."

We moved into the Bel Air house. It had so many rooms that we literally couldn't use all of them, which drove me out of my mind — I'd walk around the place, look into this or that empty room, shake my head, and close the door again. So after four years, we found a much more family-friendly house in Santa Monica. It, too, needed work, so we rented another house — which turned out to have been Cary Grant's house: Cary's widow, Barbara Grant, rented it to us.

One day while we were living there — Stacey was back East, taking a short vacation with her good friend Marcia — I got a call from Max's school, Crossroads, where he had just started a month earlier as a ninth grader. It seemed Max had just thrown up in the alley. Max got on the phone and told me that one of the seniors had given him a sip of beer. I called Stacey; she flew home.

Of course there was more to the story than Max had let on. When I talked to the dean of students, he told me that the school was going to either expel or suspend Max, because although as a ninth grader he wasn't allowed to leave the campus during the day, let alone drink alcohol, he had gone out at lunchtime with some seniors, and it wasn't a sip of beer that had made him throw up — it was Kool-Aid and vodka that these older boys were enjoying during their lunch hour.

I said to the dean of students: "You don't know us; you don't know Max. All I can tell you is that Max really is a terrific young man, but whatever you decide, we can live with."

He was suspended for two weeks; he was grounded by his parents for four. He could breathe, he could eat, he could do his homework. He was lucky water was included. His need to communicate with his friends who were not at that school was so great that he would write them letters every night and I would mail them the next day from my office. (I was producing *Hollywood Squares* at the time, with Michael Levitt. God, we had fun.)

What I found out years later was that Max would sneak my cell phone into the bathroom, lock the door, and talk to his friends from the shower (it wasn't running).

All's well that ends well — in his senior year, my son was given the Heart Award by his class at Crossroads for being a good, thoughtful, available human being, which he remains to this day.

Zoe continued to make our lives interesting. One weekend when she was about sixteen, Stacey accompanied me on one of my speechmaking trips; Terry and his wife watched the house and the kids while we were gone. When we returned, Terry came into the kitchen with a troubled look. "Sir," he said, "I am so sorry, but my wife and I saw a man on the security camera, running through the ivy at three in the morning on Saturday."

We brought Zoe into the kitchen and had Terry tell the story again. She interrupted him, full of outrage. "No!" she said. "What you saw was a ghost! You didn't see a man! I didn't have my boyfriend over! You saw an apparition running through the ivy!"

Years went by. Readers, you all know the situation: your grown kids are home for a much anticipated dinner, you're seated cozily around the table, and all of a sudden the truth comes out about so many stories. They're sitting there laughing hysterically: "Hey, Dad! Remember that time a tree jumped out in the road and hit my car?" Or, "Remember that time when there was a ghost running through the ivy? That was Brandon!"

We will now pass over my participation in the worst movie ever made by human beings, a picture where my name *was* in the credits *and* on the poster.

The film was called *Ground Control.* Never heard of it? Good!

Ground Control. They fired the writer; they fired the director. Kiefer Sutherland, who starred in it, even got to direct for a day. Then they brought in a new director. What makes a bad movie bad? People not knowing what they're doing. People not knowing how to do it, but somehow getting the money to do it. It happens more times than you can imagine.

Out of ten directors, two and a half will be good. The others will direct you, the actor, to do something so wrong that it sets your stomach on fire. You say, "Wow. Let me try that." And then you do — not the thing they just told you, but the thing that you know, from your years of training and experience, is right. And the director will say at the end of the take, "Didn't I tell you it would work?"

"Yes, you did," you say. "Thank you very much."

Those are the terrible directors. Then, on the other hand, you get Jerry Paris. You get Bill Hader. Alec Berg. Bill Hader's ex-wife, Maggie Carey, is also a really good director. You get all the other incredible directors in my life. You don't get *Ground Control.*

The best thing about *Ground Control* was that one day during the shoot, I went to the men's room, and as I was washing my hands my agent called and said that Adam Sandler would like me to play the coach in *The Waterboy.*

I'd first met Adam a couple of years earlier, not long after he sang his wonderful "Chanukah Song" on *Saturday Night Live.* Listing celebrities who were Jewish or part Jewish, the song contained the delicious lines:

Guess who eats together at the Carnegie Deli
Bowser from Sha Na Na and Arthur Fonzarelli

At the time, Jed had a job at the management company Brillstein-Grey, where Adam was a client. So I took the opportunity to call Adam and tell him, "I just want to say that I'm thrilled to be in your song." And Adam thanked me, and invited me to his house. And I went, and it was awkward.

Adam hosted basketball games at his house on the weekends, and there were a lot of celebrities there: it was the first time I met Brad Pitt, the first time I met Jim Carrey. Chris Rock was there; Kevin James was there. I spent a lot of time talking with Jim. Carrey was being Carrey, talking rapid-fire about his anxiety, Catholicism, guilt; without benefit of a degree, I was trying to psychoanalyze him — and I realize now that I was talking through my hat. I thought this was the way to relate to him, but I now see that a film like a lizard's had descended over his eyes; clearly he was thinking, *What the fuck is this guy talking about?* All the guys at Adam's were old buddies and good athletes, and I was once again eleven years old and chasing the cool kids at school. I did not play basketball. I stood on the sideline, feeling left out — even though I had left myself out.

But Adam didn't see my awkwardness, or was nice enough not to mention it. And he offered me the part in *The Waterboy* anyway.

To work with Adam Sandler was to form a huge admiration for him. He didn't direct the picture — that was Frank Coraci, who is another fine director. But Adam really is in charge of every one of his movies. He knows every detail about everything that's happening on his production. Everything. And he knows how to bring everyone in. He has a whole orchestra of musical instruments in his trailer — anybody who plays can come in and jam with him. In between scenes, he would get an easel and a canvas in there, too, and a paper bag filled with cans of spray paint, all different colors. Everybody gets a can. If an eleven-year-old walks up to him on a location and says, "Adam Sandler, I love you," Adam says, "Hey, here's a spray can." Now that kid goes from being wide-eyed and overwhelmed to being part of the pack, spraying red paint on the canvas. Adam pulls everybody in: "You know what? Maybe a little more yellow right here. What do you think? Hey, red — right here." That's the genius, and the humanness, of Adam Sandler.

With the work finally completed on the Santa Monica house, we moved into the cozy and just-right-sized home we've now happily lived in for twenty-seven years. Of course, what I didn't realize at the time was that our departure from Toluca Lake had nothing to do with air quality, and we were now living exactly eight minutes from Stacey's mother and father.

It takes me a while to catch on.

9.

The Waterboy was the best thing I did for a long time. By which I mean I completely enjoyed working in what turned out to be an excellent — and very successful — Adam Sandler movie, and what came next for me was . . . whatever I could get. People still weren't breaking down my door with film and TV roles, but I kept working.

Keep working!

Then an amazing and very frightening opportunity came my way. In 1999 I was asked to read for Neil Simon, for a new play, *The Dinner Party,* that he was doing at the Mark Taper Forum in downtown Los Angeles. And my first thought was, *I can't do that.*

Acting onstage is what I was trained to do, but I hadn't done it in a long time. A very long time. I wasn't sure I still knew how. In 1973, about six months before I flew to California and changed my life, I'd costarred in the Broadway play I mentioned earlier, the one that opened and closed on the same night. The (scathing) *New York Times* review didn't even mention my name, for which I was grateful. My mother, however, kept saying, "What is wrong with this reviewer? The play was funny!"

Acting onstage? *I can't do that.* I can't read this play out loud. I can't read, period. I certainly can't read Neil Simon's play in front of Neil Simon.

I had baggage with Neil Simon. Or maybe more correctly, I was afraid he had baggage with me. While I was still doing *Happy Days,* he had invited me to dinner. He really liked my portrayal of the Fonz — he thought it was great. So Stacey and I went to dinner at Neil Simon and Marsha Mason's house, and it was a disaster. Disaster, how?

I was uptight. I was manic. I couldn't shut up. This was the great Neil Simon, America's foremost comic playwright — one of the first plays I ever saw was *Come Blow Your Horn,* and I'd laughed so hard I couldn't breathe. How did I deserve to be invited to Neil Simon's house? My level of intimidation and self-consciousness was off the charts. As a result, I could *not* shut up. "Oh, this is the typewriter on which you typed *Come Blow Your Horn*! Oh my goodness! Oh!" And this was when I was smoking, and nobody else was smoking, and I'm smoking so much — out of sheer nervousness — that the ashtray is overflowing with butts and ashes, and Neil Simon's dogs are lying by the kitchen door, and I become obsessed that when dinner is served, the kitchen door is going to hit the dogs, so — of course — I speak up about it, and . . .

Oy.

When the evening was finally over, Neil Simon was walking me to the door with his arm around my shoulder, and you could've driven a truck between us: that's how warm and comfortable he was feeling about me. And when Stacey and I walked to our car, I said, "Boy, I really fucked that up, didn't I?"

"Yes, you did," my bracingly honest wife said.

And that wasn't all! After that night I kept thinking, *How can I make this right? I've got it — we have to reciprocate!* So I spend months, literally months, working up the courage to call up Neil Simon and invite him and Marsha Mason to dinner. I'm working up the courage and rehearsing the call in my mind. The situation takes me back to high school. I'm in my apartment in New York City, and it's August, and I want to ask this girl out. And it's hot out and the air conditioner in the window is on, and I'm sweating, but I'm shivering, can't stop shivering, because I'm going to make this call, and I put on my winter overcoat to try to stop shivering. In August. Inside my apartment in New York City.

I finally work up the courage to call Neil Simon. I have rehearsed the words I am going to say; I have prepared the casual and friendly attitude I will adopt while making the call. And I call. "Hey, hey, how about if we take you out to dinner next Saturday?"

"I'm so sorry, we're busy," he said.

"How about the following Saturday?"

"Then too."

"Don't you worry," I told Neil Simon. "I'm gonna call back with more dates."

Never happened.

So: baggage with Neil Simon. And yet I am invited to read for his new play. "Yes!" I said. And then the thoughts returned. *What are you, crazy? You can't read. You're going to* read? *Out loud, off the page? You've never been able to do this your entire life.*

The script arrives at my house. *The Dinner Party* is a dark comedy about marriage: it takes place in a private dining room at a fancy restaurant in Paris. Three couples dine together, and trouble ensues, along with a lot of great Neil Simon jokes. I am to play

Albert Donay, a somewhat dim-witted used-car salesman. I start to underline my lines with yellow highlighter. And as I'm underlining, I'm starting to think of ways to get out of the whole thing. And then as I always do, I come to the point where I say to myself, "Shut the fuck up. Walk to the edge of the precipice and fly."

So I jumped out into space, and stayed aloft. I kept underlining my lines, then I read them over and over and over until they were etched in my brain. Went downtown to read, with my castmates, for Neil Simon. An amazing thing happened while this was going on. We were all sitting in a circle in the rehearsal room when in walks Dustin Hoffman.

"Hello, Doc," he says to Simon.

"Hi, Dustin," Simon said. He looked puzzled.

"I'm here for the —" he said. He pointed at us.

"Oh, I'm so sorry," Neil Simon said. "There must have been a mistake."

And Dustin Hoffman had to leave. I could barely look up.

We read. I made Neil Simon laugh! We rehearsed. I improvised! At one point my character says to Jan Maxwell, the actress playing the woman I love, "You're beautiful!" And she says, "No, I'm not." And I lifted the lid from this silver chafing dish and showed her her reflection. "Yes, you are," I said. And Neil Simon wrote my piece of business into the play.

We now come to a moment where we're leaving this rehearsal room with tape on the floor, and we're actually moving into the theater, across the street. The set is up. Somehow I had forgotten that this was actually going to happen. I'd been so enjoying rehearsing with my great castmates, Ed Herrmann and Frances Conroy and John Ritter. Now the bell was going off: this was real. And I freaked out. I panicked. I literally could not take a step toward the door. "Wait a minute," I told the director. "I cannot go across the street. I cannot do this now. I'll get somebody else for you — we'll cast him together. I'll work day and night with him on everything that I've done, and I'll go home."

"Just shut up and go across the street," the director said.

So I went across the street. And as we started to work in the place itself, on the stage where it would happen, I got more and more comfortable. And all of a sudden, I was home again.

We opened, and we got okay reviews.

262

Neil's producer Manny Azenberg came and watched the play, and said, "You know what? It's not ready. We're not taking it to Broadway." We all go home. Then, in August 1999, we get a call. There's a hole in the schedule at the Kennedy Center in Washington, DC. Could we come and do the play in Washington?

I talked to Stacey. It would mean me moving to DC, living in a hotel for a few months. She and the kids — Zoe had just finished her freshman year in Wisconsin, and was back home for the summer; Max was sixteen, a sophomore in high school — could come visit. Stacey was okay with it: she always tried so hard to understand when it came to my work. It was very difficult when I was away for extended periods: the entire responsibility of taking care of the children and the house rested on her shoulders. But that was our life.

Neil had rewritten — and rewritten and rewritten — the play. That was part of his genius. The show we did at the Mark Taper was version number four; now we were on version ten. We opened, and got good reviews. And this time Manny Azenberg said, "We're going to New York."

We started rehearsing in September and opened in October, at the Music Box, the

Broadway theater that Irving Berlin had built in the 1920s. The reviews ranged from delighted to so-so, but the critiques were mainly about the play, not the actors, and the people came to see the actors — and kept coming: John Ritter and I did *The Dinner Party* for nine months.

I always learn a lot when I act alongside such wonderful professionals as John Ritter, Len Cariou, Penny Fuller, and the very funny Jan Maxwell. But I learned an especially big lesson early on in this show's run. When you're working on a movie or TV show, the camera can always be stopped if somebody or something messes up. In theater, though, there are no mulligans. The play must go on, no matter what.

At Yale, I'd learned that before an actor makes his entrance, he needs to prepare: take a moment, concentrate, get into the mode and the mood. But one night at the Music Box, for reasons I don't remember, I did not do any kind of preparation before my entrance: I just walked onstage. And as I made my first entrance, I started to laugh. And could not stop laughing. Why? I have no idea. Maybe something got in my nose. But there I am, in front of a full Broadway audience, giggling like an idiot. And John Ritter puts his arm around my back and walks me in a circle around the stage, whispering, *"You've got the first line. We can't start the play until you speak."*

Did that make me stop laughing? It did not. Somehow, the more I laughed, the funnier I found everything — until John whispered, "Henry, come *on.*"

I came to my senses, not a moment too soon.

The whole run of *The Dinner Party* was wonderful, but two especially wonderful things happened while I was there. The first was the annual Easter Bonnet Competition, a fundraising event for Broadway Cares/ Equity Fights AIDS. For weeks, every show on and off Broadway, and all the national touring companies, auctioned off memorabilia signed by the cast. Every night, at the end of the show, John and I stood on the stage and, largely thanks to his comic skills, did an hour of shtick that got the audience going to the point where we sold the handkerchief my character wore in his jacket pocket for $15,000. And we beat every other show on Broadway — including *Annie Get Your Gun,* where Reba McEntire, who was playing Annie, sold off her earrings. We beat Reba by seventy-five dollars, and it was like winning an Academy Award.

The other magical thing was the Broadway

Show League. In the springtime when I was in high school, we used to go out during lunch and walk through Central Park: sometimes we'd go and ride the carousel. And on those walks, I used to pass the ball fields where the Broadway Show League was playing softball. There I was at sixteen and seventeen years old, every molecule in my body wanting to act, and there were these actors and actresses with charisma to burn having the time of their lives smacking softballs and running around the bases with T-shirts reading BROADWAY SHOW LEAGUE, and I wanted to play softball in that show league more than I wanted breath in my lungs. I would dream about it, but it was so far away. And here I was on Broadway in a Neil Simon play, and John Ritter, Len Cariou, and I played softball for *The Dinner Party* — and I got to deploy the skills I'd learned on the *Happy Days* softball team. . . .

Oh. My. God.

I have the softball from my first pitch on a shelf in my office, in a plastic case.

I stayed in *The Dinner Party* for most of its run, but in June I had to return to Los Angeles. I'd gotten a movie offer — not a big role, but a role — and John Kimball's long-ago words were once again echoing in my ears: *If you want to be known to New York, stay here; if you want to be known to the world . . .*

The movie, a cute rom-com called *Down to You,* written and directed by a first-timer, Kris Isacsson, would not rekindle my world-wide fame. I played a TV chef, the dad of the young lead in the picture, the very charming Freddie Prinze Jr. (Fun fact: Freddie Prinze Jr.'s child plays soccer one field over from my grandson.) The director was a nice young guy; the film came and went. But I learned still another lesson during the shoot, and it wasn't a pleasant one.

It was just this: while we were rehearsing, I came up with a little bit of comic business, saying one of my lines in a funny cadence as I joke-punched my son's arm. But during rehearsals, every time I was about to do it, the actor in the scene with me did it first — same cadence, same joke-punch. *Who do you report this to?* I thought. The same thing had happened in the second or third season of *Happy Days,* when a guest actress began imitating one of the Fonz's hand gestures: raising a finger to make a point, stealing my thunder. I didn't do anything about it then, but this time I came up with a solution. I just did my lines flat in rehearsal — no special cadence, no physical business — and saved the funny stuff for the take. My improv training came in very handy here. And I managed to keep my funny for myself.

And what did I learn? Don't work with that person again. Not much of a lesson, but hey, I stuck to it.

One night while I was away giving a speech, Stacey went to the movies with our friends Frank and Lynn Dines, and when they went back to the car after the picture was over, there was this beautiful black Lab puppy just sitting there on the third level of the parking structure. No collar, no tag. Stacey, who's so empathic that she has to cut a half-apple in half so it won't be lonely in the refrigerator, simply couldn't leave that puppy sitting in the parking structure. She took him, as the law requires, to an animal shelter — but then couldn't stop thinking about him. She phoned the shelter multiple times every day to see whether anyone had called about the puppy; once, a person at the shelter told her, "No, just this one woman who calls about six times a day." "Oh, that's me," Stacey said.

Finally, the puppy came home with us. Max named him Linus. When we took him to the vet to be examined, the doctor said, "Oh, he has a dewclaw — it's best to remove it." So Linus began his life with us with an operation. What the vet didn't tell us was that Linus was not a black Lab but a Great Dane. In no time at all, Linus grew to Shetland pony size: fortunately, he and Charlotte got along famously. We used to take them both to the dog park on the beach in Long Beach — Charlotte, who loved the ocean, would have swum to Catalina if we'd let her; Linus, the gigantoid, was too delicate to brave the surf. He would just dip his paw.

After two years away at college, Zoe came back home. She didn't want to be far away anymore, didn't want to go through another Wisconsin winter. Her dyslexia had inclined her to put more energy into her social life than academics, and she didn't want to partake in the school's courses for dyslexic students. She'd missed us; we'd missed her. She moved back in with us, and continued college classes in preschool education at Loyola Marymount in West LA.

Had we done something wrong, raising a daughter who couldn't quite leave the nest? Had Zoe done something wrong?

Nobody had done anything wrong — we

were just living our lives. Then life got very life-y.

Soon after Zoe returned, Stacey learned she had breast cancer. And although I was home and not away working when she got her diagnosis, I couldn't be emotionally present for her in all the ways I needed to be: I just couldn't process this gigantic news. I was terrified, as I know she was, but I was also scared to share my fear with her.

Not my finest hour.

Yes, I was there when Stacey's good friend the salon owner Chris McMillan came over and proactively cut all her hair off. Yes, I went with her to her doctor, dutifully carrying a yellow pad to take down all the medical information we both needed to think about. But I was distracted: fear distracted me. I was not emotionally present. I was so removed from my life, our life. I would sit with Stacey and her doctor, thinking I was listening, but not really able to take everything in. The scared little boy in me was ascendant. Lynn Arost Dines, our close friend, started coming with us to each appointment, calmly taking clear notes about each difficult detail.

Looking back, Stacey was, as so many women are with this disease, a titan. She handled it all like a warrior, going through all the physical and emotional changes without complaint, dealing with the enormous pain and discomfort. And me? I especially remember going with her to one of her chemo infusions and falling asleep in the chair by her side. Not good. It's hard to look back and admit that's who I was at the time — but that's who I was at the time.

Then I had to go away for work. I rationalized it by telling myself I was earning the money needed for the considerable part of her treatment that insurance didn't cover. In reality, our insurance covered everything. This was just the fib I told myself to allow myself to leave the house. It was a very tough time — mainly for Stacey, of course, but also for all of us as a family, and for Stacey and me as wife and husband.

"Do you need me to come home?" I asked her. And Stacey told me no.

STACEY:

Would I have liked him to come home without me having to ask? Sometimes, you bet. Would I have preferred him not to have taken some of the jobs he felt he had to take?

Sometimes, you bet.

271

And by the way, it's not exactly like I'm the strong, silent type.

But nine times out of ten, I wouldn't say anything. And that one time out of ten when everything in me wanted to scream at him — I usually didn't say anything then, either. Because I hated when we were fighting while he was away.

We'd been married for almost twenty-five years, and we had come to know each other very well. And a very big thing I'd learned about Henry was that when he wasn't working, he was absolutely miserable. Adrift. Insecure. Anxious. First of all, it's part and parcel of the profession. Right? Imagine a show-business support group: "Hello, I'm an actor and I will never work again." I've talked about this with spouses of actors and actresses. We can laugh about it — because our spouses are actors in the business. But when you're at home with this person who's between jobs, for days and weeks and months, it isn't so funny. You can start to believe them.

And then, of course, there are Henry's quirks when it comes to money. It's going to run out. We're going to be impoverished.

"Do you need me to come home?" he asked me when I had cancer. Of course I said no. Because first of all, the thought of Henry breaking a contract — he would die. And I knew he would come home if I asked him to. And he would resent me. I know he wouldn't mean to, but he would.

As the new millennium dawned, I once again found myself sitting in the brown leather chair in my home office, staring at the green tartan couch in front of my desk, waiting for the phone to ring. I was a fifty-five-year-old out-of-work actor, still defined in the public's mind by a part I'd stopped playing more than fifteen years earlier, hoping something would come along that was meaningful at all, something that could take my work to a new level. After I'd stared at the green couch long enough, my brain would start to hurt. And my imagination would start to wander. . . .

Right over there on my desk I see in my mind a hotline that no one is allowed to touch: the phone has martin engraved on it. That's the special line for Scorsese to call me. Over there is another phone for Coppola. I have no room on my desk for a printer because of these special phones for individual directors: I spend a lot of time dusting them. Boy, are they clean.

And then, after long, long periods of waiting for something deep and meaningful, I was hoping for anything at all.

There were parts here and there. I did some more voice work, including a guest spot on the animated hit *Clifford the Big Red Dog,* thanks to John Ritter, who played Clifford. On *The Practice,* a David E. Kelley show about lawyers in Boston, I played Dr. Henry Olson, a creepy dentist with a fetish for watching women in high heels crush bugs. (Yes, you read that right.) The arc of my character was just two episodes — but then, whenever I was walking through an airport, people would say, "What happened to Dr. Olson?" So I called David and told him, and he wrote me a third episode. I was nominated for an Emmy, so that was nice. But then came another long stretch of waiting for the next thing.

My friend Gary David Goldberg sold NBC a series called *Battery Park,* a sitcom about a female police captain, and wrote me a role as an incompetent lawyer, the first of many incompetent lawyers I played. The show went one season; the network didn't pick it up. That Emmy season, I was nominated for two Emmys: one in comedy (*Battery Park*) and one in drama (*The Practice*). Unfortunately, though, someone had overlooked the fact that *Battery Park* didn't air during the eligibility period, so the academy took that nomination away.

My friend Adam Sandler called me at ten thirty one night to ask me to do a cameo in his movie *Little Nicky,* in which he was to play the son of Satan. "Please, Henry," he said, "I need you to do this little favor — Sammy Sosa didn't show." He forgot to tell me that I was going to spend three and a half hours in the middle of the night in makeup, getting bee stings pasted on my face.

Big Apple was a New York City crime drama by the brilliant writer David Milch: for two episodes in the first season I played a milquetoast lawyer defending a tough gangster played by Jim Marsden — my character was always afraid his character was going to decapitate me. The show shot at the same time I was performing in *The Dinner Party* on Broadway. Every night, I would come back from the Music Box to my suite at the Regency Hotel, make myself a snack of a bagel and Zabar's nova (the advantages of working in New York!), and memorize my TV lines for the next day. One day I came in to the production office, proud that I had all my lines in my head, to find Milch lying on the floor — he had a bad back. "What do you want to say today?"

he asked.

"What do I want to say?" I said. "I want to say what you wrote — the lines I memorized last night!"

And he said, "Aah, could be better." And from the floor, he dictated dozens of new lines to a secretary who took the handwritten pages to another office to be typed, then brought back almost a whole new script.

Big Apple's first season turned out to be the only season: CBS did not pick the show up.

The Drew Carey Show. One episode.

Law & Order: Special Victims Unit. One episode.

This was my career in the early 2000s. My agents wouldn't call me; I had to call them to see what might be out there for me. There was a lot of, "No, there's nothing. I've read everything — there's nothing for you."

A more confident actor would have changed agencies. But not me. I could not leave people who were not taking care of me. What if I left those agents and nobody else wanted me?

After Jim Wiatt left ICM to lead William Morris, Alan Berger became my go-to guy at the agency — until he, too, departed ICM and went to work for Mike Ovitz at

Artist Management Group. Alan and I really got along well. So I called him and said, "Alan, I need help. Nothing is happening for me, and it's making me crazy."

"You know what you should do?" Alan said. "I'll tell you, you should write books for children about your dyslexia."

"Alan, I can't write books about my dyslexia," I said. "I *am* dyslexic. I can't even read books — you know *A Tale of Two Cities*? I read the cover — I didn't even get to the first page."

"I'm going to introduce you to a friend of mine, Lin Oliver," he told me. "She runs the Society of Children's Book Writers and Illustrators. Maybe she can help you."

I met Lin Oliver for lunch. At a restaurant at Sunset and Gower that, may it rest in peace, no longer exists. And though the fish I ate turned out to be memorable for all the wrong reasons, I liked Lin immediately. She was very accomplished — she was actually the cofounder of the Society of Children's Book Writers and Illustrators. Not only that, but she had also been a successful TV executive, producer, and writer: one of her shows was *Harry and the Hendersons,* an early-nineties sitcom about a family who adopts a bigfoot. But mainly, she was a really good listener. I told her all about my learning problems growing up, about my crazy, intolerant, constantly yelling parents, my various summer schools, and the utter impossibility of learning spelling or geometry. She'd grown up on the West Coast, so she loved my descriptions of all the characters in my apartment building at 210 West 78th. She smiled when I mentioned Mrs. Zipzer from the fourth floor — Ella Zipzer, a very big personality.

"I love that name, Zipzer," I said.

"So do I," Lin said.

"It's very zippy," I said.

But as a children's-book author, Lin really homed in on my stories about my days at PS 87. I told her about my cruel fourth-grade teacher, Miss Adolf —

Lin's eyes got wide. "Miss Adolf?" she said. "Really?"

"I think she was related," I said. "I mean to Hitler."

Lin laughed. I told her that you had to raise your hand to go to the boys' room, and I was so often in another world from whatever we were doing in class, which usually had to do with reading something I couldn't read, that I was always raising my hand, just to escape the classroom for a few minutes — until one day when I really, really had to go. And then, of course, I became the boy who'd cried wolf. "You don't have to go," Miss Adolf said.

"I do I do I do," I said. "Pleeeeease."

She just shook her head no. In a minute, Salvatore, sitting next to me, said, "You made in your pants."

"No! I did not make in my pants," I whispered.

"You made in your pants."

"Salvatore, I did not make in my pants."

"Yes, you did."

Of course I had. I had to rush home, my underwear stuck to my body, clean up, change, and get back to school before lunch was over.

Lin was smiling in sympathy. "These are wonderful stories," she said. "This is a book. This is a whole series of books."

Now I was smiling, too. "About a little dyslexic boy in elementary school," I said.

"Let's name him Zipzer!" Lin said. "What's his first name?"

"How about Hank?" I said.

Nobody had ever called me Hank, except for my best friend of forty-five years, Dr. Frank Dines. (He starts every phone conversation: "Hank? Frank!") But a lot of Henrys were called Hank, and this little boy Lin and I were thinking of was very much like me at that age, and *Hank Zipzer* had a ring to it. Hank Zipzer! It was sweet; it was sad and funny and brave and scared, all at the same time.

We wrote a book proposal. In Lin's office, in West Hollywood. She sat at a computer, at her desk; I sat in an armchair opposite her. And I was nervous, because I'd certainly never written a book, and I didn't know if I could. Lin had a miniature Zen garden in a small cardboard box on her desk, with sand, three stones, and a tiny rake, and because I was nervous and my hands had to be busy, I was constantly raking the sand. And we came up with ideas, back and forth, and a story began to form. Lin and I would find over time that if the story was alive, the ideas erupted like a volcano.

My collaborator really knew the ins and outs of children's literature. The first lesson I ever learned from Lin was: go out the door you came in — meaning, the book resolves where it began. Not all the time, of course, but that's mainly what we did.

Our first story began with Hank having to write a five-paragraph essay about what he'd done over the summer. As I sat and talked with Lin, I channeled Hank — I *was* Hank. I was sitting at my desk in my tiny room at home, realizing that I could not write five paragraphs — I could not write one paragraph — without filling it with errors. This would give Miss Adolf reason to single me out, to embarrass me (yet again) in front of the class.

While the fourth-grade me was thinking about the impossibility of the assignment, he — I — was noticing that my desk drawer was slightly open, and that it was very messy. I pulled it out a little more, and saw that everything was mixed together — the watches that I was taking apart to see how they worked were mixed together with the pencils, which were jumbled up with the pens. And the erasers were mingled with the paper clips.

Clearly this was a drawer that needed immediate straightening.

So, in lieu of writing the five-paragraph essay, I put the pencils with the pencils, the pens with the pens, the erasers with the erasers, the paper clips with the paper clips. I gave the disassembled watches their own section. Then I lined everything up perfectly, so the interior of my desk drawer was pleasing to the eye.

The essay, meanwhile, remained unwritten.

So (as Lin and I batted ideas back and

forth, and she typed away) Hank decided, instead of writing the essay, to build it out of papier-mâché and cardboard. It's a kind of mountain with a hose attached, representing Niagara Falls, which Hank had visited with his family over the summer. And when it's his turn to present his essay to the class, he attaches the cardboard hose to the sink in the classroom, and it works perfectly for four minutes. And then disintegrates. And floods the classroom. The last thing you see is Hank's tuna sandwich in a plastic bag, floating on the surface of the deluge.

Lin smiled. I smiled. Perfect ending.

But, Lin explained, this was only the ending to this episode. If it was going to be a book, more stories would be needed. So she and I devised a working schedule: Monday to Friday, 10 a.m. to 12:30 p.m. Since I didn't have another job at the moment, it was ideal. Except that every morning, as I drove to Lin's office, I was petrified. Overwhelmed. *Oh my God,* I would think. *What are we going to write? I don't have a clue.*

I had no idea that this was what all writers went through, all the time.

We'd generally spend the first forty minutes or so just schmoozing, talking about children, the world, this and that and everything. And somehow this always led into the story that was in progress: something Lin or I said would jog my memory into recalling something about my third- or fourth-grade self, usually something embarrassing. There had been a lot of embarrassments: we had plenty to work with. (Which never stopped me from being terrified the next morning.)

I would talk; Lin would type on her computer while I raked the tiny Zen garden. I would pause, then Lin would have an idea and start typing again while I waited. Then she would read me what she'd written, and we would argue over every word. (I discovered during this process that I was crazy about alliterations, which was sometimes useful, sometimes not.)

By 12:30 or 1 p.m., when I couldn't concentrate anymore, we would have four to six pages that did not exist before I arrived. Almost every time she pushed Print on her computer and we walked down the hall to the printer, where the pages we'd come up with were spitting out — you'd think I would get used to it, but I was still awed to the point of tears every time by the day's work coming out of the machine.

And then the following morning, Lin would read a couple of pages of what we'd written the previous day, in order to know where we were going. She might say, "Oh, I was thinking about this last night, and it hit me that we didn't put this in." And we'd put it in, and it would start the ball rolling.

When we finally had what we felt was a complete first book, I called a literary agent. And not just any literary agent. Since at the time I was represented by ICM, I called the all-powerful agent Esther Newberg, to tell her what Lin and I had done.

"I don't do children's books," Esther said.

"I know that, Esther," I said, "but I'm a client of your agency, and there's always a first time."

"I don't do children's books."

"But you could look at it, and maybe you'll like it."

She finally looked at it. She sent the proposal to five editors at five children's-book publishers. Three said no. One said maybe. And Debra Dorfman, at Penguin Putnam, said, "Well, you're a celebrity. I'll give you a contract for four novels."

If you'd told me then that we would actually do the four novels — and that would then turn into thirty-nine novels — I would have called you a raving lunatic.

Our first book, *Niagara Falls, or Does It?,* is finished. I am sent to a luncheon in New

York City with all the buyers for all the Barnes & Nobles across the country. I'm asked to tell the story of how I met Lin and how this book came to be. While I'm chatting with them and making them laugh, I glance down and see the book in front of me on the table. There's my name, right on the cover. My brain freezes like an orange Popsicle. I forget where I am; I stop talking; I pick the book up. I open the book and I smell the pages. I turn the book over and over in my hands. I rub the book across my chest. Then, in a flash, I'm snapped back to reality, and I see all these young men and women staring at me. I apologize and continue telling the story.

In September 2003, I was going to guest-star on John Ritter's sitcom *8 Simple Rules.* In the middle of rehearsal, John said, "You know, I'm very sweaty; I'm gonna go get some water." And I said, "I'm gonna go memorize my lines, so I don't stink up the room."

This was four o'clock in the afternoon. Everybody went home. At eleven that night, the associate producer of the show called me and said, "We lost John." It totally did not compute. I said, "What? What? Lost John where?"

"We lost John," he said again. After I'd left the soundstage, he told me, John kept sweating profusely, then began to feel chest pain. He was taken to the hospital that was right across the street from Disney Studios, where the doctors thought he was having a heart attack. It would eventually be discovered that he had a tear in his aorta that no one noticed, and when he was treated for a coronary it exacerbated the tear, and he died.

The next day, the cast and crew of *8 Simple Rules* gathered on the soundstage, numb. No one could say a word. I was one of the few people who spoke, and I told everybody what John had said to me: how important every one of them was to him.

John's death was like a tear in the fabric of the universe. For weeks afterward, I couldn't even see straight. I'd lost my friend and acting partner, and one of the funniest people on the planet. His wife Amy, his four children, and everybody who knew him were devastated.

Writing Hank Zipzer with Lin. Worrying about not working. Getting the odd TV guest shot here and there. Worrying some more. Still paying my dues with voice work, still trying hard to gain acceptance among that elite fraternity. Voice work was actually going best of all. I was cast as Norville the bird on *Clifford's Puppy Days,* a spin-off from *Clifford the Big Red Dog,* and I won my second Daytime Emmy. Now, a Daytime Emmy may not carry the prestige of a Primetime Emmy, but let me tell you: an Emmy is an Emmy. And it is very good to win an Emmy.

And then, out of left field (though working actors will tell you that almost everything comes from left field), I got a job that turned out to be a very important one for me.

Ron Howard, who'd been having major success as a director and producer (he'd just won a pair of Oscars in those categories for *A Beautiful Mind*), loved thinking outside the box, and one thing he'd been thinking about lately was a new style of sitcom, one that, instead of having a fixed set, a studio audience, and a laugh track, felt like reality television: handheld camera, voiceover narration. Ron then met with a couple of writers, one of whom was the brilliant Mitch Hurwitz, who suggested a show about a dysfunctional wealthy family who had fallen on hard times but couldn't stop acting rich and entitled. Ron hired Mitch, who then created the Bluth family and *Arrested Development.*

The show sold to Fox, and I arrived early in the first season, as Barry Zuckerkorn, who was not only the worst lawyer ever admitted to the bar but could be called some kind of sexual deviant.

I was delighted to be invited — although I was told I would appear in one or two episodes, I stayed for five years. My very first bit of business, which I improvised, was in my first scene: I'm sitting in a chair in the living room with the entire Bluth family. On the coffee table in front of me is a pile of Danish pastries. During the scene, I very slowly and surreptitiously move that pile of Danish to the edge of the table and let them fall into my open briefcase.

Thanks to the writing of Mitch Hurwitz, yet another bona fide genius I got to work with, Barry Zuckerkorn turned out to be so deliciously awful, as an attorney and as a human being, that he just kept sticking around. Great writing is so essential if a TV show or a movie is really going to make an impact. As they say, if it ain't on the page, it ain't on the stage.

And — my God — look at the amazing group of people I got to work with. Jason Bateman, who played Michael, the only sane member of the Bluth family, was in real life a lot like his character: the keeper of all logic on the show. Jason would say, "You have me saying this on page 34, but on page 22, I said completely the opposite. That doesn't track." Jason and Will Arnett and Tony Hale were not just brothers on the show, but became close friends in life, and they were lovely to me.

As was everybody else in the cast. In the course of making the show, Tony Hale got married and he and his wife had their first child, and he radiated happiness. Portia de Rossi, so beautiful. One day in the makeup trailer she confided in me that she'd met somebody the night before who turned her world upside down. And she wound up marrying Ellen DeGeneres.

Jessica Walter was so talented and so idiosyncratic. (Fun fact: her husband, Ron Leibman, was in the professional company at Yale when I was in my freshman year there.) We got along like bread and butter, though there was sometimes static between Jessica and the rest of the cast. She could literally be looking at her makeup in a mirror while the director was calling *Action*. And Jeff Tambor would remind her, "Jessica, we're acting here! They just said 'Action'!" And Jessica would calmly put down the mirror and do the scene brilliantly.

Michael Cera, just fifteen when the show started. I first met Michael when I was getting out of my car on the Fox lot, about to go into the soundstage, and there he was with his mom. They were from Canada, quiet and very polite. And the moment I shook Michael's hand, I knew I'd met a powerhouse of talent — he just had this aura. "Oh my God," I said to him, "I'm just telling you now, you are going to fly into the heavens."

I felt the same about Alia Shawkat, who happened to be a good friend of my son Max: I knew instantly that she was a star.

Thanks in great part to the brilliance of everyone involved with the show, playing Barry Zuckerkorn turned out to be the first time in twenty years that the weight of typecasting began to lift from my shoulders. And thanks to Mitch (and Ron), I got to do two blink-and-you-missed-them but perfect homages to *Happy Days* while I was on *Arrested Development.* The first happened in Season 1, when Barry was about to comb his hair in a men's-room mirror — only to realize that he didn't have to. The other occurred midway through Season 2, while I was standing on a dock with Jason, Will, and Tony, next to a dead shark that had eaten the flipper of the seal that had eaten Buster's (Tony's) hand: Barry announces he's on his way to have lunch at Burger King and, on his way out, hops over the dead fish.

Making me the only actor alive who has jumped the shark twice.

When Jed was in third grade, I found myself saying to him all the things that had once been said to me: "Come on, you're so verbal and so smart, and your schoolwork is smudgy — why don't you just do it?" He was so funny, so good with adults, but he couldn't write a sentence. So we had him tested by an occupational therapist, and we discovered that Jed was dyslexic. And it was only then, at age thirty-four, that I realized I was dyslexic, too.

When I found out that I had something with a name, that I was not just stupid and a dumb dog, I was so fucking angry. All the misery I'd gone through had been for nothing. All the yelling, all the humiliation, all the screaming arguments in my house as I was growing up — for nothing. All the taking geometry in regular school and summer school for four years and passing it with a D-minus to get into Emerson (and I couldn't have gone to Emerson had I not gotten that D-minus); all the feeling terrible about myself, my self-image plummeting to the bottom of the ocean — all of it had been for nothing. I had something that made me unable to do any of the things my parents and teachers wanted me to do, or only able to do them in a limited way — and nobody, least of all my parents, had ever understood. My mother and father were convinced that the more they punished me, the better my grades would be, and it had never, ever worked. I wasn't going to get geometry then, or in fifty years. It had all been for nothing, because I had this thing with a name.

It was genetic! It wasn't a way I decided to be!

The people who grounded me for my entire high school career *gave* it to me!

And then I went from feeling this massive anger to fighting through it.

The Hank Zipzer books were a big part of the fight, as were all the subsequent books Lin and I wrote: every book was about a kid who was an underdog, on the outside looking in, the way I had been throughout my childhood and beyond. (This is also the theme of every Adam Sandler movie: every character he plays is an underdog, on the outside looking in. Every one of his characters starts at the bottom and works his way up to great success — I think that accounts for the natural connection between Adam and me.)

From the moment I understood that I had this thing with a name, I realized how many other people were going through struggles just like mine. And in the early 2000s, I began giving talks around the country about my fight, hoping to reach as many of those people as possible. I've now given hundreds of these talks, and the joy of them is far less about me — though it is wonderful to see what a positive force the Fonz has been in so many people's lives — than it is about *us,* all the people who have felt less-than because of something wired into their brain from birth, something that was not their fault.

Once, when Lin and I were on a book tour for Hank Zipzer in the Midwest, I met an eleventh grader named David. His school had a program where students could go and apprentice with a building contractor. David helped construct rooms in new houses by putting up the drywall. When I met him, he told me about his experience and said, "I'm not really good at school, but I'm great at building a room. I could open a business."

It has always struck me that our emphasis on the top 10 percent of a class says they are more valuable than the bottom 3 percent. If this country is going to remain strong, we need every child to be great at what it is they can do.

Some of the peak moments in my life have come from writing those books with Lin, something I'd never thought I could do in the first place. I owe her a great debt of gratitude for partnering with me on this voyage.

A stray moment from one of the first of my speaking trips stays with me. Stacey and I flew to Lancaster, Pennsylvania, then drove from the airport to our hotel. And when we got there, the bellman came running out, a young man, about twenty-three years old. And I thought he was going to say, "Can I help you?" — but instead, he said, "I've read every one of your books. They got me through school."

It was one of the greatest compliments of my life.

I've always been a negative thinker. Less so today than ever before, but it's always been a strong inclination that I have to fight. Way back when I was with the Yale Repertory Theatre, I read a book by the German psychoanalyst Fritz Perls called *In and Out the Garbage Pail.* When I say *I read a book,* it tells you how important that book was to me, because I literally had to excavate my way through it, word by word. But Perls wrote in a very lively and compelling way about negative self-esteem, and he really made me think about all the bad ideas about me that had been laid on me, and that I had continued to lay on myself.

Perls led me to the philosopher George Gurdjieff, who believed humans live in a state of waking sleep, but that it's possible to wake up and literally raise one's consciousness. That idea was exciting — but then I tried reading Gurdjieff. I tried really hard, but I had absolutely no idea what he was talking about. But. Gurdjieff mentioned a disciple of his, Ouspensky. And in reading Ouspensky — difficult but not totally impossible — I came away with this idea, which became one of the cornerstones of my existence: *never finish a negative sentence.*

When you finish a negative sentence, it grows immediately into a paragraph, and then into a thesis, into so many words that grab your ankles and hold you in place.

When a negative thought comes into your mind, you have to literally say out loud, "I have no time now." People will look at you strangely, but you have to just keep saying it until it lodges in your mind. *Release the negative thought before you put a period on the end of it.* If you put a period on the end of it, you're in the morass. On the other hand, if you don't finish the negative thought, you can get it out of your brain by replacing it with a positive. What kind of positive? What I always say in my talks is that it is a moist chocolate Bundt cake with soft chocolate chips. No frosting.

With this new positive in your mind, you're suddenly changing the way you feel. Physically! Your head and your shoulders rise out of their slump and fly back, and in this new upright posture you continue walking to your goal. In my talks I always say, "And I'm here talking to you tonight — and you could be up here talking to you also. But I'm telling you, don't put a period on the end of a negative thought."

The other cornerstone of my existence came even earlier than that, in the early days of *Happy Days,* when I was living in my bachelor pad on North Laurel Avenue and bushels of fan mail were being delivered to me daily. One letter contained a strip of engraved metal, and the engraving read, in Hebrew and English, "If you will it, it is not a dream." It was something Theodor Herzl said about the creation of Israel. I gave that simple sentence a lot of thought, and I realized that this is exactly the way the universe works: that without ambivalence, a human being has the power to have an idea and literally make it happen. But if you are ambivalent in any way, you're dead in the water. The ambivalence will cut off your ability to give your dream life in the universe.

This is how I began taking photographs on my fishing trips to Montana and then Idaho. It's such amazing-looking country that I wanted to participate in its beauty somehow. I'd admired photos that other people had taken of those rivers and mountains, but then thought, *I couldn't ever do that.* I couldn't even turn a knob, let alone operate a sophisticated camera. But in thinking I couldn't do it, I realized I'd finished the sentence. So I unfinished it. I replaced it with warm chocolate Bundt cake, with chocolate chips. I bought a camera, and I started taking pictures. Just pointing and shooting. Not very good at first! Then a little better, and a little better.

I thought I could do it. Because I had

already written with Lin these books that I thought I couldn't do, and because you really don't know what you can accomplish until you try. All you have to do is try, and you will amaze yourself. So simple. But so crucial. And so true. I didn't play baseball. I didn't fly-fish. I didn't take pictures. I didn't. I didn't. I didn't. And then I tried. You try, and then you figure out how you do it. And it does not ever have to be perfect. You can cast a fly rod and not be perfect — then lo and behold, there's a big speckled trout on the end of your line.

Adam Sandler called again, and this time it wasn't to have bee stings applied to my face at 4 a.m. This time it was to play his father in the very touching *Click.* The movie was about a workaholic who alienates the ones he loves — but then gets a chance to redeem himself when he comes into possession of a magical remote control, one that can correct the mistakes he's made in life.

Click was really a drama disguised as a comedy, and Adam got to show his range as a serious actor. Our scenes together — his character is always pushing away his loving dad — moved me in all kinds of ways, made me think about the loving father I never had. I hear people say, "Oh, my parents were my best friends" — and I look at them like they're aliens. And I know Adam was moved, too, since he'd lost his own father just a year before we shot the film. (And speaking of fathers and sons, *Click* was one of the first times I worked with Max, whom Adam hired to document the making of the movie with a video camera.) I always relish the chance to work with actors I like and respect, and Julie Kavner, who played my wife (and whom I'd met at the beginning of my career when she played Valerie Harper's sister on *Rhoda*), was so original in her comic timing. But having the opportunity to see the great Christopher Walken in action, on and off the set, was something else. One night after work, he and I were having dinner at a restaurant in Bakersfield. When the waitress asked me what I'd like, I said, "I'm going to have the meat loaf, mashed potatoes, and carrots."

"Thank you," the waitress said.

Now it was Chris's turn to order, but he was staring at the menu with an alarmed expression, seeming to be in the midst of some sort of existential crisis. "Chris, what are you going to have?" I asked him.

"I —" he began.

There was a *long* pause. Now the waitress was starting to look alarmed herself.

"What do you want, Chris?" I asked. "You want chicken? You like chicken?"

"Eh . . ."

"How about fish? They have fish." I thought I saw his expression change a little. "He'll have the fish," I told the waitress. And then, "Do you like potatoes, Chris? Yeah? What kind? Do you like mashed? He'll have mashed."

Then Christopher whispered something in my ear: *"Succotash."*

Let me just tell you that ordering dinner for Christopher Walken was a rare and delightful experience.

10.

One of the first lessons I learned as an acting student at Yale was, "You must keep your space clean, because when you're acting, the theater is your temple. And if your fellow actor doesn't keep their space clean, you do it for them." I wrote it down, a very simple but very powerful rule. It literally meant that you should never throw trash on the floor where you're working — you cannot be disrespectful to the theater you're in, whatever theater it is: Broadway or summer stock or a high school auditorium. It is your responsibility to keep it pristine.

A good rule for all kinds of things in life.

The other thing I wrote down back at the beginning was that on the stage or working with a teacher, it was crucial to listen. Not to pretend to listen, but to *really* listen.

I had a hard time with this.

I thought I was listening. I wasn't. I was always so anxious, and it's hard to do anything when you're anxious. To this minute, I still live with shame when I think about all the well-known actors I worked with, failing to do justice to the scenes I did with them. Thinking, in the moment of doing the scene, *I'm doing a scene with this very well-known person,* rather than listening. Being in that moment. It's not only not taking the other person into consideration, it's giving your present self's power to the other person.

It's something Stacey said to me continually for the first thirty-five or so of the forty-seven years of our lives together: "You're giving the power away. You're giving all your power away."

For three decades and more, I had no idea what she meant. She could have been speaking Russian to me.

During *Happy Days* and after, there were men not much older than me who were network executives, and I always thought, *They know. I know nothing.* I called them "sir." They were always taken aback: "What are you — don't call me 'sir.' " It was almost like I was insulting them. (Then again, I've long had the habit of calling every male I meet, even a friend's four-year-old son, *sir.*) I turned sixty in 2005, and I was still giving away my power. Still so rarely in the mo-

302

ment with my colleagues, my wife. I think it was easier with my children, maybe because I still (at sixty!) felt so much like a child myself — a feeling that helped me so much in writing the Hank Zipzer books.

That same year, I lucked into another TV series that looked like it could really stick around. Actually, in classic Hollywood fashion, luck had both everything and nothing to do with it. *Out of Practice* was a CBS sitcom cocreated by Joe Keenan, who'd won Emmys for writing on *Frasier,* and Christopher Lloyd, whose father, David Lloyd, was in the pantheon of comedy writing for his work on *Mary Tyler Moore . . .* where I got my television start.

Joe and Christopher were two of the funniest men in the business, and to have them working in the same room was magic. *Out of Practice* was about a dysfunctional family of doctors: I was the paterfamilias, a gastroenterologist, and the sublime Stockard Channing played my ex, a heart surgeon. The equally sublime Jennifer Tilly played my ditzy receptionist girlfriend, and an amazing newcomer, Ty Burrell, played my son Oliver, a narcissistic dermatologist. Chris Gorham was my youngest son, a marriage counselor whose wife has left him.

It was a wonderful cast, the writing was

sparkling, and I loved going to work every day. I was supremely fortunate to be in twenty-one of the twenty-two episodes in the first season — and then CBS did not pick the show up for a second season. We were on Monday nights, after *How I Met Your Mother* and *Two and a Half Men,* and those shows drew a younger audience than we did . . . and CBS wanted to hold on to that younger audience. Such is the kill-or-be-killed world of network television.

You'd think that at age sixty, I'd have grown a thick skin about such things. I had not. My skin was as thin as origami paper.

Stacey's last chemo for her last bout of breast cancer was in 2003, the same year that we lost John Ritter. Stacey's mom, Belvey, died in December 2006, and two years later, her father, Ed, passed on. The early 2000s were a very emotional time.

In 2006, Max graduated from USC's film school and, with his friend David Gelb, wrote and directed a short film called *The King of Central Park.* Film-school graduates like Max and David make short movies like this as calling cards, audition pieces that studios and producers can look at when they're deciding who to hire for full-length features.

The story of *The King of Central Park* was simple: a young man is engaged to marry a young woman whose father is a big industrialist. Papa wants his son-in-law-to-be to come work for him and climb the corporate ladder; the young man (played by Max's good friend and Stacey's first husband's second son, Armen Weitzman) wants to flee to the jungles of Bhutan with his lady love and be free. Max asked me to play Dr. Bloore, the young man's childhood therapist; I asked my friend Jeff Tambor to come and play the tycoon, for zero dollars. Jeff kindly agreed, and we went into production, in Manhattan.

You could easily imagine the type of tension that could arise between a father and son working together, not to mention in a situation where the son is the boss. Not to mention in a situation where the father is a celebrity in the field the son is just entering.

There was no tension. I loved working with Max. He was a great commander of an East Coast–West Coast crew, kids from USC and NYU film schools, oil and water. Max made them a cohesive unit. One morning, walking to the set in Central Park, I came around the corner and Max was standing on a rock in the grass, giving the crew a pep talk: the bickering could no longer be tolerated, he said. Showing up late could no longer be tolerated. He pointed to the one-person prop department. "Look at her — she's got a sore throat," Max said. "She's got a headache. And she never shirks her responsibility. We can *do* this."

With the crew and the cast, he was respectful, strong, always clear about what he wanted. We shot one scene where I was supposed to stand on the high rocks overlooking Turtle Pond. It was raining, the rocks were slippery, and I was scared. "Dad," Max said, "if you don't want to do it, you don't have to do it. But it would be a great shot. But it's raining and it's slippery. I understand. You don't have to do it if you don't want to."

Which of course made me want to — but then the camera failed because of the rain. So we sat there on the wet rock, waiting for this young crew to figure out how to fix the camera. Eventually they did, we were all a little wetter, and Max got the scene he wanted.

That is a director.

When it comes to kids of well-known show-business people trying to get into the industry, there's always a debate: does their last name give them a leg up? Do their connections give them an unfair advantage? The answer always seems to be that having a mom or a dad who's prominent in the business can get them in the door, but that they then have to prove themselves like everybody else — and often have to work harder than anybody else, just to prove they're for real. Max is for real as a director, but even with his well-known last name and the charming calling card of *The King of Central Park,* he had to do his share of scrambling before getting to direct his first feature.

In 2009 Max flew to New York to try to persuade Uma Thurman to star in a movie based on a script he'd written, *Ceremony.* Uma said yes, and then Max's very good friend Jake Johnson also signed on, along with Lee Pace, Harper Dill, and Michael Angarano. Max shot the movie on Long Island, and under his attentive direction the production went quickly and smoothly. The picture was accepted into the Toronto International Film Festival — and when it opened, no one went to see it.

Soon afterward, Max and I found ourselves walking the streets of Manhattan, 28th and Broadway, to be exact. My son was sincerely distraught. He said to me, with every ounce of determination in his

307

body, "I am never going to do this again. I paid attention to every detail, and the film didn't work. It's just too hard to accept."

"Max," I said, "I know exactly how you feel at this moment — but believe me, this too shall pass. You are meant to do this. You're a very talented director and leader. It is your duty to get back on the horse."

And in 2017, he directed *Flower,* starring the amazing Zoey Deutch, along with Adam Scott and, once again, Jake Johnson. Kathryn Hahn played Zoey's mom to perfection. It was a solid, good film, and it was very well received, and it helped move along Max's directing career. And I may soon have the privilege of working with him again, on a very high-profile project.

I can say no more.

Soon after Max moved out on his own, he went to an animal shelter and fell in love with a three-legged German shepherd puppy. Max brought the puppy home and named him Hamlet. But as Hamlet grew, he had more and more trouble walking, and one day Max's girlfriend's younger sister Destry — she was fourteen — said, "That dog is completely off-balance — he has to have an operation to take more of the leg off."

So for the first time in his life, Max was facing a huge responsibility: to have to spend thousands of dollars on an operation for Hamlet. Max was just in his mid-twenties; he was also in shock. He picked the dog; now he had to figure out what to do. And he had to figure out how to do it without my help — I always thought that it was important for our kids to meet their responsibilities. Max figured it out, and Hamlet had his operation.

Like Stacey, Zoe is red-haired. Also like Stacey, my darling daughter is a strong-minded human being, with a fiery spirit. And when Zoe was at college, I had a strong-minded, fiery-spirited daughter with a credit card. Who dressed very well. Which dovetailed neatly with my persistent money worries.

When Zoe came back home to live with us, she was still well-dressed. And still strong-minded. The latter quality sometimes put her into conflict with Stacey. Conflict is perhaps putting it mildly. Zoe and Stacey would have battle royales — and I was usually called upon to mediate. I'd be in my office at home, and Zoe would come flying in, very upset. "Tell me, what's going on?" I would say, and she would tell me. She was my daughter, she was unhappy, and I listened.

But then Stacey would say, "You should have talked to me first."

Around and around it went. And it could get tricky if I was away. I remember one summer in particular: I was in Montana working on an independent movie, and Stacey and Zoe were back at it, and then it was a race to who was going to call me first. "Don't talk to Zoe before you talk to me," Stacey would tell me — but it seemed like Zoe always won the race. Which became a bone of contention between Stacey and me, every time.

Zoe had graduated from Loyola Marymount — sort of. She was actually still a credit and a half short, which she somehow failed to mention. Still, because of her dyslexia, even her incomplete academic achievement was a big victory. When she was little, she used to tell us that she wanted to be a teacher when she grew up, because she didn't want anyone else to ever feel stupid. But unlike me, she didn't have to feel stupid for long: now there were teachers who were trained to deal with the kid who learns differently. So Zoe was able to get a job as a teacher at a nursery school in Santa Monica.

Once I was stopped at a red light while I was driving to work, when a woman in the next car asked me to roll down my window. "Are you Zoe Winkler's father?" she asked.

"Yes, I am," I said.

The woman then told me that her daughter jumped out of bed every morning, eager to get to school, because of my daughter.

Wow.

Meanwhile, Zoe was still living with Stacey and me. But the truth was slowly dawning for all of us: it was time for her to leave the nest. Which, since Max was now out on his own, would leave the nest empty. Parents of grown children everywhere will recognize the dilemma: you miss them terribly, and you're so happy when they come home — and happy when they leave.

Zoe found an apartment, but going to actually live there wasn't easy. Home was so comfortable! My joke is that her fingers were superglued to the bedpost, and we had to take her bed apart and move it to her new place.

And not long after that, the mother of one of her students fixed her up with Rob — an actor. Stacey and I bit our tongues. Zoe and Rob hit it off fabulously — they both wanted to have a family — and became exclusive.

Then, in late 2007, they broke up.

He was scared of marriage. He didn't feel he could commit to a life together. Zoe was in hysterics. First she blamed Rob, then she realized that she was frightened, too. We had always taken such good care of her: now she understood she had to take care of herself — and, if she wanted this relationship to continue, she had to take care of the man she was in love with. It was an emotional yo-yo — not only for Zoe, but for her parents. Lots of crying, lots of talking, and lots of Max pacing back and forth in our living room, giving his older sister wisdom and advice. Zoe and Rob talked, they cried, he realized he had to find something more secure than acting if he was going to help support a family. He proposed. She accepted. In June 2009 they were married in the backyard of our house. Soon Rob went to work for an old friend of his family who was in the house-building business. Rob started out by parking the crew's cars every morning when they came to work. And now he and his friend Brian own a building company of their own: they've become very successful. Today Zoe and Rob have three sons: Ace, Jules, and Gus. All of them have red hair. Like Zoe. Like Stacey.

■ ■ ■ ■

Stacey and I have always loved finding TV shows we could watch together, and one we particularly enjoyed was *Royal Pains,* the USA Network series about a young ER doctor, played by Mark Feuerstein, who gets fired and winds up in the Hamptons treating wealthy private patients — kind of like a MacGyver of doctors. The writing and the acting were excellent, and there was just the right mixture of comedy and drama: as a viewer you were never exactly sure about which way a scene was going to go, and that's a compelling thing.

So I was very excited when, after the first season, I was asked if I wanted to join the show, playing Eddie Lawson, the ne'er-do-well ex-con father of Mark's character. The cocreator Andrew Lenchewski and the producer Michael Rauch wanted to meet with me: we set a date to have breakfast, at a restaurant just down the road from my house. As the date approached, I got more and more excited — a ne'er-do-well ex-con sounded like a part I could really sink my teeth into. And the more excited I got, the more nervous I got: I was realizing I wanted this part very badly.

The day arrives. We meet at the restaurant; smiles, handshakes. We settle down in a booth. I order pancakes, because I know that I am apt to wear any meal I enjoy prominently across the front of my shirt, and with pancakes you can't make that much of a mess. We start to talk about the show, and I want to make clear to them what a real fan I am, how well I know the material. I am thoroughly conversant. And as I'm talking, I pick up the little ceramic syrup jar, and I'm pouring it on my pancakes, I don't have to look at what I'm doing, I'm just talking to them — and thinking, *Wow, is that expression on their faces interest or surprise, or both?* In any case, I'm clearly making an impression! I then take a bite, and instantly realize that I have poured the cream for my coffee, which was also in a little ceramic pitcher, on my pancakes.

"Well," I say, "these are buttermilk pancakes. The cream brings out the flavor."

I got the role, and I stayed for five years, playing the dad to Mark and Paulo Costanzo.

By the early 2010s, it felt as though the frozen tundra of my acting career might be warming up just a bit. My graying hair and slightly expanded midsection had distanced me from the Fonz; *Arrested Development* and *Royal Pains* had placed me as someone who was good at playing authority figures who lacked authority. Good at keeping a straight face amid demented goings-on.

I had a manager then, Peter Principato, who had a lot of comedians and comic actors as clients. One day Peter called me and said, "Hey, the boys who are making *Childrens Hospital* — it's a very small show, it's on at twelve o'clock at night on Adult Swim, fifteen minutes per episode, it's been on a year — they'd like to call you." I said, "Sure." So I spoke to Rob Corddry, David Wain, and Jon Stern, the show's creators. "Would you play the administrator of the hospital?" Without hearing anything about the season or the character, I said, "Absolutely." And I stayed for five or six years.

Now, here's the thing — and I have admitted this very rarely: I never understood the jokes. Any of them. All I understood was that the cast was exceptional. Ken Marino, Rob Huebel, Erinn Hayes, Zandy Hartig, Malin Akerman, Megan Mullally (who was so funny that I sometimes forgot I was in the scene with her and just stood in amazement at how spontaneous she was). Lake Bell, whom I first met at a wedding in Florida, when she was eighteen. "I want to be an actress," Lake told me, and we talked about it a long time. Then all of a sudden, here is this incredible lady on the set, and soon she became a director for *Childrens Hospital* and then went on to direct movies. Her first one starred Fred Melamed, who years later would play my agent in *Barry.*

Anyway, I took the job, did the best I could working among these very funny people, and even though I wasn't understanding what was going on, I laughed watching them. When I started doing interviews, I said, "I am part of this team. I'm telling you, it's a wacky comedy." And the show's producers literally pulled me from in front of the camera and said, "You can't say 'wacky.' It's a *meta* comedy." So now, not only did I not understand the jokes, I didn't understand what meta comedy was.

But I was as happy as a pig in a blanket to be part of this ensemble: I had the most wonderful time playing the administrator, Sy Mittleman. Once, when the doctors on the show were holding a Who Can Collect the Most Urine contest, I even got to hold a vat of urine. (Spoiler: it was actually water with yellow food coloring.)

I'm not sure, but I think that may have been a meta moment.

■ ■ ■ ■

I feel very close to Adam Sandler, and truly feel he is an important citizen of the world. Adam's loyalty and generosity are a lesson to us all. So when he called me in early 2011 to speak at the unveiling of his star on Hollywood Boulevard, I didn't hesitate. It was a beautiful morning in early February, and a big crowd was there, as were Adam's lovely wife, Jackie, and their two little girls, Sadie and Sunny. Kevin James and I were to be the two speakers. I went first. "We are here on Hollywood Boulevard, where history is made, because this man, Adam Sandler, has helped to create, in recent times, the history of Hollywood Boulevard as we know it. Today his star will be cemented for history, forever. This is *bashert,* which is a Yiddish word that means 'meant to be.' I love this man, and my star is directly across the street from his." (Which is true: my star is right under the marquee of the Pantages Theatre, where I take my grandchildren to see Broadway plays. And I must admit that I have us all take a picture in front of my star each and every time we're there.)

I was speaking, not from notes — which I wouldn't have been able to read anyway —

but from the heart. I spoke the same way at Adam's wedding, eight years earlier. Everyone else roasted him; instead, I talked about the union he and Jackie were making, the life together they were embarking on. Afterward Adam told me, "You're the only one who really spoke about the event, the marriage." I was very touched.

Kevin spoke next, and he was as funny as Kevin James can be — another way of honoring Adam and the occasion. That afternoon at about three fifteen, Kevin called me. "Hey, I'm doing a new movie. You want to be in it?"

"Do I want to be in it?" I said. "My bag is packed, waiting at the door."

So we went to Boston and shot *Here Comes the Boom,* one of my favorites of all the pictures I've been in, right alongside *Night Shift.* Kevin played a biology teacher at a high school that was so strapped for funds it was going to cut all extracurricular activities — and so, to raise the money for my music department, he decided to become a mixed martial arts fighter. Crazy? Of course. I played his friend, a music teacher who became his MMA manager. Hopeless? Of course. But it all worked, because of Kevin and the script and Frank Coraci, who by now had directed three of

318

Adam's movies, including *The Waterboy.*

Kevin and Adam are good friends, and Adam executive produced *Here Comes the Boom* — and his influence on the movie felt strong, even though he wasn't present on the set: Kevin had script meetings outside his trailer at a table with a rug underneath, just like Adam does on his movies. So I felt right at home.

Since my character was a music teacher, I got to conduct this orchestra of schoolkids, which was a real music class from a school nearby. And even though it was movie conducting, and these kids were playing broken instruments, raising my arms and leading these children to a recorded track moved me to tears. It took me back to conducting Sibelius in my utility closet of a bedroom on West 78th Street. And it took me, too, to Saturday afternoons in the present, when Stacey and I and our good friends Lynn and Frank had (and still have) tickets to the Los Angeles Philharmonic, where we'd go to hear that great orchestra conducted by greats like Gustavo Dudamel. It was always so easy to feel reluctant about going — "Oh my God, we live so far away from downtown; it's Saturday afternoon, there's going to be traffic" — but then we'd get in the car anyway and go and sit down, and then we'd be transported and so grateful to be there. That's how I felt channeling Dudamel, leading these kids on broken instruments: transported. At the end of the shoot, the production bought the entire student orchestra brand-new instruments.

Frank Coraci said a lovely thing to me on *Here Comes the Boom.* He said, "You are the heart of this movie." He'd actually said it to me before, on *The Waterboy,* and again on *Click.* It was almost as though he was trying to convince me. Because each time, I thought, *Wow, I wonder if that's true.* Until very recently, I always felt so clear about being second-rate.

Oddly — or maybe not so oddly — I do really well with first-time directors. Could it have something to do with the fact that I lack self-importance? That I'm always so in touch with my own feelings of fear and uncertainty?

In the strange zigzag that has been my career, I've had the privilege of working with a number of directors who were doing it for the first time. Why? Candidly, because at various points, small independent films have been the only jobs that were available to me. And what I try to bring to these under-the-radar projects is a spirit that is as open and generous as possible. It makes me and everyone around me as comfortable as possible.

I will only work with someone who gives me a good feeling at the initial meeting. My intuition is pretty strong about that. And once those first seeds of openness and respect are planted, things tend to go well once we get on the set. I know I haven't signed on to direct the director, but first-timers often need and are open to some guidance, and if my like for them and my esteem for them are clear from the outset, they don't mind taking some advice from someone who's been around the block — a lot.

One thing I've noticed when I'm working with people who are just starting out is that they're often way more deliberate than they need to be. A lot of times on a new production (new in every way) you could have lunch — you could sew yourself a jacket — between the buzzer that signals quiet on the set and "Action." It's not fair to everyone involved to get them excited about shooting and then drag your heels. So I will, especially if it's late at night, say things like, "Anytime you want to start will be fine with everybody who's waiting to go home."

Or, after a less-than-successful take or two (or three), I might say to the director —

softly, almost in a whisper — "I heard you say what you wanted in the scene, and that person is not giving you their full energy. Maybe say to them, 'Try it this way.' " Or, the other side of the coin, I might say to an actor, "I see you're confused. Either ask for clarity, or do what you know is right." Again: trust your tummy, not your head. Your head only knows some things; your tummy knows everything, if you just listen.

I trusted my stomach when I signed on to do *The Performers,* a new play by the Canadian writer David West Read, in 2012. I thought David, who would later create *Schitt's Creek,* was very talented, and his play, a dark comedy that took place at the Adult Film Awards in Las Vegas, was terrific. My character — this wasn't typecasting! — was an adult film star named Chuck Wood, who was receiving a lifetime achievement award. The cast included the wonderful Ari Graynor, Daniel Breaker, Cheyenne Jackson, Jenni Barber, and Alicia Silverstone.

It was my dream to be on Broadway again, and I thought we were on our way. Our director, Evan Cabnet, was encouraging and insightful. The show got belly laughs in previews; we were the Pick to Click in New

York — and then Hurricane Sandy hit. Sandy, the superstorm. It was the end of October. When we opened two weeks later, the tunnels and railway lines were still flooded or damaged, and the audiences who would've flocked to our show, theatergoers from Connecticut, New Jersey, Long Island, stayed home.

It would also turn out that one of the show's backers, a guy who'd promised $400,000 to the kitty, had told a fib, and we were underfunded. The producers thought, *We'll run, it'll pick up steam, people will buy tickets, and the money will come.* And then nobody could come. We closed after seven performances, and my Broadway dream was shattered. It took me a long time to get over it.

I had a ball during rehearsals and previews, with one exception. In the show, one of the female characters was sitting on a hotel bed crying because she thought her fiancé was having an affair with a hooker, except he wasn't. And I had worked out a moment where my character reached out and touched her cheek. And every night, this actress edged farther and farther away from me. The first couple of times, I put my knee on the bed in order to get close enough to do the moment — but finally realized that she, the actress not the character, was purposefully making herself unavailable for my moment. Therefore undermining my moment, and me.

(There was another moment concerning that hotel bed. In the scene, the same actress was chasing me around the room; she grabbed on to my sport coat, and as I ran, I slipped out of the coat, leaving her holding it. I jumped up on the bed to get away from her — and during one performance, my toe got caught in the sheet. I fell forward onto the nightstand, bounced off it onto the floor, got up on all fours, and crawled to the door, raising one hand and yelling, "I'm okay!" before exiting. But oh, did that hurt.)

Acting in a company is trust and co-operation, togetherness in the best sense: *I will help you so we can both do better. So we can make the show work better.*

And then there are those actors who, for reasons of their own, just won't.

Acting in a company is togetherness in the best sense. You form this family — at least I think we're a family. I think, *Great, we're going to have dinner now.* Then, suddenly, it's all over. I don't know what it is, but most people who are not me are adults about it: you work with somebody, and then you move on. You go back to your life and you're on another project and you're working with these people now. That isn't me. There are people that I've called and I'm still waiting for the phone to ring. Michael Keaton and I did *Night Shift* together: that was 1982, 1983. I did six months with him. I called him up to have dinner. We had dinner and I never saw him again.

I don't separate well.

11.

I had a shrink for two years. Every week I'd go in and talk about my parents, Stacey, our children, my troubles getting acting work, and — when I did get work — my continuing problems getting out of my own way.

Then one day my shrink asked me to look at a script he'd written.

And so I spent a number of years shrink-less.

In spite of my raised hopes a couple of years earlier, the early 2010s were an especially tough time. On the one hand, the Hank Zipzer books Lin and I were writing were selling, and I was regularly being asked to give my talks about dyslexia. And I finally seemed to have made it in the world of voice acting, especially in *Clifford's Puppy Days* (where I won a Daytime Emmy), *Monsters at Work,* and *Rugrats.*

People wanted to hear my voice on-screen. It just seemed nobody wanted to see my face on-screen.

It was great to be the heart of the piece in Adam's movies — but Adam could only make so many movies. It was lovely to be treated so warmly by so many people, but if you don't feel the warmth toward yourself that people are showing you (*They can't possibly be talking about* me, I'd think), then your happiness is fleeting: you need to keep feeding this beast with outward approval. And though it was fun to play the kind of unauthoritative authority figures I played on *Arrested Development* and *Royal Pains* and *Childrens Hospital*, good writing like that (or in the case of *Childrens Hospital*, very interesting writing) came only once in a while.

Meanwhile, my phone wasn't ringing.

I've never thought a lot about age — or maybe a better way to put it is that I've tried not to think a lot about it. I'd felt for a while . . . okay, I'd *known* for a while that my age was working against me in the business. It's a young person's game: that's a given. I definitely didn't look young anymore — my hair had gone from black to gray to mostly white. (I still liked my hair.) But I had also developed a kind of mound of fat on my throat: at one point one of my agents brought it up. "You should get rid of that," he said. "It might be stopping you from getting work." And I took umbrage. I thought that was rude. At first I wasn't even thinking about the possibility that what he said might be true.

But eventually it dawned on me: he might not have phrased it very diplomatically, but he was right. I went to a plastic surgeon and had the thing removed. And it not only made me look better, but made me feel better.

And I still wasn't getting any work. (But what a neck!)

My agency, a big agency, kept passing me down to whoever was brand-new. That wasn't so good. Every pilot season I'd call and ask what was out there, and this new young person, whomever he or she happened to be, would say, "Sorry, I've read everything; there's nothing for you." I'd say, "Come on, there's got to be *something*. At least a meeting. Get me a meeting, and I'll go in and maybe they'll change the fifty-year-old to a sixty-five-year-old."

"Sorry."

When I tried going over my agent's head to see if I might do better with someone else, I'd hear: "You know, I gotta ask if anybody wants to take you on."

Not so encouraging.

But instead of standing up for myself, I'd just say, "Oh."

Now, my wonderful son Max is a go-getter. Max doesn't let moss grow beneath his feet. And he kept saying, "What are you doing? You've got to get a new agent — these people are doing nothing for you."

I dismissed it each time. "Nah, I'm okay."

Then Stacey and Zoe would say it: "Why don't you get a new agent?" And I'd think, in my typical way, *At least I have somebody. I don't know who else would want to take me. I don't want to try to see if someone will take me and they won't.*

At some point, when I got passed along to the latest new person at the agency, she turned out to be Leigh Brillstein, the daughter of the legendary manager Bernie Brillstein. I liked Leigh a lot: she was funny. And made great brownies.

I still wasn't getting any work, though — just getting chubby.

Then Leigh left to go to Resolution, a brand-new agency founded by Jeff Berg, one of the founders of ICM. And, thinking that maybe a new company might work better for me, I decided to go with her.

Then, in very short order, Resolution

closed. And for a while I had no agent at all.

As Max traveled more and more for directing work, his German shepherd, Hamlet — now fully grown — began staying with us. And when Hamlet stayed with us, he became territorial and aggressive. This despite the fact that Linus, who was still with us, was bigger than anybody.

In the meantime, Zoe and Rob, who now had two little boys, Ace and Jules, got Scruffy, a goldendoodle. And when Zoe and Rob went on vacation, Scruffy stayed with us.

So at times, we had Hamlet, Scruffy, Linus, and Charlotte — now I'm no longer in show business; I'm a kennel. And it's my responsibility to make sure all these dogs stay safe and fed.

With four dogs on the premises, we were a three-ring circus. Maybe a four-ring circus. Where Hamlet was concerned, if you were in the pack you were golden; if you weren't, watch out. And Scruffy, as the latest arrival, was under immediate suspicion. Growling, lifting his lip, Hamlet chased poor sweet Scruffy all over the yard (and after his operation, he could really haul ass on three legs), until she jumped into my protective arms. Linus and Charlotte watched with interest.

But that only happened once. The second time Hamlet began to growl at Scruffy, Linus got up from his comfortable bask in the sun and placed his large bulk between the two of them, his eyes telling Hamlet, *Don't even think about it.*

Hamlet thought about it for about one second. He backed off.

Jed had married his beautiful Amanda in 2008, and now they had two beautiful little girls, Indya and Lulu. And a French bulldog, Ringo. When Jed and his family went on vacation, Ringo stayed with Stacey and me, increasing the kennel population by one. All okay in theory — except that Ringo was one of the few dogs I'd ever met who would not warm up to me. Maybe he was just homesick, I thought at first; maybe he was distracted by the unfamiliar surroundings. Nope. When I leaned down to pet him, he edged away.

My solution to the problem was rather brilliant. I duct-taped slices of deli turkey to my shoes, and Ringo came up and snacked on my loafers. And we made friends.

In 2013 Max introduced me to his manager,

Cliff Murray. Cliff was young, early thirties, went to Harvard. Smart, direct, ultrapractical. He worked with Eryn Brown, who was also very smart, and the equally smart Chris Huvane. And they took me on.

Now, they were taking me on for two reasons. One, I think, was as a favor to Max. The other was, "Yes, of course — it's *Henry Winkler.*"

If I hadn't been Henry Winkler, capital H, capital W, I'm quite sure I wouldn't have gotten anywhere near their roster. Because the rest of their roster was people more like Max's age.

Working with these three managers, I was definitely in new territory. Soon after we began, Chris called me and said, "Be careful on Twitter. You said something anti-gun — watch yourself." And he was absolutely right: after tweeting what I thought had been a very thoughtful gun-safety tweet, I got forty-eight hours of, "You should crawl back under the rock you came from" — and worse.

One day I asked Cliff if the silence of my telephone was due to my age. Somebody else might've tried to sugarcoat it; Cliff didn't hesitate for a nanosecond. "Oh, absolutely," he said.

So when I was asked to play the

obstetrician-gynecologist Dr. Lu Saperstein on one or two episodes of a new sitcom called *Parks and Recreation,* I jumped at the opportunity. Not only had the creators, Greg Daniels and Michael Schur, done brilliant work on another mockumentary, *The Office,* but *Parks and Rec*'s cast was equally stupendous: Amy Poehler. Nick Offerman. Chris Pratt. Aubrey Plaza. Aziz Ansari. Adam Scott. Rashida Jones, who had been friends with our children and in our backyard for years. Rob Lowe. And on and on. Wow. But best of all was the fact that my character was the father of Jenny Slate's and Ben Schwartz's characters, and these two are just incredibly inventive and funny people in their own right. Jenny and her husband, Ben Shattuck, created the amazing Marcel the Shell — if you don't know it, I won't try to explain it; you just have to see it — and Ben Schwartz is part of an improv team with Thomas Middleditch and Zach Woods. And though I did improv in New York a hundred years ago, Middleditch and Schwartz are on another planet entirely.

They invited me to come and be part of an evening of improv at the Upstanding Citizens Brigade's theater on Franklin Avenue in Hollywood, and in the spirit of Try (Almost) Anything Once, I accepted.

There was a little stage backed by a brick wall, some lights overhead, and the audience on three sides. I was onstage, standing against the brick wall as Thomas, Ben, and Zach started their act, and as I watched them being unbelievably brilliant, knowing I was going to somehow participate, I was thinking, *I've never seen anything quite like this. I'm crazy. I have to leave now.* I was not only out of my league, I was underwater. All I wanted to do was melt into the brick.

Then Ben grabbed my wrist and pulled me into the scene. I think I said something that made him laugh, and he was very kind. But basically I had no business being on the same stage with those guys. This was like the time I saw the Royal Shakespeare Company in London and understood why I could never do Shakespeare.

But *Parks and Recreation* was such fun. And after being asked to do one or two episodes, I stayed for three years. I delivered all the stars' babies. I delivered Rashida Jones and Rob Lowe's baby. I delivered Aubrey Plaza and Chris Pratt's baby. I delivered Amy Poehler and Adam Scott's baby. I mean, of course, that my character did. As clueless in general as Dr. Lu was, he kept answering the call.

When I was doing the ultrasound on

Amy's tummy, I congratulated them on triplets. The spots on the screen, however, turned out to be cream cheese from my lunch.

I never truly felt that I understood who my character was, but I guess something I did at the beginning was funny, because, to my surprise and delight, they kept bringing me back. I'm sure Amy Poehler was in on that decision. Because when I did scenes with her, I could see that she was completely in charge: it was really her show. She would direct, act, crack amazingly funny jokes. She truly was the commander in chief.

I should say here that I've always worked well with women in charge. My first insurance broker was a woman, Betty. (Who knew I even needed insurance? Tom Bosley knew.) My most recent lawyers, Wendy Heller and Jamie Cohen. Eryn Brown is one of my managers; Shauna Perlman is one of my major agents at CAA. (I signed with CAA after my long unagented period.) I've never felt in anything but good hands with each of these women.

The Hank Zipzer books were so successful so quickly that the idea of turning them into a TV series, live-action or animated, seemed irresistible. Lin Oliver and I had the books sent to Disney, and the first reaction there was, "Oh my gosh, these are so funny; he's such a great character."

That was nice to hear. We wrote him funny first. And resourceful, and tenacious.

But then they said, "Kids want aspirational heroes, and he's got a problem."

Well, first of all, call it a challenge, not a problem. And one-sixth of the children in the world have Hank's kind of learning challenge — except that there is resistance, and ignorance, everywhere to simply acknowledging this fact. Once, when I was touring in Europe with the books, and speaking at a town hall meeting in Italy, a man stood up and told me that there's no such thing as a learning challenge — these children are just lazy.

"Oh," I said. "One of my parents has come back to life! Do you actually think the kids are lying about their struggle to learn?"

He sat down.

After Disney, we sent the books around to every children's-television outlet in the country, but we met the same kind of resistance everywhere: the nitty-gritty of Hank in the trenches, dealing with his challenge in all kinds of humorous ways, just wasn't aspirational enough. Not uplifting enough. But apparently the books' fans felt differently. Lin and I wrote the twenty-eight Hank novels to be entertainment reading for the reluctant reader. And the greatest compliment I ever got came from the many, many fan letters we received. Children wrote the same thing, over and over, in seven languages: "How did you know me so well?"

Curiously, though, when we took the idea across the Atlantic to the UK, the BBC was very interested. Walker Books published the novels in England, with great success. And so it was that *Hank Zipzer,* the (live-action) TV series, debuted in January 2014 on CBBC, the children's-programming branch of the BBC. The production was under the banner of Kindle Entertainment, a tasteful production company headed by Anne Brogan. Nick James, as Hank, headed an excellent all-British cast — the wonderful Nick Mohammed, also of *Ted Lasso,* played the principal, Mr. Love. (Actually, the cast was all British with one exception: a certain American television legend played Hank's music teacher, Mr. Rock, who was of course based on Donald Rock, my music teacher back at McBurney, the only teacher who ever encouraged me.) Maddie Holliday was Hank's annoying younger sister; she was ten at the time, and this was one of her very first acting jobs. During a scene in the pilot, I threw her an ad lib as I exited, and she threw an ad lib right back, as if she'd been doing it for years. The casting pièce de resistance was the sublime Felicity Montagu. She re-created my real fourth-grade teacher, Miss Adolf, as Lin and I had dreamed her: she was pure perfection. And bringing it all to life was the very talented young director Matt Bloom, who went on to do multiple episodes over three years, and a holiday movie.

I had a ball.

Zoe and her husband, Rob, and their little baby son, Ace, moved in with us for about a year and a half while their house was being made livable. It was the cutest thing in the world: the padding of Ace's footsteps running down the hall, coming to our room, still echoes in my ears. So in 2014, Max, who is a writer-producer along with being a director, and Rob, the former actor who is now a successful builder, came together and developed a series called *The Winklers.* Aka *The Winklers: The Son-in-Law, the Baby, My Daughter Living with Us, and the Sturm und Drang That Came Out of That.* Then they went to Phil Rosenthal, the cocreator of *Everybody Loves Raymond.* Phil took over and wrote a script, directed a pilot — and ultimately disagreed wholeheartedly with ABC's take on the show. So we almost got it on, but it never actually came to life. Judith Light played my wife; Domenick Lombardozzi was my son-in-law: who knew that this bald, heavyset, kind of menacing-looking guy from *The Wire* could be so funny? Susan Sarandon's daughter, Eva Amurri, played my daughter. There were some great scenes in it. And we ate very well because Phil Rosenthal invests in and nurtures new restaurants and new chefs in LA. So lunch was always an adventure. His sixteen-year-old daughter, Lily Rosenthal, was Phil's assistant and creator of good cheer on the set. The Winkler family's relationship with Lily lasted, and during the pandemic, she helped tutor Ace, Jules, and Gus.

The show never saw the light of day. But if it had seen the light of day, it is very possible that I would not have been available for *Barry.* Maybe somebody up there had bigger plans for me.

One day during the first season of *Happy Days,* Ron Howard and I were walking down a street on the Paramount lot when I spotted Robert De Niro standing in a doorway, in 1920s clothes, taking a break from shooting *The Godfather Part II.* "We gotta go say hello," I said to Ron. So we walked up and introduced ourselves. De Niro was very taciturn. "How you doin'," was all he said.

"I just want to tell you before we leave you," I said, "you use the word 'fuck' better than anybody on the planet in *Mean Streets.*"

He gave a tiny nod, never changing his expression. "Thank you."

Cut to forty years later. Stacey and I are in New York, at a premiere party for *The Intern,* starring De Niro and Anne Hathaway, directed by Nancy Meyers. We're at the party because our daughter is best friends with Nancy's daughter Annie. And De Niro is at the party. I go up to him and say, "I have to ask you the same question people always ask me — can I take a selfie with you?"

"Yeah," he says. Forty years later, he's still taciturn. But really warm. A tiny smile comes to his face. "You said I use the word 'fuck' better than anybody on the planet."

Oh, man. Had I caught up to the cool kids at last?

But deep down I knew that the part of me that was chasing after the cool kids (and never catching them) — that was the part of me that had to change. The ten-year-old in me. Who took up most of the space inside me.

Not so easy.

We still had our dog visitors from time to time, but our in-house contingent was fading away: first Linus passed on, then Charlotte. Linus was so brave, but cancer shattered his leg, and he couldn't survive it. I felt every dog's passing as a painful loss.

Then while I was at a Comic-Con in Virginia, Stacey and I picked up Sadie, a chocolate-brown labradoodle, and she flew home with us. But when Hamlet stayed over, as regularly happened while Max was working, he and Sadie had to stay in separate rooms. Sadie needed a friend she could be in the same room with.

Maisie, a goldendoodle (white with brown spots), came from Georgia to join us. And happily for everyone — except maybe Hamlet — she and Sadie bonded as sisters.

Sometime around late 2015 or early 2016 I felt I had come to a crossroads. Despite all I had done — and there was some good work, with both my family and my profession — I knew, if I was being honest with myself, that I was still uncooked. A little boy inside. Who felt he didn't know as much as other people. Who felt he wasn't as educated as other people. I was this little kid, and everybody else knew more than I did.

My wanting to be perfect, with no room for mistakes, was standing toe to toe at the O.K. Corral with the knowledge that there had to be another way for me to be.

But what was it?

Though being a scared little kid inside made it easy for me to get along with children and animals, it did not help me to get along with my wife. It was very, very difficult for me to be vulnerable with Stacey. She had been dealing with the effects of my inner immaturity forever, but I couldn't — it felt like I was physically unable to — share the causes with her. She and I bumped up against this again and again, and it was corrosive to our marriage. After almost forty years together, something in me still couldn't let her in, and this was causing intense pain to both of us.

There was also this: after more than a dozen years working with Lin Oliver, she and I were also encountering bumps in the road. It happened whenever we disagreed about a plot point in one of our books, the kind of thing that's bound to happen with collaborators — except that I was unable, again physically unable, to hold up my side of an argument: I would just cave, then keep quiet about it and build a thunderhead of resentment. I was bottling things up to an unhealthy degree. To this day, there is a word in chapter 3 of the second book that I so resent, I leave it out every time I read the book aloud.

Something had to change.

One night Frank Dines and I were going to the theater in LA, and I asked his advice about how I could change my working partnership with Lin. I knew deep down that whatever was going on with her and me was of a piece with what was happening with Stacey and me, but the professional relationship was easier to talk about than the personal.

Still, Frank was looking at me as if he knew I might be talking about more than I was talking about.

"Well, partnerships are tough," he finally said. "You've got to give and take, give and take, all the time. And really getting into it can be scary."

Oh boy, did I know what he was talking about. Across the board.

We went in and saw the play, and I didn't

say anything else to Frank, but on Monday he called me to say that if I was interested, he could refer me to an excellent therapist. If I was interested.

I was interested.

And I went in to see this woman, and that's when my life began to change.

Very early in my treatment, I asked my new shrink in a casual way if she had children.

She looked me in the eye. "How would my telling you help what you and I are doing here?" she asked.

That was an interesting moment. I am famous, I am charming — famously charming. How could she resist answering this perfectly normal, perfectly innocent (I thought) question from me, the charming Henry Winkler?

She resisted. And by resisting, she was showing me that she wasn't going to be impressed by my being famous and charming — nor was she going to hold it against me. She was simply showing me that she was there to work — to really help the human being in front of her — and that I had to be willing to work, too. Without deploying any of my usual crutches. I slowly realized there was still a lot of little boy in me, desperately trying to make everyone in the world love me, because my parents didn't seem to. The little boy who knew less than everyone else.

I had to cut that idea off my bones with a bowie knife. I had to saw that little boy out of my being.

Oh, it was hard at the beginning. A lot of the time, I had absolutely no idea what my doctor was talking about. It didn't compute. Where do I look? What do I do? Am I doing it right? Am I attacking the right problem? Am I saying the right thing?

Then, very, very slowly, I began to understand.

It was the fall of 2016, and Stacey and I had just come from a long meeting with our business managers Steve Bills and Jodie Munoz and our attorney Paul Hoffman about estate planning. I mean a long, *long* meeting — our advisors could literally have been speaking Turkish. Stacey and I understood a little bit here and there. We got that our three children would all share equally after we passed on . . . but there was a lot besides that. I mean, a lot.

So our heads were buzzing, and we were driving down Ventura Boulevard in the Valley, through a whole area that was kind of historic for us — where our first house was, the house that was home to our children when they were small. We were reminiscing a little . . . and my phone rang.

It was my latest agent calling. Iris. She had the happy-agent sound in her voice, so I began to get excited. After a quick couple of pleasantries, she started saying something about Bill Hader and a new show and HBO. "Well, you're on a short list," she said.

"Bill Hader?" I said.

"Yeah."

"HBO?"

"Yeah."

Oh my God. Bill Hader. HBO. I've never worked with HBO — I've never been asked.

"Oh my God," I said. "I'm on a short list — wait. Is Dustin Hoffman on that list?"

"I'll find out," my agent said.

"Okay," I said.

She put me on hold. I looked at Stacey. She looked at me.

Two, three, four . . . we came to a red light. Stayed there awhile. The light turned green. A couple of blocks later, another red light. I looked at Stacey again. She raised her eyebrows.

My agent finally came back on the line. "No, he is not."

"Dustin Hoffman is not on the list?"

"Right. Not on the list."

"All right, I'm in," I said. Because if Dustin Hoffman is on that short list, they're going to go with an Academy Award–winning movie star — I have no shot. I'm not even going in.

We get home. I get the script. It's called *Barry.* Created by Hader and Alec Berg. The story of a professional hit man, to be played by Bill, who bumbles into an acting class and feels he's discovered his true calling. I can tell immediately that the writing (by the two of them) could not be more perfect: so perfect that it's almost shocking.

Now I'm sitting with my pages at the desk in my home office. This is the very first piece of furniture I ever bought — in 1975, for my first house, in Studio City. A big, tall doctor's desk with a lot of drawers and wings of cubbies that open from the center. I'm sure that back in the day, each cubby was used for a different bottle of medicine. Me, I have tchotchkes from the first time I brought the desk home: Swiss Army knives; every patch that was given to me at appearances, even the patch I wore on my jacket at the McBurney School; a Best Dad Smurf award given to me by Jed. I'm sitting at my desk, and my son Max, the director, is directing me. My audition is tomorrow. I'm saying my lines, and Max is looking puzzled.

"What are you doing?" he asks.

"I'm just doing the lines," I say.

"What you're saying isn't in the script," Max says.

"No, no, no, I'm improvising," I say. "I'm making it my own."

"Respect the writer, Dad," Max says. He gives me a look. I give him a look. He knows what I know: reading, for me, is like pulling my own teeth. So I'm doing the same thing I've always done: it's mostly worked pretty well for me.

"Max," I say, "I've been doing it for forty years. It's okay."

He looks at me. "Not this time, Dad."

All right, so now I memorize my lines, verbatim — which adds an extra layer of anxiety on top of the thick layer that's already there. I drive to the audition. I get lost. It's in some Sony building not connected to HBO or the studio, somewhere on the way to LAX, near the cemetery where my in-laws were laid to rest. I find the place but miss the driveway. I turn around. I turn around again. I finally get into the parking lot and park, and walk into the building. I go up the stairs, find the office, go in. I sit down in the metal chair that is known to every actor in every audition that has ever occurred. The folding chair at your school dance, or at the Passover table when you've run out of furniture and there are more guests. I'm sitting there in the chair, and all of a sudden, Bill Hader walks up. He's carrying all kinds of things — a script, a coffee, his bag. He now has to juggle all of this and open the door to the casting office. He looks over and spots me. "Oh," he says. "I'll be right with you."

"Have your coffee," I say. "Relax. Enjoy. Sit down. Take a bath. I'll be right here."

He goes inside. Now I'm really waiting. Because the waiting I did before he arrived was nothing. Now the waiting is, he's here, and I've got to go in front of him.

Finally, someone opens the door and invites me in. The casting people's young assistant is sitting at a desk outside the inner sanctum. "Good morning," I say. "Nice to see you." I walk in. Sherry Thomas, the casting director, says hello. She's standing behind the smallest videotape camera I have ever seen, mounted on a tripod. Bill Hader stands to the left of her.

"Okay, Henry," Sherry says.

I do a scene. It's a monologue. My character, the acting teacher Gene Cousineau, is making a presentation to his class, demonstrating how acting is done, performing a couple of lines from *Hamlet,* from *A Street-car Named Desire,* from *Serpico.* He's an incredibly bad actor — a failed actor who thinks he's God's gift to teaching — but of course he doesn't know it. Bill is laughing. The more he laughs, the more I get into it. Stacey and I have watched this man for years on *Saturday Night Live,* and *I* just made *him* laugh.

Now I have another scene, one where I'm talking to an acting student named Sally, telling her everything that she did wrong in the scene she just performed. I could perform it solo, but I sense it's going to be better if I do it with somebody. And in my work I've always had the nerve that I've never had in life, so I turn to Sherry Thomas and say, "Excuse me, Sherry. Come on up here with me. The camera is pointed correctly — you don't need to zoom in or out."

So Sherry stands next to me, and Bill starts to direct me. "You're a teacher and you're full of shit, but you think you're the greatest teacher in the universe," he says. So I put my arm around Sherry and do the scene with her standing in for Sally. Gene bullies her, browbeats her until she bursts into tears. He's monstrously full of himself, egomaniacal. Bill is laughing. I finish my speech and give Sherry a hug. "Thank you for playing with me," I tell her. "And it was a pleasure to meet you, Bill." I shake his hand and leave, and I drive home. I'm feeling pretty good. I made Bill Hader laugh. Twice.

And that good feeling dissipates slowly, then disappears completely, because I hear nothing back from my manager Cliff — nothing the next day, or the next. Or the next week, or the week after that. Or the week after that. The wait is excruciating. It's as if I'm being cut by a scalpel. Finally I can't take it anymore. But I can't call my agent, because we don't have that relationship. For all the weeks and months and years that I wasn't working, they — they, because I get handed off from agent to agent at this big agency — have never called to see how I was. To say, "How are you doing? We're looking. Don't worry. We're trying." Nothing. I had to call them. They'd say, as if I'd just woken them from a nap: "Oh, hey! How are you?"

So I phoned Cliff again, who of course is in the loop.

"Henry, I know," he says. "If there was any news, I would've called you."

"I know, I know," I say. "But please — is there any movement you can detect? The slightest tremor? I've fallen off their radar, haven't I? Because this is way too long. This is, like, crazy long. They've gone in another direction, I'm sure of it. Could you please call and find out?"

Cliff calls Bill's agent. Calls me back. "No, you're still in the mix," he says.

This gives me about three seconds of relief, then I'm sweating bullets again. I don't want to be in the mix. I want to be the main ingredient.

A couple of more weeks creep by.

Once again I reach my absolute limit. I don't want my manager to get exasperated with me, but I can no longer control myself. The anxiety has grown to such a point that it has shot out the top of my head, which forces my fingers to phone him. He phones Bill's agent. Phones me back. "No, they're meeting other people, but you're still in there."

Another week. Another week. It's like I'm under the ocean and my air hose is being crimped — somebody has put a safety clip on my air hose. And I'm gasping and trying very hard to be cool. I'm trying to talk myself down. Stacey tries to talk me down. My puppies try to talk me down by dropping a ball at my feet. I'm trying so hard just to live my life and go about my business and forget about Bill Hader and HBO, and be like, "Hey, it's okay — I'm throwing it up to the heavens, it's up to God . . ." Yes, I talk to God, in the garden, like Emily Dickinson.

But oh my God, so long. I have sat in this chair at my desk for so many years, waiting for this phone, or one like it, to ring. My Scorsese phone is covered with cobwebs. The push buttons don't work anymore.

Another week goes by. Then — bang, out of the blue — Bill himself calls.

"Hey, how you doing?" he says.

"How am I doing? So great, Bill. How are you?" *I'm just sitting here and I'm so relaxed. Wow, I'm so surprised to hear from you. I wasn't thinking about this at all.*

"You want to come in and play?"

"Do I want to come in and play?"

In my mind: *No! Are you kidding? If the first audition was good, I don't want to fuck it up. No, I don't want to come in and play.*

Instead, I say, "Yes, of course I will, Bill. As a matter of fact, I can't think of anything I'd rather do."

"Hey, I just wrote two scenes last night," Bill says.

"You wrote two scenes last night?"

"Yes, I did. I'm going to email them to you."

"Great, Bill. Thanks. Can't wait." Very

casual. "Standing by, Bill."

I run downstairs to my computer. Almost break my neck. Get the scenes (once again, by Bill and Alec, once again incredibly well written), email them to Max with a note: "Oh my God. I have another audition tomorrow." He directs me over the phone this time.

I drive down to the same building again, managing this time not to get lost. Walk upstairs, where the first thing I see, in the hallway, is a girl — pardon me, a young woman — with script pages in her hand, pacing up and down, up and down, semi-audibly practicing her lines as (I know from my pages) Sally, Barry's fellow acting student. This young lady is deep, deep into these pages: she's practically eating the paper in order to become Sally.

"Hello," I say. "Nice to see you."

She gives me a quick surprised look, blinks a couple of times, then goes back to her lines. I sit down in a chair outside the office door, trying to sit quietly and be in my own space — which is impossible, because I have an entire opera going on here with this young woman — *Rigoletto* is going on in the hallway.

The door opens. "Hi, Henry," the young

assistant says. "Come on in."

I go in. Same wonderful assistant. But this time, along with Bill, both casting directors, Sherry Thomas and Sharon Bialy, are there, as is Alec Berg, sitting on the couch. There are introductions all around. I'm particularly fascinated by Bill's cocreator Alec, who seems so quiet, cool, and self-contained (self-contained is an understatement) that I immediately have the fantasy that he is Norwegian. I will later find out that he is not in any way Norwegian. (At one point I asked Alec if I could continue to refer to him as Norwegian. "Yes, you can," he said.)

I will also discover that Alec has a rep. Not only is he considered the crème de la crème of comedy writing in Hollywood, but he's so close to the vest, I think the vest is tattooed on.

I do the scene with Bill. Once again I am the acting teacher Gene Cousineau, and this time I'm instructing Barry, the hit man / acting student, in how to summon intense emotions. "If I want pure sorrow," I say, passionately, as Gene, "I call up Princess Diana's death. Or the day that my dad fell off the roof when I was a kid" — I mime the fall with my hand — "ka-plunk."

Bill is laughing, breaking the scene. I have made Bill Hader laugh again. And — I can't help glancing over at the couch — Alec (The Norwegian) Berg is actually smiling.

Oh my God. I just made Alec Berg smile. I nearly wet myself.

Bill, shifting from actor to director, is giving me his notes on the scene. Because Bill is so good, because Bill and Alec's writing is so good, because this piece we're doing is in such a different stratosphere from so much that I've read before, I absorb every syllable he's saying, like a man in the Mojave Desert, dying of thirst, absorbing water.

Alec is still smiling. The casting people are smiling. Bill is smiling. I shake everyone's hand and leave.

Out in the hallway, *Rigoletto* is still going on — it's the third act. Now another young lady is sitting on the stairs, also holding script pages, saying the lines, gesticulating, feeling Sally's words in the most intense way possible. I walk past her down the steps, excuse myself. Then something makes me stop and back up.

"Hi," I say. "Are you going in to see Bill and Alec?"

"Yes, I am," she says. "Yes, I am."

"Wow," I say. "Where are you from?"

"Brooklyn," she says. "I'm living in Brooklyn."

"Great pizza," I say. "Well, I have a feeling

you're going to have a great time, and you're going to do really well. I wish you the best. Break a leg."

She thanked me. She looked surprised and delighted. And I went down the steps and out to the parking lot. Later I found that this young lady was the wonderful actress Sarah Goldberg — and Sarah told me she saw me, through a window in the door at the bottom of the stairs, walking back and forth, back and forth. I had lost my car in the parking lot. I was pushing the button on my key, but not hearing the *beep-beep.* That's what Sarah saw.

Finally I found my car and went home.

12.

Another six or seven years go by (maybe six or seven days in everyday time, but I am feeling very far from everyday time). I'm waiting, waiting, waiting. *Oh well,* I think, *the fulcrum has somehow shifted; I've slid out of their imagination. These things happen.*

The phone rings. I jump involuntarily.

It's my new agent, Jim. (Iris has left the agency.) He tells me that a certain fried-chicken chain wants me to play a certain trademark character in a commercial — they're making a series of TV spots where a different recognizable person plays this character in every one. They're offering a lot of money.

I mean, a *lot* of money.

I turn it down.

It killed me to do that. But my stomach had spoken: *You shouldn't do that.* So I just couldn't.

A day or two later — I've totally lost track

of time by now — the phone rings again, and I jump again.

It's Bill Hader.

"Hi, Bill," I say, in my calmest voice.

"You know," he says, "I can't get you out of my mind. Would you like to play Gene Cousineau?"

"Oh yeah," I say. "Sure." I say it so casually, I should get an award just for the acting I'm doing on the phone. Meanwhile, if my skin wasn't attached, I would have exploded all over the room.

Now we're at HBO, doing the first reading: the pilot script. A big table in a big room. Michael Lombardo, HBO's president of programming; Casey Bloys, the network's chief content officer; and Amy Gravitt, the coexecutive vice president of programming (who would become the fairy godmother of *Barry* at HBO) are at the head of the table. Bill and Alec are at the other end. Sherry and Sharon, the casting directors. And the rest of the core cast: Stephen Root; Anthony Carrigan; the young woman who was sitting on the steps practicing her lines, Sarah Goldberg, who has been cast as Sally; and D'Arcy Carden.

We're reading. Sarah does a scene as an acting student doing a poor job in a class exercise, then I come in as Gene, her teacher. My first line is, "Bullshit!" I slam the table. "Bullshit!" And out of the corner of my eye, I see the HBO executives jump. Later on, I was told that Michael Lombardo said, "I had no idea Henry Winkler had that in him."

It was one of the greatest compliments I've ever gotten.

Also later on, Sarah told me, "You know, when you walked down the stairs as I was practicing my lines, and I looked up, and you were standing there, giving me encouragement, I thought, *Wow, I guess this really is Hollywood. I'm just sitting here waiting to audition, and the Fonz is talking to me.*"

Bill and Alec told me which acting teacher Gene Cousineau was based on — a very famous teacher in LA, whose name I can't tell you. A most unpleasant fellow, though everyone went to his classes. I watched a video of him teaching: it gave me something to start with.

I thought about all the acting teachers I'd had, then I imagined what my life would have been like if I had gone that route myself. One detail about the unpleasant guy in LA was useful: he painted, and he wanted his students to buy his artwork. And I thought, *Now, that is the craziest thing I ever heard. These people are scraping together a few dollars to pay for rent, gas, and food, and then on top of that they feel they have to pay for this class in order to be good actors, so that they might be able to put together a career — and then on top of* that, *he wants them to buy his art.*

And pay cash, no doubt.

That part actually got into the script. Gene to his students: "As long as you pay cash and on time. . . . You're so talented! I personally have never seen anything quite like it!"

We shot the pilot, where Barry is established as this hit man who follows his target, Ryan, to an acting class where Ryan is a student — Gene's class — and winds up doing a scene with Ryan. And gets invited to come back and take the class, as a paying student, of course. And meets another student, Sally, who encourages him, stirring his interest in acting — and in her.

We shot the pilot, and I loved every minute of it. And loved every person in it.

And then we waited, month after month — it felt like a year — to see if we were picked up.

Zoe was watching the news one night in 2017 when she saw a story about immigrant children being separated from their parents and put in these very stark facilities down by the Mexican border. "Those could be my children," she said. And having watched her mother her whole life, she snapped into action.

Together with two friends, Zoe started a charity called This Is About Humanity. They hire buses and invite members of the community here in Los Angeles to go with them down to the border and visit the children in these facilities to see what they need — anything from toothbrushes to a new roof — and then they spend the money to get it done. Just as one example, the interior designer Nate Berkus and his partner, Jeremiah Brent, went on the bus one day with Zoe, and rented a house for young LGBTQ detainees, and committed to completely refurbishing it. To date, Zoe and her partners in TIAH have raised $2 million for all these kids, with zero overhead — not a single paper clip, not one secretary.

I did voice work — and then a lot of voice

work. Lin and I kept writing our books. I gave my talks around the country. I made a Hank Zipzer TV movie for CBBC, *Hank Zipzer's Christmas Catastrophe.* I read an assortment of Hank Zipzer, Alien Superstar, and Ghost Buddy books on tape, which was the hardest thing I've ever done. And every Monday morning I sat with this insightful woman who was helping me to jackhammer the Chernobyl-like barrier of concrete that sheathed the tiny kernel of human that was me.

It was hard work, drilling all that concrete.

I knew there was a wall, but I didn't know what it consisted of. So slowly, slowly, I — we — started breaking it down. Not being able to be intimate. Wanting to be perfect. Not being able to handle that I was not who I wanted to be or thought I wanted to be. Needing to put my problems on the other person — that was a big one. In any given situation, I couldn't clearly see my responsibility to the problem at hand. I had trouble telling myself, "You know, it doesn't really matter what the other person is doing. What are *you* doing?" When you stop looking outside yourself, clarity comes like cream to the surface.

And then the shame.

Shame for being disconnected to the reality of the life I was living. Shame for not being there for Stacey when she needed me most.

I'd never felt seen or heard by my parents, but had I ever really seen or heard *them*? When I was young, I heard some stories about my mother and father escaping Nazi Germany. Some stayed with me. Some were very dramatic. But I never asked, really. I never pursued it. What did my mother's mother look like? What was she like? My grandfather on my mother's side was a pharmacist; my mother worked at the pharmacy. But I never asked, "Where was it? What did it look like?"

I was disciplined constantly, sometimes I didn't even know why. And I didn't really fucking care who my parents were. All I saw was what was in front of me, and I had to negotiate that and survive.

Then *Barry* was picked up.

HBO ordered twelve episodes, but Bill and Alec, not wanting the story to be diluted, decided to do eight instead. They went off and started writing.

The next thing that happened was that the whole cast — not just the core people, but everyone — met in a big empty room, a rehearsal hall. The sheer mass of talent in this room was breathtaking. We'd all read the seven additional scripts Bill and Alec had written. We had lunch and talked and talked. We were really bonding. And then all of a sudden, Bill took half of the cast away to rehearse — because, of course, the Chechen mobsters and Barry's other life as an assassin had nothing to do with the acting class. And it never dawned on me that I was never going to see these people again. As always happened with me, it felt like a real loss — I loved these people. Bill left me with our half of the cast and said, "Henry, you're the teacher. Teach a class."

So I took all these wonderful young actors — Sarah Goldberg, D'Arcy Carden, Kirby Howell-Baptiste, Rightor Doyle, Darrell Britt-Gibson, Andy Carey, Alejandro Furth — and treated them as a class, doing the kind of exercises with them that I did in drama school and that I still do with actors sometimes, when I'm directing. Some could improvise; some were nervous. I made them move around the room, embodying their favorite automobile. Soon I had a veritable showroom: there was a jalopy, a Camaro, a Rolls-Royce, a Lamborghini. Every one of these people was a home-run hitter. Each could be the star of his or her own show. And I was lucky enough to have them as actors in Gene Cousineau's class.

I worked so hard at listening to Bill and Alec and trying to go where they wanted me to go, but this was just writing on another level than I'd ever seen before.

Imagine: I'm at home, memorizing my lines. Reading them over and over and over, giving them the attention that's literally physically painful for me, but that this writing deserves. I learn my monologues; I know the scenes. I'm here in LA, comfortable; I know exactly what I'm going to do the next day. Then I go to the set — and Bill has a vision in his head that I never saw coming, and all of a sudden I'm in Peru. But we're still using the foundation of the work I've done at home.

It's mind-bending.

During the first year, some of the episodes were directed by Hiro Murai. I first met this young man in Max's film class at USC, as I watched screenings of the films that the second-year students had made. Hiro's film was amazing. I went up to his parents and said, "Your son is going to be very successful." And now here he is directing *Barry* after he created the tone of another hit show, *Atlanta.*

■ ■ ■ ■

One day on the set, a light bulb clicked on over my head. I turned to Bill and Alec and said, "Oh, wait a minute. I'm an asshole. Gene is an asshole."

They looked at me, smiling at my late-arriving enlightenment. "Yes," they said. "Yes, he is."

Bill and Alec originally wrote Gene as very cold and tough, but as I played him from episode to episode, different tones emerged. Was Gene self-deceiving? Massively. Was he grandiose? Impossibly. Was he a bad actor himself? Outrageously. But was he a bad teacher?

Pretty bad, yes. Yet at the same time, Gene Cousineau can't help loving his students. Even when he's telling them that the acting they've just shown him is so nauseating that he's about to vomit all over their shoes, he feels for them. I think. At least I felt for them. I identified with them.

I remembered the time Stella Adler came to our class at Yale and shot me down while I was doing her exercise, vividly imagining the flowers I was seeing in the imaginary garden. I remembered — vividly — how she denied my very worth as an actor. ("Sit down! You see nothing!") And I mentioned it to Bill, and he let me improvise a scene with him, where Barry and Gene are doing an exercise in front of the class.

"The primary responsibility of any actor is to create the reality and let the audience *live* there," Gene tells him. "So — where *are* we?"

And this hit man who's never acted in his life, who's never done anything but kill people, who has zero idea what acting even is, is stumped. And terrified. "I don't know," he whispers.

"Anywhere," Gene says. "You've been *some* where — come on. Where have you been?"

"Uh — grocery store."

"Are you asking me or are you telling me?"

"Grocery store."

"All right, we're in a grocery store. All right, here we go — this is great. What do you see up there on the shelves?"

Barry's breathing hard. Really scared. "Gum," he finally says.

"Gum is at the register, Barry," Gene says, scornfully. "All right — here we go." He mimes pushing a grocery cart. "We're walking down the aisle. Get your cart. You feel the handle? Here we go."

They're side by side, pretending to wheel

their carts.

"Now. Take a look around — what do you see?"

"Soup."

"You see soup! What kind of soup?"

"Um —" He's stumped.

"Chicken noodle? Consommé!"

"I don't know."

"What do you mean, you don't know?"

"I don't know."

"Just look at the shelf."

"I can't."

"Why?"

"Someone bought it?"

"No one bought it — that's a lie! Take your hands out of your pockets. Don't slouch. You're stuck. Barry, I need you to surrender."

But Barry is paralyzed with self-consciousness. He has no idea what to do with his hands.

"No no! Stay in place, don't move. Take your hands out of your pockets! Just surrender. Surrender to the soup, Barry."

But Barry was unable to surrender to the soup — the same way I was unable to surrender to my own imperfect perfection until my therapist and I had drilled away a few more inches of the cubic yards of concrete that covered me.

■ ■ ■ ■

Barry's first season began in March 2018, and the show was an immediate success with audiences and critics. And in July, we got a boatload of Emmy nominations: for Outstanding Comedy Series, Outstanding Lead Actor in a Comedy Series (Bill), Outstanding Directing for a Comedy Series (Bill again), twice for Outstanding Writing for a Comedy Series (Bill, for Episode 1; Liz Sarnoff, for Episode 7), and Outstanding Supporting Actor in a Comedy Series (me).

Me.

I had done some good work with some amazing people over the years, but there was something about *Barry* that put it in a different sphere altogether. It was fun and often very funny, but it could turn quite dark in a millisecond. Barry was a killer, after all, and the killings weren't soft-pedaled. A strange and unsettling and brilliant show, thanks to those strange and brilliant men, Bill and Alec.

A month after we premiered, HBO renewed us for a second season.

The only time I ever get tired of award

ceremonies — the red carpet, the interviews, the salmon dinner, the long, long speeches, the suspense about when the band is going to start playing the person off for babbling on and on — the only time I ever get tired of all that is when I don't win something.

And I'm positive that every other nominee feels exactly the same.

The 2018 Emmys were held on September 18, at the Microsoft Theater in downtown LA: a huge auditorium, and totally packed for the occasion. The nominees get to sit down in front. Stacey was next to me, and we were holding hands: Outstanding Supporting Actor in a Comedy Series was to be the first award of the evening.

Michael Che and Colin Jost, those two very funny guys whom I look forward to watching every week on *Saturday Night Live,* announced the nominees: Tituss Burgess, for *Unbreakable Kimmy Schmidt;* Louie Anderson, for *Baskets;* Brian Tyree Henry, for *Atlanta;* Tony Shalhoub, for *The Marvelous Mrs. Maisel;* Alec Baldwin, for his stinging Trump imitation on *Saturday Night Live;* Kenan Thompson, for being the rock of *Saturday Night Live.* Heady company. And me.

The Crown's Matt Smith and Claire Foy, handsome and beautiful and elegant, came out onstage to present. "We are thrilled to present the first award of the night," Matt said. Claire: "And if we don't sound thrilled, that's just because we're very, very British."

And then she opened that big blue envelope and, with a sweet and genuine smile, said my name.

What the fuck? I thought.

And a millisecond after, *Oh my God, I won an Emmy.*

I embraced my ecstatic wife. I stood. I gripped my heart for a second; it was pounding at a hundred miles an hour. I could barely breathe. I saw Bill and Alec jump to their feet — and dear Kenan Thompson. Thank you, Kenan! And then everyone else in the theater. The sound of applause was oceanic. Standing ovations aren't rare at award ceremonies, but this one felt very, very special to me. And different, somehow. I think I can honestly say, without blowing my own horn too much, that I felt the same kind of sweetness emanating from this audience as I had seen on Claire Foy's face: it felt like they knew there was some kind of justice to this.

Matt handed me the statuette. I immediately started telling him and Claire how much Stacey and I loved the second season of *The Crown.* They looked at me in shock. Claire stage-whispered, *"You have a speech."*

I whirled to the mike. "I only have thirty-nine seconds," I said. "I wrote this forty-three years ago. Can I just say, Skip Brittenham said to me a long time ago, 'If you stay at the table long enough, the chips come to you.' And tonight, I got to clear the table. If you get a chance to work with Bill Hader or Alec Berg, run, don't walk. Thank you for producing us, for creating us, for directing us; and Bill, for acting with us, and all of our wonderful writers . . ." — I thanked Sherry Thomas and Sharon Bialy and my extraordinary publicist Sheri Goldberg; I thanked Cliff and Eryn and Chris — "Almost for the first time, I feel represented. I can't stop yet. My wife, Stacey — oh my God, my cast and crew. And the kids, Jed, Zoe, and Max — you can go to bed now, Daddy won!"

Now, in a certain way, this wasn't my first rodeo. It was my third Emmy — there was the one in the daytime category for voicing Norville in *Clifford's Puppy Days* in 2005; twenty years before that I won my first daytime award for directing an after-school special.

But primetime is something else. I'd started out in primetime, and stayed there for eleven seasons. I'd been Emmy-nominated three times for *Happy Days,* but never won.

I wrote this forty-three years ago . . .

And then came my long, long in-between. Very often working with wonderful people, in very worthy movies and shows, but —

But. When you have the kind of success I had right out of the gate, it's very hard to think that it might never come again. And so this Emmy was a validation, not only of the kind of work I could do, but of the kind of work I could do at seventy-two.

If you stay at the table long enough . . . It's a nice thought, and it sometimes comes true. But not always. Not always. People who do great work don't always get rewarded for it. But may I just say, this felt like sweet redemption.

And the one person I couldn't thank on camera, the one who, every Monday morning, helps me jackhammer off just a few more centimeters of this concrete sheathing around me — well, I've thanked her in person, again and again. I say, "If I were to give you a gift for all you have done for me, it would have to be the size of a skyscraper."

In the late nineties, Bob Daly married his second wife, the Academy Award–winning songwriter Carole Bayer Sager, and love really was lovelier the second time around: Carole has made Bob unbelievably happy. And Bob and Carole have made Stacey and me unbelievably happy by being such good friends and taking us on some of the most amazing vacations of our entire lives. The four of us travel so well together, no matter where we go in the world. And no matter what restaurant we dine in, whether it be in Italy, Spain, France, or India, Bob's mealtime routine never varies: he has a few bites of his dinner, then switches my empty dish for his almost full one — thus I've wound up having two dinners all over the world.

One summer, the Dalys took Stacey and me to Italy's Amalfi Coast on a yacht that was owned by the Getty family. I had never experienced that kind of luxury, nor have I since. When we first walked onto the boat, both Stacey and Carole welled up at the sheer beauty and elegance that surrounded us. Sitting on the rear deck in a soft sum-mer breeze, or outdoors at a restaurant onshore, we had to pinch ourselves to make sure we weren't dreaming the gorgeousness of the scenery, and the deliciousness of the meals — except for Bob, who tried as hard as he could to have pasta and tomato sauce wherever he was. Which I got most of anyway.

One amazing thing that happened after the first season of *Barry* was that the South by Southwest festival in Austin invited me to hold a class as Gene Cousineau. "I can't do that," I told them, "but I can do the best I can as Henry."

I've had some very wonderful teachers along the way, people — like Bobby Lewis, Carmen de Lavallade, Dr. Thomas Haas at Emerson — who have done a remarkable service and been so important to my craft and my life. In my own brief experiences teaching, I've tried to pay that service forward, and give young actors something that will let them walk away feeling a way they've never felt before.

I'd taught a few times before: first at Garry Marshall's alma mater, Northwestern; a couple of years later, my good friend Lynda Goodfriend, who played Richie's girlfriend on *Happy Days,* invited me to guest-teach her acting class at the New York Film Academy's Burbank campus. And Vulture.com invited me to teach a class. Then, while making *Here Comes the Boom* in Boston, I visited my alma mater, Emerson, and held three master classes: one in musical comedy, one in scene work, and one in Shakespeare — which scared the hell out of me, because I'd always avoided Shakespeare like the plague. Iambic pentameter didn't trip lightly from my tongue — to put it mildly. The only thing I did well when it came to Shakespeare was wearing the tights.

But, I thought to myself, *okay, you're here — just listen very hard to the scenes the kids are doing, and make sure they're clear about what they're saying and who they're saying it to.* And it went great. In the end, at Northwestern and at Emerson, I think every student who did a scene or a monologue for me really did come away with something fresh and new — and I think I got as much from the classes I taught as the students did. I truly enjoy working with young actors.

So when my PR rep Sheri Goldberg called me back and said that South by Southwest would like me to do two classes, one in acting and one in improv, and could I bring someone from the cast? I didn't hesitate for a second — hands down, it had to be D'Arcy Carden, who played Sally's friend Natalie on *Barry,* and who is an improv master.

Stacey, D'Arcy, and I flew down to Austin, and it was fun — there were a lot of other actors representing their movies and TV shows; I enjoyed running into some people I knew. (I would also like to tell you that the next time you're in Austin, you absolutely have to eat at Loro: the fusion of Japanese cuisine and Franklin's barbecue will make you think you've died and gone to heaven.)

I was looking forward to the teaching, but I was also worried. Whenever I talk with young actors about their work, it's so important that what I say is constructive, that it really makes sense to them. And as much as I love the experience, it never gets any easier.

The improv class came first. D'Arcy and I are onstage, and as we bring volunteers up from the audience to participate, I begin to realize I'm in way over my head. Slowly, I move to the side of the stage and let D'Arcy run the class, which she does brilliantly.

Now it's time for the acting class. This'll be great, I think: there are so many South by Southwest events, there'll be fifty or sixty people; I can handle that. And I walk into the room, and there are six hundred people.

I was moved and amazed that so many people would show up, believing that I would have something to tell them. So I called volunteers up to the stage, and worked with actors at various stages in their pursuit. There was a couple who'd prepared a scene; there was a young lady who'd flown from halfway around the world, having prepared a monologue she'd written: she sat in a folding chair and transformed herself into a woman driving a car, having a conversation with her husband, who didn't understand her. She was nothing short of magnificent.

The life-affirming high of winning a major award lasts for a while, then it fades. But there are results that are much longer lasting. The ad copy for your next project will read, "Starring Henry Winkler, Emmy Winner."

I was no longer just a nominee. I was a winner, and oh God, that felt good.

Winning, as opposed to just being nominated, also makes a difference in the way people in the business treat you — fellow actors, everyone. It's not something that's spoken, overtly. It's something in the air: a vibe. A very good vibe.

I never for one second felt that I was a better actor than any of my fellow nominees. But with this seal of approval, I could at last feel I was as good.

■ ■ ■ ■

In 2019, Lin and I started on a new series of young-adult novels, Alien Superstar, about a six-eyed extraterrestrial who lands on the back lot of Universal Studios and winds up starring in a popular TV series. It reminded me of myself, as I lived through *Happy Days* and the sheer weirdness of becoming a big star.

People think you're more than you are; they think you're taller, smarter, and wiser. And you want so badly to believe it, but it is very important that you don't allow that belief to pervert who you really are — because if you do, that fantasy will come back and smother you. It dawned on me early that if you use the power other people think you have, it turns out to be a mirage.

The other amazing thing that happened that year was that Max directed his third feature, *Jungleland,* one of whose stars was the delightful British actress Jessica Barden, who first appeared on the scene as the star of the British TV series *The End of the F***ing World.* Max and Jessie started dating, and in March, smack in the middle of the pandemic, they were married in our living room. The masked officiant, Max and

Jessie, Stacey and I (also in masks), and as the witness, Hamlet, Max's three-legged, idiosyncratic German shepherd, who was on trazodone (and not masked). And that October, Jessie and Max became parents to the enchanting Frances Joan. Stacey and I were now proud and adoring grandparents six times over.

We shot the second season of *Barry.* In the continuing plotline, Gene falls in love with Janice Moss, the detective — beautifully played by Paula Newsome — who is investigating a murder committed by Barry. The scene that fans would later talk to me about the most was when Gene and Janice have a romantic restaurant dinner of chicken à la king: a lovely little sonata of reluctance (hers) and persuasion (Gene's). The second season's writing was as brilliant as the first, and, with Barry having been forced to kill two people he really didn't want to kill, and face up to the consequences, the story dug down deeper; the comedy grew darker and darker. Gene's relationship with Barry became more and more fraught. HBO quickly renewed us for a third season, and once again the show was nominated for a boatload of awards. Bill and I won Critics Choice Awards for acting, and Bill won his second Primetime Emmy for Outstanding Lead Actor in a Comedy Series. I did not take home another Emmy. Wished I had; didn't.

Then Bill and Alec went off to do their writing magic once again.

In early March 2020 we did our first table read for Season 3. We read the first three scripts — wow. As funny as ever, but also darker than ever. I looked at all the things Gene was going to say and do, and some deep-down part of me was afraid. Which wasn't necessarily a bad thing: my fear energized me for the challenges to come. During my Monday mornings I had come to understand my limitations — and at the same time to feel limitless. An interesting razor's edge to tiptoe on.

After we read I took Sarah Goldberg, D'Arcy Carden, and Jessy Hodges, who played Sally's agent, to lunch, to celebrate the beginning of Season 3. We had a delightful time, all of us looking forward to coming back the following morning to read more scripts.

Then Covid struck, and we were out for the next year and a half.

We all went home. And there were tough times and nice times. One nice thing was that my usual worries about not working evaporated. Nobody was working.

Stacey and I had a lovely time together during the pandemic, even though we rarely got to leave the house. We had wonderful little adventures. Stacey sat at the dining room table for hours putting together a jigsaw puzzle. I would walk through the room, pick up a piece, put it in, and make myself a sandwich. And we saw television from all over the world.

Let me just say that South Korean television is pretty great.

We discovered that James Pickens Jr., a terrific actor on *Grey's Anatomy,* and his beautiful wife, Gina, had opened a restaurant, Black Bottom Southern Kitchen, in North Hollywood. Grits, fried chicken, shrimp. We would order the chicken, and we would take towels and condiments, and we would have the piping hot southern fried chicken in the car. We would have hamburgers at the Win-Dow, down in Venice. We would take our ketchup, our towels, and our Diet Cokes, and we would eat like that, enjoying not having to wait till these things came home and congealed.

We would have dinners on our front lawn with Lynn and Frank: we each got our own picnic blanket, we all sat eight feet apart.

We would call to each other across the lawn, telling stories, laughing, talking about world events. Twice a week, the grandchildren would have sports class on the lawn with Coach Cooper, and the girls had a dance class with their friends. The kids' happy noise made isolation so much more palatable.

Funny how tough times can bring people together, and make for lasting memories.

And we were always grateful for the good fortune that allowed us to enjoy all these things.

We love being grandparents. Oh my God, do we love it. We spent delicious times with Jed and Amanda and their two dancing daughters, with Zoe and Rob and their three boys, and with Jessie and Max and Frances Joan. Our cup runnethed over. Is "runnethed" a word? Ranneth? You know what I'm talking about. We felt, and feel, blessed.

And how did Bill and Alec spend their pandemic? Finishing the writing of Season 3 of *Barry* and doing all the writing for Season 4. I was dying to get back to work, and I know everyone else involved with the show was, too.

■ ■ ■ ■

Nobody could announce that Covid was over, because it wasn't over. But by the summer of 2021 the pandemic had diminished enough, and enough protocols had been established, that it was agreed we could safely go back into production. And in August we began shooting Season 3.

At the beginning of the series, Barry's killings could almost be glossed over; comedy reigned. Gradually, though, and then with growing momentum, the human cost of his slayings came more and more to the forefront. Gene Cousineau's realization of who exactly Barry is and what he does for a living set the third season's very dark tone. (Although there were some bright comic highlights, including Gene's scenes with his equally full-of-himself agent, delightfully played by the deep-voiced Fred Melamed.) Comedy had made me the actor I was, but the Monday mornings with my therapist were giving me the confidence to dig deeper into my toolbox and find strengths I never knew I had. Encouraged by Bill and Alec, who between them directed all eight of the season's episodes, I now found myself playing scenes that were more dramatic than anything I'd ever done before in movies or on TV.

In the season's climactic episode, Gene is interrogated by Jim Moss, the father of Gene's late girlfriend, the police detective Janice Moss. The powerful Robert Wisdom had been cast as Jim, who would not stop until he had solved his daughter's murder. On the morning we were to shoot the scene, Robert and I had an elaborate rehearsal in the garage it was set in. Afterward, we went and got made up, got into costume, and came back to the garage, which was now completely empty except for a camera on a crane: Bill would direct the scene by video from behind the garage's wall.

Robert and I sat in two folding chairs, face-to-face, two feet from each other. As the scene proceeded, Robert pulled his chair closer and closer until we were literally nose to nose. As he interrogated me, his power seemed to blow through my hair like the wind. And Gene's emotional breakdown as Jim Moss grilled him was simply beyond anything I'd ever been able to achieve. Robert took me there, my therapist took me there, and I owe them both beyond measure.

The same was true with Bill. When he and I acted together, he was both actor and director: I'd see him mouthing the words I was saying, and I would have to remind him that he was in the scene. We had an incredible rapport on-screen — it was so easy to create my scenes with Bill. And I owe him so much for choosing me.

Back when my manager Cliff gave it to me straight, telling me that my age was preventing me from getting work, he moved on quickly to the next subject. Though he was young, he was wise enough to know how crazy actors are, no matter what the exterior looks like.

When I'm sent directions to drive to a location, I always say, "You know, I look like an adult. But I'm a four-year-old who can drive." So the directions had better be very precise: "There's a blue pebble on the sidewalk. And eleven feet later, you make a right turn."

There's a woman who works on *Barry*, a second second assistant director named Chalis. She's in charge of the base camp when we shoot exteriors. I call her almost every time I'm driving there, because I get lost almost every time. I say, "Okay, Chalis, I took the wrong freeway."

"All right," Chalis will say. "Where are you?"

I look for an exit sign, a landmark, anything. I tell her what I see.

"Okay," she says. "All right, get off the freeway at the next exit, turn around, go five miles, take Exit 67" — and she stays with me on the phone until I pull into the base camp.

This is the four-year-old with a driver's license. But this is the tightrope I'm always walking: to exorcise the little boy inside who held me back in everyday life, and to keep him around, always on tap, for my work.

STACEY:

I always used to say to Henry, "You made history. What are you looking for? Don't expect that to repeat." But it's very hard, when you have that kind of success early on, not to hold that as the bar you're supposed to rise to again and again. He would always say, "I don't want to be a flash in the pan. I don't want to be small potatoes." Now, all kinds of people say things like that. Henry, though, meant it from his heart. From his gut. What did small potatoes mean to him? It meant unseen, uncared for, unheard.

Used-to-be.

Has-been.

Then he started with this therapist.

Back when he began, I was very interested to see what would happen. Interested, and worried. I thought, *Oh, maybe he's going to come home and hate me.* A shrink of mine once told me, at the beginning of my treatment: "You're going to be great, but the people around you might be a little pissed off." When someone changes, it can be very threatening.

Now, I have been Henry's biggest fan for forty-five years. But in the past, I could always see his self-consciousness in the characters he played: I had a unique perspective on that. To watch him act now — it's really like he had this whole other person inside him, waiting to come out. I watch him on this show and think, *This is amazing.* He's willing to try to climb that fence and fall flat. The rawness, the exposure, are like nothing he's ever done before.

Yes, someone could argue that this material — *Barry* — is just better than what he had before. Okay. It's great material. But Henry had to be able to rise to it. And yes, I'm prejudiced, but I think he also lifted it.

It all makes him feel wonderful. I am so proud of him, and so happy for him — and

389

selfishly, happy for myself. Because when someone is feeling good about themself, they're a lot easier to be around. He had moments of self-satisfaction in the past, but they were brief. This time I'm not waiting for the other shoe to drop, for all his self-doubt to come flowing back in. This time, I really think he knows he's good. Living with an actor can be challenging: nobody knows that the way I do. But Henry is a fuller person now.

I went with him to his shrink once. She's great. I know he was embarrassed — maybe even stunned — when he asked her at the beginning if she had children, and she said, "How will knowing that help you? What would that add to why we're here?" Because he's not used to being told no. He can charm the pants off anyone: people adore him. But I think he came to realize that her saying no to him showed how deeply committed she is to looking past the star and helping the human being.

In May 2022 HBO ordered the fourth and final season of *Barry,* and we began shooting it in June. Bill directed all eight episodes. We finished in December.

We had a wrap party at a wonderful restaurant on Sunset Boulevard. Everybody was there; I don't think anyone was missing. Funnily, it was hard to recognize people on the crew, first because everybody was dressed up, and second because they'd always worn masks on set. Everyone had to take a Covid test before we could enter the party: Fred Melamed found his son hadn't been tested, so we all hugged him outside.

Bill gave me a big hug and said thanks for being a great collaborator. Then I tapped my glass and said a few words to the crew. The actors get to go home, I said; the crew has to restore whatever space we're in back to the way it looked, rolling up miles of cable and cleaning the trailers before they can even move to the next location — I don't know when those men and women sleep. Because at seven the next morning, we start all over again.

I've adored almost every crew I've ever worked with. When you're on the set, if there is a connection between you and them, they take care of you within an inch of your life. And the look on their faces when you do a good scene, when it really crackles, is an Emmy all unto itself.

For a long time after *Happy Days,* I was saddened that the world could only see me as the Fonz. But I never lost sight of what the character gave me — a roof over my head, food on the table, my children's education — and how much it gave me in terms of introducing me to the whole world. And I gradually came to accept how much that character meant to people everywhere. As a matter of fact, for years, in interviews, I would joke that I built a bungalow in the back of our house for the Fonz, where he would work on neighbors' cars.

Then came levels and levels that I hadn't understood before.

A few years back I was the honorary chairman of the Very Special Arts Festival, at the Music Center. All the mentally and physically challenged students from the Los Angeles school system converged there for two days, singing, acting, painting, dancing with and without wheelchairs. It was the most amazing event. And one afternoon I was standing there, and I heard a little voice behind me say, "Fonz." I turned around to see a little girl with her mother, and the mother was weeping and shaking. "What's happening?" I asked.

"My daughter is autistic," the mom told me. "She just said her first word, and it was 'Fonz.'"

I gave that little girl my very best hug.

When I go around the country speaking

publicly, a lot of children with challenges come with their parents, and especially if I see them in the audience, I speak directly to these kids and the parents about the universes we all have inside, and how people so often focus on the outside instead of the inside. I pose for pictures everywhere. At one of these events I put my arm around Richard, who was in high school and taller than me. Everybody's taller than me. His father was very emotional. I said, "Tell me what's going on." And the dad said, "My son doesn't allow people to touch him. Even the family really can't touch him, except on very rare occasions. And you, without a blink of an eye, put your arm around him and he put his arm around you."

It was the Fonz who unlocked that moment, and it was moments like that that unlocked me.

People come up to me all the time. I hold their hand. I look them in the eye. They say, "My father and I watched you, I can't believe I'm meeting you." Or, "Oh my God, my daughter and I watched you," or, "Oh my God, my grandmother —" Or, filming you with their phone, "Could you say hello to — ?"

"Of course," I tell them. "Sure! Melody! How you doin'?"

But for so long, all of that was off to the side of me somewhere. I heard it, it made me feel good, but somehow I wasn't connected to it. It wasn't a reality. I couldn't take in the chatter of, "Oh, you're my favorite," "Oh, I love you," "Oh, you're so great," "Oh my God. Oh my God." It was like white noise. My lack of self, not knowing where I really fit on the earth as Henry, made me unable to enjoy all that. But these challenged kids gave me a warmth that felt so different than what I usually have gotten in my life, a gift that led me so much closer to understanding my real place in the world.

People come up to me, and I go up to people. I walked up to Joaquin Phoenix at the SAG Awards. He said, "I can't believe I'm meeting you." I said, "You can't believe you're meeting me! You!" He said, "Summer, come here." His sister. "How important was this guy when I was growing up?" he said. Oh my God.

Brad Pitt was there.

"Brad."

"Henry."

"Brad, could you just stay here for one minute? Because I'm just going to get my wife over here. She needs to just say hello to you."

I've posed for a million selfies. And there I am taking a phone movie of Stacey talking with Brad Pitt.

One night I was in my car, stopped at a traffic light on Ocean Avenue in Santa Monica, and a man pushing a rolling suitcase containing all his worldly possessions slowly crossed the street in front of me, and I thought, *I am this far away from that person.*

And if you said to me, "But Henry, that could never, ever be you; everybody in the world recognizes you and loves you" — I would say, "Well, you know what? I've thought about that." And I have. I have literally thought that if it ever came to that, if I lost everything and there I was with my rolling suitcase, I could roll up to somebody's house and say, "Hi. It's Henry Winkler. I know this is crazy, but do you have leftovers?" And I would get leftovers. They would invite me in, I would take a bath and sit at the table. I have literally plotted out that scenario and consoled myself with it: "Oh, there's a solution!"

The revelation I had back when I was at Emerson, as I walked up the steps to the Back Bay Brooks Brothers in my painful new Bass Weejuns, came and went just like that. My 360-degree awareness vanished into thin air. But the fruit of it stays with me, and that fruit is gratitude. I have gratitude for everything. I love being on the earth. I love everything.

Are you skeptical?

Michael Eisner was. Michael, when he was head of Disney (I was always very careful to call him "sir"), once asked our very good friend the uber-manager Sandy Gallin the following question about me: "Is he real?"

What did Eisner mean?

I suppose it had something to do with me being thought of as a nice guy. Am I a nice guy? Maybe it's my pride talking, but I bridle a little bit at that characterization — we all know the saying about where nice guys finish. Still, as I walk around on this planet, I am grateful. And out of that gratitude, I am able to be patient. Now, I am not patient all the time. I'm impatient when people are disrespectful of others. I'm impatient with people who are so stupid emotionally that they accuse others of doing what they themselves are doing, without understanding that we are all the same.

No matter where we come from, no matter what the color of our skin is, we all want exactly the same thing. We want a house, we want food to eat. We want our children not to be malnourished and die from hunger. We want clean water.

We want love.

I have had all these things — and still have them — in abundance. And my gratitude is abundant, too.

Fly-fishing in Idaho. My solace, my meditation. My connection with something so much larger than me — something pointing toward what may be my form of religion.

We wear waders, Stacey and I, even though we're mostly in the boat. But sometimes you get out and stand on the rocks that the water is passing over. This is the riffle. You now know, after years, where the fish are. You stand on the rocks and let your line go, and they're waiting in the shallows below for the food that is coming off the riffle. The dark brown of the rocks, the light green of the shallows, the dark green beyond. If you can cast your fly into the light green, you have a shot of catching a fish.

Let the rod help you make the cast. You bring it up to twelve o'clock, hold for a second, and let the line load behind you. Then you move the rod forward with a gentle whip, to two o'clock, and the line floats like an angel onto the water.

And that is serenity.

ACKNOWLEDGMENTS

The adventure of writing a book is filled with people along the way without whom the book would never have been possible.

SO:

This space is filled with thank-yous that could never be big enough or loud enough.

Without Esther Newberg — my fierce, fearless, and tasteful agent since the beginning of my writing journey — I could never have arrived here at this moment.

A very special thank-you to Deb Futter, who, without hesitation, embraced the idea of me writing this autobiography and said "Yes!" immediately upon hearing the concept.

I must thank Alan Berger, who pointed me in the direction of writing in the first place. Without Alan, I would not be writing these acknowledgments at all.

Thank you, Deborah Dorfman, for giving Lin Oliver and me our very first "YES!" as a team to write Hank Zipzer.

After thirty-nine children's novels, I sincerely need to thank Lin Oliver, who has been a wonderful writing partner and guide.

Thank you to the editors throughout my writing career, Bonnie Bader, Maggie Lehrman, and Randi Kramer, for their constant contributions and support.

James Kaplan: THANK YOU for helping me shape my life story AND bringing it to the page with your patience and extraordinary talent.

Thank you to the entire team at Celadon, who make me feel like anything is possible. And whose tireless energy brought this book to the world.

Thank you, Sheri Goldberg, for helping the world know that this book exists.

I really must acknowledge Cliff Murray, Eryn Brown, Shauna Perlman, and Harrison Waterstreet, who keep my professional life on track.

Leaving my everyday life behind so I could pay proper attention to writing this book stress-free became the responsibility of three incredible people: Dana Vines, Leticia Perez, and Ricardo Perez. Thank you, thank you, thank you.

You can't choose your family, but you can choose your friends. Thank you to Bob Daly and Carole Bayer Sager Daly; Frank and Lynn Dines; Daniel Silva and Jamie Gangel; Maxine and Gary Smith; and Margaret and the late Howard Weitzman for all of your support. Always. And to all my friends whom I forgot to mention, thank you for your forgiveness.

Thank you to my family. Thank you to my children — Jed and Amanda, Zoe and Rob, Max and Jessie — and my grandchildren — Indya, Ace, Lulu, Jules, Gus, and Frances Joan — for constantly cheering me on, not only as a writer but also as your dad and grandfather.

And then, there is my secret weapon: my wife, Stacey, my personal editor in all things Henry. Your counsel, your insight, your taste, and your caring are the threads that hold these pages together.

ABOUT THE AUTHOR

In 2023, **Henry Winkler** celebrates fifty years of success in Hollywood and continues to be in demand as an actor, producer, and director. He costarred as the acting teacher Gene Cousineau on the hit HBO dark comedy *Barry.* For this role, he won his first Primetime Emmy Award in 2018 for Outstanding Supporting Actor in a Comedy, as well as two Critics Choice Awards for Best Supporting Actor in a Comedy Series. A graduate of the Yale School of Drama, he was cast in 1973 in the iconic role of Arthur Fonzarelli, aka "the Fonz," in the TV series *Happy Days.* During his ten years on the popular sitcom, he won two Golden Globe Awards, was nominated three times for an Emmy Award, and was honored with a star on the Hollywood Walk of Fame. In recent years, Winkler appeared in a number of series, including *Medical Police, Arrested Development, Childrens Hospital, Royal*

Pains, New Girl, and *Parks and Recreation.*
He is the *New York Times* bestselling author
of numerous children's books, including the
Alien Superstar trilogy and Hank Zipzer:
The World's Greatest Underachiever, a
twenty-eight-book series inspired by Winkler's own struggle with learning challenges.
Of all the titles he has received, the ones he
relishes most are husband, father, and
grandfather. Winkler and his wife, Stacey,
have three children — Jed, Zoe, and Max
— and six grandchildren. They reside in Los
Angeles with their two dogs.